Visual Reference Guides

Guitar

RICHARD CHAPMAN

METRO BOOKS
NEW YORK

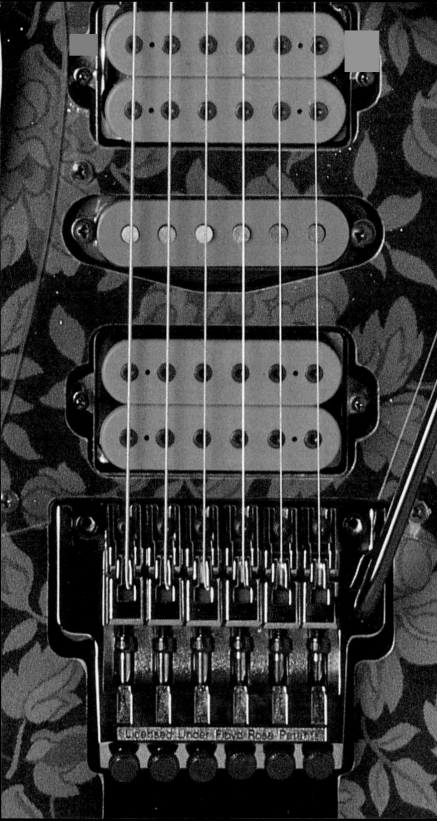

This 2010 edition published by Metro Books,
by arrangement with Dorling Kindersley
Limited, London.

Art Editor	Jenisa Patel
Editor	Matthew Milton
Managing Editor	Miranda Smith
Managing Art Editor	Karen Self
Art Director	Bryn Walls
Publishing Director	Corinne Roberts
DTP Designer	Karen Constanti
Production Controller	Luca Frassinetti

Produced for Dorling Kindersley by
Project Editor	Angela Baynham
Designer	Edward Kinsey

Metro Books
122 Fifth Avenue
New York, NY 10011

ISBN: 978-1-4351-2129-4

A Cataloging-in-Publication data is available from
the Library of Congress.

Color reproduction by Colourscan, Singapore
Printed and bound in China by LRex

3 5 7 9 10 8 6 4 2

CONTENTS

THE GUITAR IS USED FOR PLAYING ALMOST EVERY TYPE AND STYLE OF MUSIC. IT EXISTS TODAY IN A VARIETY OF FORMS, RANGING FROM SIMPLE NYLON STRING ACOUSTIC TO FUTURISTIC ELECTRIC MODELS WITH SOPHISTICATED ONBOARD ELECTRONICS.

Classical

The classical guitar has been in existence for more than 3,000 years. Early guitars had small bodies with four courses of gut strings and they were used in Europe to accompany songs and dances. Hardly audible for prominent musical roles, the guitar was used on its own to accompany singers and occasionally in small ensembles. It evolved acquiring a standard six-string in the third quarter of the 18th century tuning and a larger body in the mid-19th century. Today, the classical guitar is well established, and there is also a large repertoire of material written specifically for it, that ranges from early music to modern atonal compositions. The instrument continues to develop, with new arrangements and fresh works being written all the time. Technique has evolved over hundreds of years and tends to be orthodox. The great popularity of steel string acoustic and electric guitars has led to the classical guitar being somewhat overshadowed, yet the classical instrument is capable of producing some of the most appealing of all guitar music.

Spanish guitarist *Dioniso Aguado (1748–1849) produced a wide range of material for the guitar.*

Entry of the guitars
In the 16th century, the guitar was played both solo and in harmony at all levels of society.

Flamenco

The classical guitar has always been closely associated with Spain and is still often referred to as the Spanish guitar. While the classical guitar and its music were developing in Spain in the 19th century, flamenco music derived from folk and Arabic traditions was also emerging in that country, with guitarists accompanying singers and dancers in a highly energized rhythmic style using scales and harmonies that have a Middle-Eastern flavor. Flamenco guitar playing became established in the 20th century, and although related to the classical guitar, it uses a whole range of different techniques including rasgueado strumming. Characteristic musical pieces that often have regional Spanish roots are played as a set of inventions with variations or as vehicles for improvisation. Flamenco exists both as a highly traditional form and as a modern evolving fusion, with South American and jazz influences.

This instrument, *made by René Voboam in Paris in 1641, is richly decorated with ivory and ebony.*

Blues

Based on African scales, rhythms, and inflections, and evolving within church music and other European influences, blues was the music of African-Americans, and its highly expressive power and immediacy came into focus with the guitar in the 1920s and 1930s. Acoustic styles on steel string guitars, with percussive picking and exotic slide techniques, were used to support emotional lyrics. In the 1940s, blues began to be played on electric guitars, and riffs, solos, and chords were melded to form a singular vocabulary that is catchy, appealing, and highly poignant. This in turn helped to pave the way for rock 'n' roll and the explosion of pop and rock developments in the 1960s. Blues still exists as a music in its own right and as part of the template for much of today's popular music on the guitar.

Country and folk

The unique identity and flavor of country music evolved in the US, from roots that derived partly from British and European folk music. Songs and dances were accompanied by sophisticated fingerstyle techniques on acoustic steel string guitars. Fast virtuoso fiddle and banjo styles helped to lay the foundations for playing styles such as bluegrass. The electric guitar slowly became popular after the 1940s, and virtuoso country-style chord melody

The musically sensitive *French guitarist Ida Presti (1924–67) played in a duo with Alexandro Lagona (1929–99) and made outstanding recordings.*

and electric soloing started to emerge. Today, country is a diverse music, with both traditional and rock influences.

In North America, folk guitar styles were almost indistinguishable from country until the 1950s and 1960s, when the guitar started to be seen as a vehicle to accompany singer-songwriters. Folk also produced an interesting and diverse range of guitarists in Britain, where the guitar was considered a new vehicle for reviving lost traditions, as well as a way of exploring indigenous styles from around the world. On the electric guitar, folk rock emerged as a vibrant synthesis of tradition and innovation. In recent years, folk has spread around the world to explore and reveal a heritage of indigenous cultures on acoustic and electric guitars.

Gillian Welch (b.1967) *plays the guitar in a particularly sensitive way to support her crossover folk- and country-style songs.*

Jazz

The word jazz has come to be seen as an umbrella term for a wide range of musical styles that range from Dixieland to the avant-garde. Originating in the US and linked to blues, ragtime, and classical music, early acoustic jazz styles with rich harmonies and virtuosic pick techniques emerged in the 1920s and 1930s. The invention of the electric guitar in the US in the 1930s led to the guitar becoming an instrument that could rival the saxophone, trumpet, and piano when played in a group.

Jazz developed at an astonishing pace, from swing to bebop and modal areas, and the guitar absorbed ideas from other instruments. It has been used for many years to realize advanced musical concepts, with compelling harmonies, complex linear solos, and open improvisation. Jazz has produced many of the greatest guitarists in the last 100 years, and with its multilevel stylistic crossover areas and futuristic experiments, it continues to lead the way in musical development.

Rock and pop

Today, the electric guitar maintains an unfailing appeal to every generation. This is largely due to the advent of rock 'n' roll in the 1950s and pop and rock in the 1960s, which led to the guitar dominating large areas of the world of music. The electric guitar in rock 'n' roll merged blues, country, and pop influences to become highly potent, and it has continued to form the basis for the launch of innumerable guitar-based groups. Amplifiers and effects such as echo and distortion are used to enhance the sound, and the guitar continues to create entrancing and infectious rhythms, harmonies, and melodies, and soaring solos that give the instrument a charismatic and seductive power.

Today in pop and rock, there are various approaches with roots in blues, rock 'n' roll, pop, soul, funk, and other hybrid and world music areas. Solos can be based on simple melodies, blues-based

Today, the electric guitar still maintains an unfailing appeal to every generation

Buddy Guy (b.1936), *the great American blues guitarist, uses a Fender Stratocaster to create a range of emotional solos and fills.*

pentatonic vocabulary, classical ideas or jazz. And it is still appealing to back vocals simply with basic chords. In recent decades, synthesizers, midi, and computer-generated sounds have opened up unlimited possibilities for playing "sonic" guitar parts, where sounds and textures can be created that range from mimicking other instruments to unearthly futuristic soundcscapes. Today, rock and pop is played on both steel string acoustic and electric guitars, with pick and fingerstyle techniques and a wide range of styles and approaches, and it continues to be hugely popular.

I recommend the guitar as a wonderful medium for personal expression and fulfillment

Playing the guitar
I recommend the guitar as a wonderful medium for personal expression and fulfillment, or even just as an object for simple enjoyment. For me, playing the

guitar has been an essential passion and a life-enhancing occupation. The possibilities for musical development and invention have never ceased to increase. I could not imagine life without the guitar. It has been a matrix for connections and a touchstone that has given my life meaning. Inspired at first by jazz musicians such as Eric Dolphy and John Coltrane, and classical composers including Claude Debussy and Belà Bartok, I often found guitar music limited and stylized. Today, I have come to realize that the guitar has incredible potential and unlimited possibilities and I like to remind myself of that every day.

RICHARD CHAPMAN

A big country star, *Garth Brooks has brought country music into the pop mainstream in the 1990s.*

One of the biggest rock bands *in the world today, the Red Hot Chili Peppers were originally formed in Los Angeles in 1983. Guitarist John Frusciante (b.1970) joined the band in 1988.*

GREAT
GUITARISTS

THERE ARE MANY STYLES AND APPROACHES WITHIN GUITAR PLAYING, AND IT IS ILLUMINATING TO SEPARATE THE ROLES OF PLAYERS BY DIVIDING THEM ACCORDING TO THE TYPES OF INSTRUMENTS THEY PLAY FOR VARIOUS KINDS OF MUSIC.

Nylon string

With nylon string guitars there are four main areas of musical activity: classical, flamenco, Brazilian, and jazz. In the 20th century, the Spanish guitarist Segovia dominated the classical guitar world and he was followed by outstanding figures such as Julian Bream. In flamenco during the 20th century, Ramon Montoya and Sabicas paved the way for Paco de Lucía's brilliance. Brazilian music is a synthesis of native, African, Latin, classical, and jazz influences, and has produced players such as Baden Powell and Rafael Rabello who have

One of the world's *leading classical guitarists, Manuel Barrueco was born in Cuba and is now resident in the USA.*

produced beautiful and inventive music. In jazz, the classically influenced Ralph Towner and Egberto Gismonti developed new sounds, and virtuoso soloing with a pick was pioneered by John McLaughlin.

Steel string acoustic

Steel string guitars are played in many areas of music. Early recordings feature blues legends Blind Lemon Jefferson and slide players using resonators such as the Hawaiian virtuoso Sol Hoopii. The first great jazz guitarist, Django Reinhardt, played acoustically in the 1930s. In the postwar years, amazing

In the 1980s, *some of the most vibrant music emerged from Africa, from groups such as the Bhundu Boys.*

country players such as Merle Travis appeared, and in the 1960s and 1970s folk legend Doc Watson and bluegrass player Tony Rice created exceptional music. In the 1960s folk guitarist Davey Graham developed world music approaches. The singer-songwriter Joni Mitchell created dozens of open tunings and Pierre Bensusan has specialized in using DADGAD (*see* p.22). Today, players such as Adrian Legg pioneer the use of effects. Around the world, there are many fascinating areas of music, from the slide playing of India to the vibrant music of Africa.

The first great jazz guitarist, Django Reinhardt, played acoustically in the 1930s.

Electric

The first major figure to adopt an electric guitar was the jazz guitarist Charlie Christian in the 1930s. His single-line solos opened up the potential of the instrument. Chuck Berry's rock 'n' roll playing in the 1950s and the advent of The Beatles made the electric guitar a worldwide phenomenon. When Jimi Hendrix appeared in 1966, his brilliance shone out. In the 1970s, innovative jazz fusion soloing with players such as John McLaughlin and Allan Holdsworth pushed the boundaries, and in rock, Eddie Van Halen and Joe Satriani displayed formidable technical skills, and sonic boundaries have been explored by Bill Frisell in jazz and Tom Morello in rock.

In a long and successful career *the singer-songwriter Bonnie Raitt (b.1949) has produced a great deal of fine blues-based guitar music, including melodic slide playing.*

Chet Atkins

Born June, 20, 1924, in Luttrell, Tennessee **Died** 2001

A major figure of 20th-century guitar-playing, Chet Atkins' country style formed part of the basis of pop and rock styles from the 1950s onward.

Growing up in the South, Chet Atkins was a prodigy on the guitar who was influenced by country styles and a wide range of other genres. He assimilated ideas from instruments including the violin and banjo, and idolized the American country guitarist Merle Travis. This led to him developing a tremendous technical control, enabling him to play with the versatility of a classical guitarist. Atkins' use of the thumbpick gave his playing a hard-edged, chopped bass sound that lent a rhythmic propulsion to chords and melodies played with his fingers. Atkins mainly adopted the electric guitar. Among many classic early instrumental tracks are "Black Mountain Rag" (1952) and from 1953, "Oh By Jingo," "Kentucky Derby," and "Dill Pickle Rag."

CAREER HIGHLIGHTS

1940 Starts working on the radio at WNOX, Knoxville, Tennessee.

1947 Begins a long association with RCA in Nashville as an artist and producer.

1954 Hit with "Mr. Sandman."

1956 Plays as a sessions musician for Elvis Presley and the Everly Brothers.

1965 Hit with "Yakety Axe."

Derek Bailey

Born January 29, 1930, in Sheffield, Yorkshire, England

The revolutionary Derek Bailey has been at the forefront of modern improvisation for more than four decades. His atonal playing has broken down barriers and challenged musical orthodoxies.

Derek Bailey played conventional jazz until he began to experiment with new forms of music in Sheffield in the early 1960s. In the late 1960s, he moved to London and abandoned conventional scales, chord sequences, and meter to give himself the freedom to improvise in radical, free music groups such as the Spontaneous Music Ensemble. Bailey concentrated on forming short, angular lines, atonal clusters, and percussive textural effects. These can be heard on the recording *Karyobin* (1968). He also developed solo playing, and a mixture of minimalist, compositional material, and free improvisations are featured on his recording *Solo Guitar* (1971). Bailey has played all over the world with musicians from different genres.

CAREER HIGHLIGHTS

1965 Plays with Tony Oxley and Gavin Bryars.

1967 Plays in the Spontaneous Music Ensemble with John Stevens, Paul Rutherford, and Evan Parker.

1970 Incus Records formed.

1980 Runs annual Company Week festival.

2002 Releases jazz standards album *Ballads*.

Jeff Beck

Born June 24, 1944, in Wallington, Surrey, England

One of the great guitarists, Jeff Beck has forged an innovative style, which has developed throughout his career. His soaring solos and melodic interpretations are exceptional.

In his formative years, Jeff Beck was influenced by rock 'n' roll, blues, and classical music. His playing is a highly individual synthesis of melodic elements. With the Yardbirds, highlights such as the instrumental 12-bar "Jeff's Boogie" (1966) show off his ability to use an array of techniques to create textures and shifting moods on the guitar. Beck's use of sustain, his cutting rhythmic incisiveness, and his blending of metallic heavy sounds and electronic effects influenced future rock and heavy metal.

After leaving the Yardbirds in 1968, he formed the Jeff Beck Group and continued to lay the foundations for modern rock on the album *Truth* (1968). This album and the following one, *Beck-Ola* (1969), are full of exhilarating, heavy, bluesy rock playing, with effective arrangements and elements of suspense and surprise.

He was later influenced by jazz rock fusion, producing the instrumental albums *Blow By Blow* (1975) and *Wired* (1976). Over the years, he has continued to produce high-quality recordings such as "Jeff Beck's Guitar Shop" (1989). Beck is particularly noted for his live playing where his sense of touch and ability to communicate a range of emotions transcend the instrument.

The Yardbirds
Beck used distorted rock riffs on "I'm Not Talkin'" (1965), and was featured on singles such as "Heart Full of Soul." Jimmy Page joined the group in 1966.

CAREER HIGHLIGHTS

1963 Joins the Tridents and starts to make an impact on the London scene.

1965 Replaces Eric Clapton in the Yardbirds.

1967 First single "Hi-Ho Silver Lining" charts at No.14 in the UK.

1968 Forms the Jeff Beck Group with Rod Stewart on vocals and Ron Wood on bass. Releases first solo album *Truth*.

1969 *Beck-ola* album reaches No.15 in US charts.

1972 Forms new group with Carmine Appice and Tim Bogert from Vanilla Fudge.

1975 Releases jazz-rock fusion album *Blow by Blow* produced by George Martin.

1980 Releases *There and Back*, introducing Tony Hymas on keyboards.

George Benson

Born March 22, 1943, in Pittsburgh, Pennsylvania

George Benson is unusual in being both an exceptional jazz guitarist with a sophisticated bebop vocabulary and a singer who reached a mainstream audience in the 1970s, combining vocals with bubbly guitar playing.

Brought up with blues and rock 'n' roll as well as jazz, George Benson was influenced by the vocabulary of modern jazz, and guitarists such as Charlie Christian and Wes Montgomery. His debut album *New Boss Guitar* (1964) instantly placed him in the mainstream as the best new jazz guitar soloist. His music shows an openness to various influences with the use of fast heads and unison riffs, and funky rhythms and pentatonic blues flavors on tracks such as "Shadow Dancers." The album *It's Uptown* (1965) showed Benson as an artist who could both sing and work with a popular touch, while retaining the ability to produce virtuosic jazz on standards such as "Willow Weep For Me."

In the early 1970s, Benson made albums with lush arrangements, such as *White Rabbit* (1971), aimed at a middle-of-the-road audience. By the mid 1970s, he began to alter his approach and emerged as a pop star, achieving commercial success with the single "This Masquerade" and the album *Breezin'* (1976). Benson continues to lead a high-profile career as a performer and recording artist.

CAREER HIGHLIGHTS

1962 Plays with organist Brother Jack McDuff.

1964 Releases debut album *New Boss Guitar.*

1965 Meets main influence Wes Montgomery.

1976 Hit single with "This Masquerade."

1977 Hit single with "Nature Boy."

Pierre Bensusan

Born October 30, 1957, in Oran, Algeria

Pierre Bensusan has forged his own type of music, which is melodic and ethereal as well as percussive and rhythmic. His approach paved the way for New Age, ambient, and crossover styles.

Brought up in France, Pierre Bensusan was influenced by Celtic folk, jazz, Brazilian, classical, and Arabic music. He has concentrated on playing in a fixed alternative tuning DADGAD, which gives the guitar more depth, and makes it possible to invent rich and unusual voicings. He writes all his own material, and his compositions have their own Gallic flavor and charm. Bensusan started recording in the 1970s and one of his first outstanding albums, *Solilai* (1981), features material full of interesting juxtapositions and ideas on tracks such as the bright and optimistic "Nice Feeling" and the courtly "Au Jardin D'Amour." Bensusan's music is ahead of its time. He is a major figure in guitar-playing and an outstanding individualist with a cult following.

CAREER HIGHLIGHTS

1974 First recording contract.

1975 His album *Près de Paris* wins Grand Prix du Disque.

1981 Album *Solilai* earns him international recognition.

1987 Album *Spices* features Bensusan in group context, with instruments including saxophone and bass.

2001 Releases *Intuite* album.

Chuck Berry

Born October 18,1926, in St. Louis, Missouri

The founding father of rock 'n' roll guitar, Chuck Berry is a legend who forged the template for three-chord rock in the 1950s. He helped to establish the electric guitar as the premier instrument in popular music.

Chuck Berry sang in a Baptist church as a child and took up the guitar while at school. His formative influences stem from the blues tradition and guitar motifs introduced by figures such as Robert Johnson and T-Bone Walker. Berry was also molded by country music, and absorbed and rearranged ideas from jazz and calypso music. Early on, Berry was able to create a simple and effective technique where he uses powerful, piano-style boogie chords on the guitar. His early hit "Maybellene" (1955) has a primeval simplicity and the guitar has a throaty distortion. "Roll Over Beethoven" (1956) introduces one of his hallmark devices, an exclamatory intro with double-stopped notes. On Berry's most well-known composition, the famous "Johnny B. Goode" (1958), he created a memorable chord riff-type solo intro, and breaks that have become an integral part of the vocabulary for aspiring rock 'n' roll guitarists.

The father of rock 'n' roll
Berry is credited by many musicians and admirers with inventing rock 'n' roll.

CAREER HIGHLIGHTS

1941 Performs at his school musical stage performance, accompanied by his friend Tommy Stevens on guitar. Inspired to learn to play the instrument himself.

1952 Starts playing in the Sir John's Trio with pianist Johnnie Johnson and Ebby Hardy on drums.

1955 Lands a recording contract with Chess records in Chicago. First songs include "Maybellene" and "Wee Wee Hours."

1956 "Roll Over Beethoven" reaches No.29 in the US pop chart.

1957 Releases first album *After School Session*. "School Day" single is No.3 in the US.

1958 Hit with "Johnny B. Goode."

1972 First UK No.1 hit with "My Ding-A-Ling."

1984 Wins a Grammy for Lifetime Achievement.

Julian Bream

Born July 15, 1933, in London, England

Julian Bream is a musically sensitive interpreter of classical repertoire. He has encouraged mainstream composers to take the guitar seriously, and has commissioned and premièred many important works.

Julian Bream grew up listening to Django Reinhardt and Andrès Segovia. At an early age, he devoted himself to mastering classical music, and in the 1950s and 1960s he emerged as one of the world's outstanding performers and recording artists. His repertoire ranges from early music and Bach through to Sor, Giuliani, and Aguado, as well as Rodrigo Albeniz and Villa Lobos.

Bream championed the guitar with British classical composers. One of his first commissions was Malcolm Arnold's "Guitar Concerto" from 1959. Benjamin Britten's beautiful, rich and complex piece "Nocturnal" (1963) has eight sections reflecting different moods and states of mind during the night time. For example, the episode "Dreaming" has a quiet beauty with magical lines and harmonics. Other highlights include William

Modern works
Bream's rich legacy includes a role in helping to extend and modernize the repertoire of the classical guitar in the 20th century.

Walton's inventive and exuberant "Five Bagatelles" (1971) and Peter Maxwell-Davies' "Hill Runes" (1981).

Bream has continued to encourage the writing of new material, notably works by the Japanese composer Toru Takemitsu. During the 1970s, Bream produced outstanding recordings of well-known pieces, such as the "Five Preludes" by Villa Lobos.

CAREER HIGHLIGHTS

1944	Receives a classical guitar from his father for his 11th birthday.
1951	Debut London concert at Wigmore Hall.
1955	Starts to record first albums for RCA on the lute and guitar.
1959	Première of Malcolm Arnold's "Guitar Concerto."
1964	Receives OBE for services to music.
1967	Releases innovative album of modern guitar works *Twentieth Century Guitar*.
2001	Anniversary recital at Wigmore Hall celebrates 50 years since his debut.

Lenny Breau

Born August 5, 1941, in Auburn, Maine   **Died** 1984

One of the most brilliant jazz harmony virtuosos, Lenny Breau produced a style that is an amalgamation of jazz and classical ideas with his own type of country-style technique.

CAREER HIGHLIGHTS

1948 Takes up the guitar at the age of seven.

1968 After being discovered by Chet Atkins (*see* p.20), he signs a recording deal with RCA. Releases debut album *Guitar Sounds Of Lenny Breau*.

1977 Releases solo albums *Five O'Clock Bells*, with five of his compositions, and *Mo' Breau*.

1995 The tapes from an outstanding live concert in 1983 are finally released as *Live At Bourbon St.*

Brought up by parents who were Canadian country music singers, Lenny Breau was influenced by the playing of country guitarist Chet Atkins, and assimilated jazz guitar and piano music. He developed a right-hand fingerstyle technique on both acoustic and electric guitar that combined a thumbpick with all four fingers, and he used a seven-string guitar to add range. His impressionistic, close voicing chords echo the work of pianist Bill Evans, and his luminous plucked artificial chord harmonics create a cascade of color.

Breau played with energy and drive, creating independent guitar parts, soloing over supporting chord tones, and switching the improvisational flow to fast bass lines. On the album *Live at Bourbon St* (1983), his mastery of well-known standards "All Blues" and "On Green Dolphin St." is breathtaking. Breau worked outside the jazz scene and received little recognition. His recordings stand as a lasting testament.

Charlie Christian

Born July 19, 1916, in Dallas, Texas   **Died** 1942

The key figure in the emergence of the electric guitar as a single line instrument, Charlie Christian's inventive swinging solos became the templates for jazz guitar.

In his early years, Charlie Christian was influenced by blues and jazz, and absorbed the advanced linear approaches of saxophonists such as Coleman Hawkins and Lester Young. Christian adapted his style to the electric guitar brilliantly. It gave him newfound volume and projection and enabled him to work on an equal basis with brass instruments. In 1939, he joined Benny Goodman's group. There, Christian's riffs and solos were showcased with great effect. "Flying Home" has arcing lines and rhythmic subtlety. "Seven Come Eleven" has memorable catchy riffs and "Stardust" has melodic inventiveness and variety. On his most famous solo, the exceptional "Solo Flight" (1941), Christian plays with an uplifting gracefulness and assurance, long supple lines, and inventive turns of phrase. As his solo unfolds, he builds momentum and responds to the Goodman Orchestra with an incisive attack. Christian died tragically at the age of 25 from tuberculosis.

CAREER HIGHLIGHTS

1934 Plays bass with Alphonso Trent.

1937 Starts playing the electric guitar after meeting guitarist Eddie Durham.

1939 Auditioned by swing bandleader Benny Goodman in Los Angeles and joins his sextet.

1941 Records *Solo Flight* in New York. Plays at Minton's in Harlem with musicians such as Thelonious Monk and Dizzy Gillespie.

Eric Clapton

Born March 30, 1945, in Ripley, Surrey, England

One of the world's most famous electric guitarists, Eric Clapton captured everyone's imagination in the 1960s when he became one of the first people to develop a powerful and assured blues rock soloing style.

After taking up the guitar at the age of 11, Eric Clapton became fascinated by the blues, and listened to artists ranging from Robert Johnson to Muddy Waters. His break came when he joined the Yardbirds in 1963, and his developing soloing technique can be heard on tracks such as "Got To Hurry" (1964). He joined John Mayall's group where his rich, reedy tone, soaring sustain, and string bending can be heard on tracks such as "Steppin' Out" on John Mayall's album *Bluesbreakers* (1966).

Later in 1966, Clapton joined Cream and his playing was extended into jazz and progressive rock. "The Sunshine Of Your Love" (1967) became one of the seminal guitar riffs of this era. His famous live solo "Crossroads" from the album *Wheels Of Fire* (1968) is a vehicle for his inventive playing and showcases his ability to drive his solo in waves of tension release to reach a passionate climax. Other highlights include the wah-wah solo on "White Room." In 1968, the group split up and Clapton pursued a solo career, concentrating on his singing, and playing shorter solos. He had success with the gritty and emotional "Layla" (1970), and albums such as *Slowhand* (1977) with its tasteful laid-back arrangements.

Fingerstyle playing
Clapton's acoustic playing in the early 1990s is heartfelt, and his writing can be heard on tracks such as "Tears from Heaven" on *Unplugged* (1992).

Cream
One of the first "super groups," Cream featured three highly talented individuals.

CAREER HIGHLIGHTS

1963	Takes the place of Top Topham in the Yardbirds.
1966	Forms Cream with bass player Jack Bruce and drummer Ginger Baker.
1968	Plays the solo on George Harrison's song "While My Guitar Gently Weeps" on the double album *The Beatles*.
1969	Forms Blind Faith with Stevie Winwood, Ginger Baker, and Rick Grech.
1970	Plays with Delaney and Bonnie, and forms Derek and the Dominoes.
1970	Releases first solo album *Eric Clapton*.
1974	Releases his album *461 Ocean Boulevard* and has a US No.1 with "I Shot the Sherriff."
1992	The *Unplugged* album becomes a huge commercial success and helps to bring about an acoustic renaissance.
1993	Wins six Grammies for *Unplugged*.

Guitar legend
Clapton has had one of the longest and most successful careers of any guitarist, spanning more than 40 years.

Kurt Cobain

Born February 20, 1967, in Seattle, Washington **Died** 1994

Kurt Cobain's raw energy and irreverent wildness brought back an element of honesty to mainstream rock. His intensity and non-technical approach have made him an icon.

An outsider who grew up listening to The Beatles as well as heavy metal, Kurt Cobain was inspired by little-known indie punk bands. A true rebel, he sought to express himself by playing the guitar with abandon, using a primeval electric sound. The album *Nevermind* (1991) includes tracks such as "Smells Like Teen Spirit," which has guitar parts with an appealing vocal contour as well as a simmering fuzzy tone. Tracks such as "Breed" have a bright guitar sound with seething electricty, and "Territorial Pissings" has angry punk-style guitar. Cobain died at the age of 27, yet continues to inspire those who feel alienated by overproduced pop and rock.

CAREER HIGHLIGHTS

1985 Meets bass player Chris Novoselic.

1987 Forms Nirvana.

1988 Band signs to Seattle label Sub Pop. Records album *Bleach* for just over $600.

1991 Releases *Nevermind* on Geffen Records label.

1993 Releases album *In Utero*.

Ry Cooder

Born March 15, 1947, in Santa Monica, California

A guitarist whose role has been based around playing slide and using open tunings, Ry Cooder is a songwriter, and an expert on the history of blues and many areas of world music.

Having started playing the guitar at the age of four, Ry Cooder listened to music that included the classical guitar. He developed a great interest in the rich heritage of American music, such as folk, country, and the different styles of blues on acoustic and electric instruments. He was a prodigy with a highly developed knowledge of open tunings, the vocabulary and heritage of blues, and other styles of slide, such as Hawaiian. In the 1960s, Cooder started working with bands ranging from Captain Beefheart to the Rolling Stones.

His own albums feature gritty, driving, abrasive compositions that often have surging rhythms and interesting textures. Cooder juxtaposes licks and motifs in fresh and inventive ways. He also uses a glass slide which gives him a smooth, full tone. His sophistication and originality can be heard on *Into The Purple Valley* (1971), with tracks such as "On A Monday." *Chicken Skin Music* (1976) uses Hawaiian music on "Yellow Roses" and Tex-Mex rhythms on "He'll Have To Go." Cooder has created a high-quality body of work, and is an innovator and a custodian of tradition.

CAREER HIGHLIGHTS

1966 Works with Captain Beefheart on the album *Safe As Milk*.

1971 Releases *Into the Purple Valley*, featuring traditional material.

1979 The album *Bop Till You Drop* brings his music to a wider audience.

1980 Records *Bloodlines* in Hawaii with musicians that include Shoukichi Kina.

1984 Composes music for the film *Paris Texas*.

Tal Farlow

Born June 7, 1921, in Greensboro, North Carolina **Died** 1998

The first great postwar bebop-influenced jazz guitarist, Tal Farlow brought a new sophistication to the guitar. Playing with a hard-edged swinging tone, he set the standard for the future.

Tal Farlow taught himself to play the guitar and developed his ear by listening to the radio. After moving to New York in the 1940s, he became influenced by Charlie Parker and Bud Powell. Farlow joined vibes player Red Norvo's group in 1949, where he was required to play standards at fast tempos. He developed his virtuoso linear technique, playing soaring, inventive lines with tremendous drive. In 1953, he started leading his own group and his playing can be heard on *The Swinging Guitar of Tal Farlow* (1956), where his solos are inspired on standards such as "You Stepped Out of a Dream." Throughout his life, Farlow developed voicings and reharmonizations of standards and played mesmerizing passages of improvisation using artificial harmonics.

CAREER HIGHLIGHTS

1949 Joins Red Norvo's Trio.

1953 Starts recording as a leader for Blue Note.

1958 Leaves the music scene and works as a sign-painter.

1969 Makes a comeback with *The Return Of Tal Farlow.*

Robert Fripp

Born May 16, 1946, in Wimbourne, Dorset, England

Robert Fripp brought elliptical solos, attractive arpeggios, and rhythmic motifs to electric guitar music and, with electronic sound processing, added a new dimension to popular music.

Robert Fripp applied himself to the development of a mastery of lines and arpeggiation with a pick. He absorbed classical, jazz, and pop motifs with harmony ideas. His breakthrough came with King Crimson and the album *In The Court Of The Crimson King* (1969). Fripp takes an astonishing solo on "Twenty-First Century Schizoid Man," using effects to create an eerie sustain and color with bending pitches, and a unique melodic flavor. Fripp's challenging and subversive approach have helped move the guitar toward the future.

Sonic innovator
Fripp has pioneered the use of unusual effects and futuristic guitar parts.

CAREER HIGHLIGHTS

1969 Forms King Crimson with Ian McDonald, Greg Lake, and Michael Giles.

1973 Collaborates with Brian Eno on *No Pussyfootin'*.

1981 Releases innovative new King Crimson album *Discipline*.

1982 Works with guitarist Andy Summers and records *I Advanced Masked* and *Bewitched*.

Bill Frisell

Born March 18, 1951, in Baltimore, Maryland

A sonic architect on the guitar, Bill Frisell is a jazz revolutionary whose sounds and crossover ideas are highly innovative. He is the master of assembling rich collages of sounds.

CAREER HIGHLIGHTS

1979 Records with bass player Eberhard Weber.

1981 Releases first solo album for ECM *In Line*.

1985 Releases *Rambler* with Kenny Wheeler, Bob Stewart, Jerome Harris, and Paul Motian.

1988 Releases *Lookout for Hope*.

At an early age, Bill Frisell was inspired by rock and blues, and as he developed his playing, he discovered jazz fusion artists such as John McLaughlin. Instead of imitating current styles, Frisell concentrated on building a technique using space in which to place understated lyrical melodic phrases, and tasteful harmonic inventions with mobile chord voicings. These are all heavily processed with electronic effects, taking the overall result well away from a normal guitar sound.

On his recordings, Frisell has established himself as a master at creating thoughtful, poignant, and often startling compositions. His albums are full of bizarre and curious elements, and he has been at the forefront of jazz crossover developments in the last 20 years.

Egberto Gismonti

Born December 5, 1947, in Carmo, Brazil

Egberto Gismonti is a progressive Brazilian guitarist and composer who has created a style of music with classical, crossover jazz, and native traditions.

CAREER HIGHLIGHTS

1967 In addition to piano, starts playing guitar.

1968 Leaves Brazil for France where he studies under Nadia Boulanger.

1969 Releases first album *Egberto Gismonti* through Elenco.

1976 Releases *Danca Dos Cabecas* for ECM.

1981 Releases outstanding album *Sanfona*.

1989 Releases *Danca Dos Ecravos*.

Egberto Gismonti grew up with classical and Brazilian music, playing piano and guitar, and studied classical composition with Nadia Boulanger in Paris. His visionary music can be reflective as well as spirited, driving, and muscular. He has used classical guitars with anything from eight to 14 strings to play music with a dramatically wide range of register, texture, and expression. The album *Danca dos Cabecas* (1976) demonstrates his sophisticated playing with percussion. Gismonti's wide range of register and inventive acoustic techniques transcend limitations, and place the guitar in a varied central role. His refreshing synthesis of serious compositional ideas, incorporating music from around the world, continues to be a vehicle for his mesmeric guitar voice.

Jon Greenwood

Born November 15, 1971, in Oxford, England

Using sound-processing to create contrast, Jon Greenwood's guitar-playing adds an experimental edge to Radiohead, conveying atmosphere with his layering and fills.

Growing up with pop and rock influences, Jon Greenwood developed his style of guitar-playing by enhancing material in the recording studio. On Radiohead's album *The Bends* (1995), his futuristic playing has a sci-fi quality. "Planet Tex" has shaking, pulsating guitar chords and strange tone effects. His progressive guitar touches add variety and mood to the group's songs.

CAREER HIGHLIGHTS

1993 Breakthrough single "Creep" reaches No.7 in the UK charts.

1995 The band releases the album *The Bends*.

1997 Album *OK Computer* reaches No.1 in the UK, and the single "Paranoid Android" reaches No.3.

George Harrison

Born February 25, 1943, in Liverpool, England **Died** 2001

As a member of The Beatles, George Harrison recorded many varied and memorable melodic guitar parts that have become central to the history of pop and rock music. He played classic intros, solos, and fills, and forged his own style, adapting to new instruments and studio sound-processing.

With The Beatles, George Harrison added important parts to many of the group's finest compositions. He adopted an electric 12-string on tracks such as "Eight Days A Week," and on the album *Revolver* (1966), he created atmospheric riffs for "I Want To Tell You," and used Indian influences on "Love To You." He also plays part of the exceptional intro and fills for "And Your Bird Can Sing." On *Sgt. Pepper's* (1967) he uses inventive sound-processing to mask the guitar and create exotic sonic soundscapes. On *Abbey Road* (1969) his composition "Something" features a solo full of emotional melodic phrasing.

CAREER HIGHLIGHTS

1958 Plays in the Quarry Men with Lennon and McCartney.

1963 First Beatles UK No.1 "From Me To You."

1969 "Something," first Beatles hit written by Harrison, reaches No.3 in US charts.

1970 Releases solo album *All Things Must Pass*, which reaches No.1 in the US, and the single "My Sweet Lord" reaches No.1 in the US and UK.

1971 Plays on John Lennon's album *Imagine*.

Playing live
A brilliant showman,
Hendrix produced
electrifying
performances
that enthralled
his audiences.

Jimi Hendrix

Born November 27, 1942, in Seattle, Washington **Died** 1970

One of the all-time greats, Jimi Hendrix was a brilliant performer and an inspired recording artist. He redefined the sound of the electric guitar and gave it an elemental potency.

Jimi Hendrix started playing the guitar in the mid-1950s and was influenced by rock 'n' roll, blues, and soul music. In England, he started to experiment with new effects units and amplifiers, and created a scintillating guitar sound. Hendrix developed his new rock sound for "Purple Haze," a surging rock number that opens with a dramatic tritone motif followed by sweeping melodic curves, crunching chords, and octave fills.

Hendrix could convey gentle intimate moods and this can be heard on "The Wind Cries Mary," a haunting ballad with rising chord figures and a sensitive, delicate solo. On his first album, Are You Experienced (1967), "Manic Depression" has start-stop cutoff riffs which build tension, and he breaks into a wild careering solo. Hendrix also plays expressive blues on "Red House." His exceptional album Electric Ladyland (1968) features an array of highly developed guitar sounds including wah wah. "All Along The Watchtower" has a solo broken into four contrasting sections that builds to a climax, and "Voodoo

The Jimi Hendrix Experience
In 1966, Hendrix was discovered in New York, and taken to England where he formed his group with Noel Redding and Mitch Mitchell.

Chile" takes the guitar to its limits with crashing power and screaming, rasping notes.

Hendrix died tragically in London at the age of only 27, but his transcendent presence lives on.

CAREER HIGHLIGHTS

1962 Tours on the black music circuit.

1965 Forms his own band, Jimmy James and the Blue Flames.

1966 Taken to England by Chas Chandler. Forms the Jimi Hendix Experience.

1967 Breaks into the UK singles charts with "Hey Joe" at No.6, followed by "Purple Haze" at No.3 and "The Wind Cries Mary" at No.9. Plays the Monterey Pop Festival in California in June.

1968 Electric Ladyland double album reaches No.1 in US. Forms the Band Of Gypsys.

1969 Plays at the Woodstock Festival in New York State.

1970 The single "Voodoo Chile" charts in the UK at No.1.

Jimi at Woodstock
In 1969, Hendrix put in a stunning performance at the Woodstock Festival in New York State, with highlights such as a savage "The Star-Spangled Banner." His legacy is enormous and his recordings continue to have a tremendous influence on guitarists throughout the world.

Allan Holdsworth

Born 6 August, 1946, in Bradford, Yorkshire, England

An important innovator and an exceptional improviser, Allan Holdsworth created his own vocabulary of lines and chord voicings, taking him way ahead of his contemporaries.

Allan Holdsworth is a self-taught individualist who grew up with jazz and rock, and was inspired by saxophonist John Coltrane. He came to prominence through working in the British jazz scene in the 1970s, and joined jazz rock groups such as Tempest and Soft Machine.

Holdsworth plays his solo lines with his left hand sounding the notes, and he often uses four fingers per string as well as large fret stretches. He uses minimal right-hand picking, which gives him a smooth, floating sound. His solos incorporate large interval movements with rippling sheets of advanced melodic inventions, and he uses effects to give the guitar a sustaining violin or keyboard synthesizer-like sound and a tremolo arm for pitch movements.

In a duo with the jazz pianist Gordon Beck on the album *The Things You See*

(1980), he matches the intensity of the piano, using acoustic guitar on the unison heads and exuberant solos. On his solo album *Road Games* (1984), his astonishing solo on "Three Sheets To The Wind" has lyrical passages, complex phrasing, and unusual harmonic detours that culminate in a swirling, passionate climax.

Holdsworth adopted a SynthAxe guitar controller in the 1980s to extend his range of textures, and on his album *Atavachron* (1986) his composition "Non-Brewed Condiment" opens with a futuristic linear head, followed by a solo full of expression and explosive improvisation. Holdsworth continues to create original solos and harmonies using his unique voice and technique.

Flowing virtuosity
Holdworth's stretch-fingering legato soloing has been at the cutting edge of fusion.

CAREER HIGHLIGHTS

1969	Records album with band Igginbottom called *Igginbottom's Wrench*.
1971	Joins progressive rockers Tempest.
1973	Joins Soft Machine.
1975	Records the album *Bundles*.
1975	Joins Tony Williams' group Lifetime led by ex-Miles Davis drummer, and records the album *Believe It*.
1976	Records first solo album *Velvet Darkness*.
1982	Releases rock-influenced album *IOU*. Moves permanently to the US.
1983	Records solo album *Road Games*.
1992	Releases album *Wardenclyffe Tower*.
2003	The album *Then!*, featuring his band playing live in Tokyo in 1990, is released.

Blind Lemon Jefferson

Born July 11, 1897, in Couchman, Texas **Died** 1929

One of the first popular male country blues artists, Blind Lemon Jefferson accompanied himself with a sophisticated picking style, creating variations on blues, ragtime, and traditional harmonies.

CAREER HIGHLIGHTS

1917 Becomes established as a performer at house parties and moves to Dallas, Texas.

1925 Starts recording tracks for Paramount including "Black Snake Moan."

1927 Records tracks such as "Matchbox Blues" and "See That My Grave Is Kept Clean."

Blind Lemon Jefferson grew up within a vibrant traditional musical heritage and absorbed a wide range of influences from ragtime to blues and gospel music. He traveled in order to work and was for a time part of the music scene in Dallas, Texas, where he performed in the street as well as playing for dances and in bars. His primeval song themes and strong voice are accompanied by an intricate and imaginative fingerstyle. From 1925, he started making recordings and quickly achieved commercial success.

Jefferson was one of the first singers and guitarists to overcome racial barriers and break into the mainstream. He was astonishingly versatile, playing percussive ragtime on "Hot Dog" and slide on "Jack O' Diamond Blues." Jefferson showed how the guitar could become a vehicle for powerful musical expression, superseding the voice and providing rich accompaniment with countermelodies.

Robert Johnson

Born May 8, 1911, in Hazlehurst, Mississippi **Died** 1938

A legendary figure whose life is surrounded by myth, Robert Johnson brought together blues traditions, and produced a powerful focused style with picking and slide.

Robert Johnson grew up in an environment where he was able to distill elements from musicians such as Charley Patton, Son House, and Lonnie Johnson. He evolved within the repertoire and created new songs based on variations of traditional material.

Johnson's passionate and emotional vocals are supported by lucid and direct guitar parts. He uses open tunings, and his tone and sharp, acidic attack can be heard on the famous "Cross Road Blues." "Hellhound On My Tail" has wavering microtonal slide to convey persecution and fear, while a highlight is the shimmering slide on "Come On In My Kitchen." Johnson creates insistent rhythms and urgent high-register fills for "I Believe I'll Dust My Broom," "Sweet Home Chicago" rolls beautifully with the voice, and "Terraplane Blues" has a sophisticated funkiness.

CAREER HIGHLIGHTS

1930 Meets Son House; is inspired to develop his guitar playing.

1931 Begins to travel around the Mississippi Delta playing at juke joints and picnics.

1936 Starts recording a body of work in San Antonio, Texas.

1937 Makes his last recordings in Dallas, Texas.

B.B. King

Born September 16, 1925, in Indianola, Mississippi

The key figure in the development of electric blues guitar soloing, B.B. King forms a link between Delta traditions and the modern era. He has influenced blues and rock soloists from the 1950s to the present day.

B.B. King grew up playing guitar and singing in the blues environment of the Mississippi Delta. In 1946, he went to Memphis where he was influenced by his cousin, the blues guitarist and singer Bukka White. Molded by blues and gospel as well as jazz, King derived elements from figures that included Blind Lemon Jefferson, Lonnie Johnson, T-Bone Walker, and the jazz guitarist Charlie Christian.

King of the blues
B.B. King's guitar phrasing and melodic breaks are now part of the fabric of blues.

King concentrated on developing a linear guitar technique and largely avoided using block chordal playing. His unique style is based on using the guitar as a counterpart to his lyrics, answering his vocal phrases, and taking sensitive, emotional solos that are melodically accessible. He weaves subtle phrases in a unique way, and his string bending and vibrato add to his powerful presence. King also uses varied tones and controlled dynamics to add expressiveness to his electric guitar.

A superb showman, his classic album *Live At The Regal* (1965) highlights his fluent playing in an atmosphere where he takes long solos with abandon and energy.

CAREER HIGHLIGHTS

1946 Goes to Memphis. Helped by his cousin Bukka White in the art of the blues.

1948 Starts out as the Beale Street Blues Boy; later changes name to Blues Boy King, and finally shortens it to B.B. King.

1949 Signs a recording contract with RPM, part of Modern Records. Releases first single "Miss Martha King."

1952 "Three O'Clock Blues" becomes a No.1 hit on the US R&B charts.

1952 First national tour opens at Howard Theater in Washington D.C.

1970 The single "The Thrill Is Gone" reaches No.15 in the US charts.

1975 First guitarist to be chosen for *Guitar Player* magazine's Gallery of the Greats.

1987 Receives Lifetime Achievement Grammy.

Albert Lee

Born December 21, 1943, in Lingen, Herefordshire, England

A virtuoso country guitarist whose inventive, improvisational style has an effevescent edge, Albert Lee's playing blends a whole array of technical devices and licks.

Influenced by such virtuoso figures as the electric country guitarist Jimmy Bryant and the rock 'n' roll guitarist Cliff Gallup, as well as jazz musicians, Albert Lee developed a high level of technique and a tremendous command of country guitar music. He has reinvigorated country and fiddle vocabulary with twangy, rhythmically propulsive playing, and his sparkling, metallic tone made him stand out in the British music scene.

Lee enhanced his reputation as a guitarist with his solo album *Hiding* (1979), which features "Country Boy"—a signature instrumental full of scintillating variations that showcases his technical dexterity. Using a sharp, snappy tone, he plays melodic lines, fast skittering motifs, passages of highly controlled double-stopping, and uses textures such as muting and echo. Lee has worked with a variety of musicians, from the Everly Brothers to Eric Clapton. His incisive articulation and musicality carries on the heritage of traditional electric country playing at its best.

CAREER HIGHLIGHTS

1958 Picks up his first guitar, a Hofner President acoustic archtop.

1976 Replaces James Burton in Emmylou Harris' Hot Band.

1978 Plays on Harris' album *Quarter Moon In A Ten Cent Town*.

1979 Releases solo album *Hiding*.

1980 Tours with Eric Clapton.

1983 Plays with the Everly Brothers at their reunion concert.

1987 Releases instrumental album *Speechless*.

Adrian Legg

Born May 16, 1948, in London, England

An individualistic acoustic guitarist with a superb technique, Adrian Legg draws from every area of music without sounding derivative.

CAREER HIGHLIGHTS

1972 Tours UK and Europe with country and western band New Frontier.

1977 Releases first album *Requiem For A Hick*.

1985 Records album *Fretmelt*, and starts to gain wide recognition.

1990 Releases *Guitars and Other Cathedrals*.

1993 *Guitar Player* readers' poll in the US votes Legg top acoustic player for four consecutive years.

2003 Records album *Guitar Bones*.

With a unique fingerstyle technique, Adrian Legg uses an array of open tunings and original chord voicings, creating variations with a smooth articulation, fast arpeggiation, melodic control, and counterpoint. He is also able to add devices such as two- and three-string bends. His music is played with spirit and he generates ideas that range from crossover classical pieces to eclectic vignettes. His album *Technopicker* (1983) illustrates his style, with "Pass The Valium" using both liquid legato lines and a biting incisiveness. "Een Kleyne Komedye" is a futuristic folk-style technical tour de force incorporating country-style techniques and sounds.

Paco de Lucía

Born December 21, 1947, in Algeciras, Spain

The great flamenco virtuoso Paco de Lucía brought a new level of technical brilliance to the genre, and incorporated ideas from other styles, including jazz and Brazilian music.

Growing up within a family who played flamenco, Paco de Lucía was encouraged to practice the guitar fervently. Heavily influenced by Niño Ricardo and Sabicas, he was a prodigy. During his teens, his fast, inventive playing, bright tone, and physical attack won competitions. He continued to develop his razor-sharp articulation and improvisational abilities throughout the 1960s, adding power and depth. On his album *Fuente y Caudal*

Guitar techniques
With rasgueao strumming, picado, tremolo, and alzapua thumb-picking, De Lucía has developed one of the greatest techniques.

(1973), the title track is an atmospheric Moorish-flavored taranta, played with a dark intensity using crystalline harmonies, expressive lines, and tremolo. For the rumba "Entre Dos Aguas," a popular hit in Spain, de Lucía applied a modern popular approach, using a rhythm section with electric bass and percussion.

De Lucía continued to incorporate new approaches on *Almoraima* (1976). The title track, a buleria, features chopped rhythms, a delicate melody and Latin-jazz influences. The rumba "Rio Ancho" has a seductive rhythmic backing and features a mixture of lyrical themes and explosive passages of invention. On the live album *Castro Marin* (1979), he played in a guitar trio

with jazz musicians John McLaughlin and Larry Coryell. The album mixes flamenco with jazz and other influences, and led to the formation of a trio with McLaughlin and Al Di Meola, which featured high-energy rhythmic chordal backdrops and virtuoso exchanges of soloing.

De Lucía has continued to develop group and solo work, using a sextet lineup on *Solo Quiero Caminar* (1981). He also recorded sublime traditional flamenco, with pieces such as the inspired "La Barrosa" (1987) and the heartfelt tribut "Tio Sabas" (1990). His speed, power, and improvisational skills have kept him at the top.

Musical horizons
De Lucía has introduced the use of open thematic arrangements in flamenco and pioneered the use of a modern rhythm section.

CAREER HIGHLIGHTS

1961 Starts touring with the flamenco troupe of dancer José Greco.

1967 Releases first solo album *La Fabulosa Guitarra de Paco de Lucía*.

1968 Meets premier flamenco singer Cameron de la Isla. They go on to produce 10 albums together.

1973 Releases the album *Fuente y Caudal*, which includes the track "Entre Dos Aguas." This becomes a hit in Spain.

1976 Releases *Almoraima* album, featuring group tracks, including "Río Ancho."

1979 Forms trio with John McLaughlin and Larry Coryell.

1981 Releases the album *Solo Quiero Caminar*, featuring a sextet including three guitars.

1991 Records Joaquín Rodrigo's classical work *Concerto de Aranjuez*.

Johnny Marr

Born October 31, 1963, in Manchester, England

One of the finest pop guitarists to emerge in the last 20 years, Johnny Marr's inventive way of writing and layering ideas within songs has brought different textures to the creative side of popular music.

CAREER HIGHLIGHTS

1982 Writes songs with Morrissey and forms The Smiths.

1983 "This Charming Man" charts in the UK at No.25.

1984 The group's debut album *The Smiths* reaches No.2 in the UK.

1985 No.1 in the UK with *Meat Is Murder.*

1987 The Smiths split up.

1989 Works with Bernard Sumner of New Order.

Developing an original approach based on pop, soul, and folk music, as well as strands from African guitar styles, Johnny Marr has built his thoughtful guitar-playing style around the creation of carefully layered melodic parts and supportive harmonies for his songwriting. With the singer Morrissey in The Smiths, he produced the engaging ideas heard on the album *The Smiths* (1984). Marr uses pairs of notes in thirds and other intervals for melodic breaks and underlying countermelodies. On the album *The Queen Is Dead* (1986), Marr's detailed touches abound. He blends acoustic and electric guitars effectively and sets up attractive contrasts.

After The Smiths split up in 1987, Marr continued to explore experimental pop, funk, and soul styles. He recorded with The The on the album *Mind Bomb* (1989), and collaborated with Bernard Sumner to produce the album *Electronic* (1991). Marr has produced an extensive body of fine songs, and sophisticated and musically intelligent guitar work.

Pat Martino

Born August 25, 1944, in Philadelphia, Pennsylvania

A jazz guitarist who bridges bebop, modal jazz, and fusion, Pat Martino creates intense improvisation based around long lines of extended phrasing. He is one of a small band of exceptional guitar soloists.

Pat Martino developed a jazz vocabulary at a young age. Influenced by Wes Montgomery, among others, he adopted elements from blues to modal jazz. He was inspired by saxophonist John Coltrane and created a synthesis of bop licks and open-ended, scale-based thinking. At the end of the 1960s and into the early 1970s, his playing was innovative. On *Desperado* (1970), he plays Sonny Rollins' composition "Oleo" and his solo consists of a series of soaring, extended bop lines played with an insistent swing while retaining a metronomic accuracy. His mesmeric flow can be heard on Coltrane's *Impressions* (1974), where he builds a solo of bluesy minor phrases, intervallic motifs, and repeating cyclical ideas. Martino's individual sound has great momentum and inventive content, and his playing is part of the heritage of modern soloing in jazz.

CAREER HIGHLIGHTS

1967 First solo album *El Hombre.*

1972 Releases *Live!* album.

1974 Releases album *Consciousness.*

1984 Starts remarkable comeback after losing his memory following an operation on a brain aneurism in 1980.

John McLaughlin

Born January 4, 1942, Kirk Sandall, Yorkshire, England

A musical visionary, John McLaughlin has created new virtuoso playing styles on the electric, steel string acoustic, and nylon string guitar, paving the way for the future.

John McLaughlin grew up with classical music and the blues, and as a teenager was inspired by jazz. He moved to the US in 1969 and joined drummer Tony Williams' group recording the album *Emergency* (1969). Here, his fast articulation and original playing style can be heard on "Spectrum." He also recorded with Miles Davis on *In A Silent Way* (1969) and other albums. McLaughlin takes driving emotional solos using steel-string guitar on *My Goal's Beyond* (1970) and explores open-ended Indian-flavored ideas.

He formed the Mahavishnu Orchestra, and their ground-breaking jazz-rock album *The Inner Mounting Flame* (1971) features surging electric solos on "Meeting Of The Spirits" and "Noonward Race." He plays an innovative steel-string acoustic guitar on the album *Natural Elements* (1977), which uses ringing drone chords, fast heads, and takes cutting solos with Indian-style inflections and bending. He put together a guitar trio with Paco de Lucía and Al Di Meola in 1979, and their blend of acoustic jazz and flamenco music can be heard on *Friday Night In San Francisco* (1980).

CAREER HIGHLIGHTS

1969 Records first solo album *Extrapolation*, then moves to the US to join Tony Williams' group Lifetime. Records with Miles Davis.

1970 Plays on Miles Davis album *A Tribute To Jack Johnson.*

1971 Forms his own group the Mahavishnu Orchestra, with Jerry Goodman on violin, Jan Hammer on keyboards, Rick Laird on bass, and Billy Cobham on drums. Records the album *The Inner Mounting Flame.*

1975 Forms the group Shakti with Zakir Hussain on tabla and L. Shankar on violin.

1979 Forms guitar trio with Paco de Lucía and Lary Coryell (who was later replaced by Al Di Meola).

Modern virtuoso
One of the most important guitarists in the last 40 years, McLaughlin has mastered jazz and incorporated Indian and classical ideas.

Pat Metheny

Born August 12, 1954, in Lee's Summit, Missouri

One of the foremost jazz players, Pat Metheny is also a highly regarded composer who has created material that ranges from dreamlike pastoral impressions to driving fusion. He uses a range of different settings and contexts for his own individual style.

Pat Metheny has been molded by influences that range from guitarist Jim Hall through to classical music. His first album, *Bright Size Life* (1976), conjures gentle soundscapes with ringing harmonic movements that use carefully thought-out voicings. He formed a new quartet and released albums including *American Garage* (1979), where he creates orchestral sounds using a guitar synthesizer, and takes solos that range from lyrical to complex.

CAREER HIGHLIGHTS

1976 Releases first solo album *Bright Size Life*, featuring Jaco Pastorius on bass.

1978 Forms Pat Metheny Group with Lyle Mays on keyboards, Mark Egan on bass, and Dan Gottlieb on drums.

1979 Releases *American Garage*.

1982 Releases *Offramp* on which he uses a guitar synthesizer.

1985 Plays free jazz on *Song X* with saxophonist Ornette Coleman.

Wes Montgomery

Born March 6, 1925, in Indianapolis, Indiana **Died** 1968

The embodiment of jazz guitar tradition, Wes Montgomery was one of the most expressive guitarists. He played with a bop style and an intuitive genius.

Surrounded by a musical family and inspired by Charlie Christian and Django Reinhardt, Wes Montgomery started to develop his own technique by using his thumb to create a jazz vocabulary with a rich, full tone and driving swing, as well as chord melodies and rhythms. His album *The Wes Montgomery Trio* (1959) features a magical version of Thelonius Monk's "Round Midnight," where his solo is profound with sublime flourishes of invention. Montgomery made a breakthrough with his album *The Incredible Jazz Guitar Of Wes Montgomery* (1960). This features his composition "West Coast Blues," with its attractive melody and an inventive melodic solo. Montgomery was one of the major figures in jazz guitar and his influence is still felt today.

Invention and emotion
Montgomery had a great feel, ranging from sensitive playing on ballads to hard-driving riffs and ebullient solos.

CAREER HIGHLIGHTS

1959 Releases *The Wes Montgomery Trio*.

1960 Releases the album *The Incredible Jazz Guitar Of Wes Montgomery*. Briefly works with John Coltrane.

1965 Makes live recordings for the album *Smokin' At The Half Note*.

Gary Moore

Born April 4, 1952, in Belfast, Northern Ireland

One of the finest blues rock soloists, Gary Moore's work ranges from fast and incendiary to slow and lyrical, and he has created a range of memorable guitar solos.

Brought up with the influences of 1960s blues and rock, Gary Moore was a prodigy able to play with a surging intensity and articulation. He played on and off with the group Thin Lizzy, with highlights including tracks such as "Still In Love With You" (1974), where he plays attractive emotional phrases, and "Toughest Street In Town" (1979). Moore also played in jazz rock fusion groups such as Colosseum II in the mid-1970s. Under his own name, "Parisienne Walkways" (1979) has a rich sustaining melody sound and a solo that uses space, with touches such as string-bending, slides, and hammering to create variety and expression. At the same time, he produced tracks such as "Hurricane" (1979), which have an effervescent velocity. He plays metallic rock on "Out In The Fields" (1985), and his blues roots can be heard on "Still Got The Blues" (1990). Moore has produced an exceptional blend of traditional blues and rock.

CAREER HIGHLIGHTS

1973 Releases first solo album *Grinding Stone*. Joins Thin Lizzy.

1979 Records *Black Rose* with Thin Lizzy. Solo single "Parisienne Walkways" reaches No.8 in UK.

1990 Releases album *Still Got The Blues* featuring classic blues tracks.

1992 Releases album *After Hours*.

1995 Releases tribute album to guitarist Peter Green *Blues for Greeny*.

Tom Morello

Born May 30, 1964, in New York City

One of the few innovative guitar voices to emerge in the 1990s, Tom Morello has created a challenging sonic palette with the guitar. He has also developed techniques to control sound-processing so that it sits across driving rock rhythms and alongside hip hop and rap vocals.

Tom Morello was influenced by rock, heavy metal, and funk. With Rage Against The Machine, he created a fresh approach to the capacities of the guitar. He uses turntable-style interjections and makes the guitar generate sounds like synthesizers and samplers. On the album *Rage Against The Machine* (1993) "Killing In The Name" has crunching resonating decay, uneasy lines, declamatory fuzzy distortion, and a high-pitched, seesawing solo break with a whistling sound. He has created his own futuristic language that combines rock with imaginative solo breaks, distorted harmonized parts, and wild pitch shifts and registers.

Sonic approaches
Morello forged a new voice for the guitar by combining heavy rock with funk and rap.

CAREER HIGHLIGHTS

1992 Formed Rage Against The Machine. Releases first single "Killing In The Name" and album *Rage Against The Machine*.

1994 The band plays at the Glastonbury Festival.

1996 The album *Evil Empire* goes to No.1 in the US charts.

Jimmy Page

Born January 9, 1944, in Heston, Middlesex, England

Jimmy Page redefined studio sounds and rock arrangements, and created a template for heavy metal. His solos, riffs, and chordal playing are part of the vocabulary of modern electric guitar.

Jimmy Page took up the guitar at the age of 15 and became interested in rock 'n' roll and blues, as well as folk. He worked as a session musician first, then in 1968 formed the group Led Zeppelin. On their first album, *Led Zeppelin* (1969), Page sets up hard-edged, innovative guitar sounds in the studio. "Good Times Bad Times" has power chords, and the guitar plays cascading lines and has a violinlike sustain. He plays acoustic folk-influenced guitar on "Black Mountain Side" and creates adventurous, shifting, and colorful textures for "Dazed And Confused." On *Led Zeppelin II* (1969), Page created a unique tone for the guitar with the catchy riff "Whole Lotta Love," which also has

Page and Plant
The combination of Robert Plant's voice and Jimmy Page's guitar gave Led Zeppelin an intense, hard-driving edge as well as lyricism.

dramatic power chords and lead breaks. Page takes an explosive bluesy solo on "Since I've Been Loving You" (1970).

One of the most famous tracks, "Stairway To Heaven" on the untitled *Led Zeppelin* album (1971), features layering and changes of pace, with acoustic guitar, electric 12-string guitar, fanfare-type effects, and a graceful, inspired solo full of soaring melodic phrases.

Guitar riffs
Page created magnetic guitar riffs such as "Heartbreaker" (1969).

Rock legend
Page produced some of the most enduring material in rock. He is shown here (right) in the 1970s with his Gibson double-necked guitar.

CAREER HIGHLIGHTS

1966 Joins the Yardbirds and plays alongside Jeff Beck.

1968 Forms the New Yardbirds, which changes its name to Led Zeppelin, with Robert Plant on vocals, John Paul Jones on bass, and John Bonham on drums.

1969 Release of the first Led Zeppelin album. *Led Zeppelin II* is released in the fall and goes to No.1 in the UK and US.

1970 *Led Zeppelin III* is released and goes to No.1 in the UK and US.

1979 Release of last Led Zeppelin studio album *In Through the Out Door*.

1988 Releases solo album *Outrider*.

1993 Releases *Complete Studio Recordings*.

Joe Pass

Born January 13, 1929, in New Bruswick, New Jersey   **Died** 1994

The figure who established solo jazz guitar-playing, Joe Pass developed a hard-swinging style of playing standards with chord melodies, improvisation, and bass lines.

Joe Pass was inspired by figures such as Django Reinhardt and Charlie Christian and absorbed ideas from jazz piano playing. His solo album *Virtuoso* (1974) established him as a major voice in jazz guitar. Pass plays infectious versions of jazz standards as chord melodies with a driving rhythm and uses mobile partial chords, bass lines, and linear breaks. On "Night And Day" his playing bubbles with enthusiasm. He plays up-tempo on "How High The Moon," which has highly charged strumming and improvised passages that run between different registers.

CAREER HIGHLIGHTS

1964 Releases album *For Django* playing Django Reinhardt material.

1973 Records the first of a series of *Virtuoso* albums on which he plays solo guitar.

1974 Records album *Ella and Oscar Peterson* with Ella Fitzgerald.

Rafael Rabello

Born October 31, 1962, in Petropolis, Rio de Janeiro, Brazil   **Died** 1995

A guitarist who stood out as one of the great emerging virtuosos of the nylon-string guitar, Rafael Rabello blended traditions with innovative techniques on six- and seven-string guitars.

Rafael (spelled Raphael after 1991) Rabello came from a large musical family. Drawing from Brazilian choro and samba traditions, the approach of Garoto and Baden Powell, and classical and flamenco influences, he became a technically brilliant prodigy. His control with each finger, and independent movement with counterpoint, arpeggiation, and tremolo were exceptional. His talent and sensitivity can be heard on the album *Rafael Rabello* (1988). "Lamentos Do Morro" features recurring tremolo with moving chords and punchy staccato. On "Comovida" he improvises with a sensuous legato string tone and color, delicate arpeggiation, and altered scales to create a tangled beauty. "Ainda Me Relondo" weaves inventive low bass figures beneath rhythmic, bouncing chords.

CAREER HIGHLIGHTS

1982 Releases *Rafael Sete Cordas*.

1988 Records *Rafael Rabello*, playing seven-string solo guitar.

1990 Releases *À Flor da Pele* with the singer Ney Matogrosso.

1992 Releases *Todos os Tons* with Paco de Lucía, Tom Jobim, and Jack Morelenbaum.

Baden Powell

Born August 6, 1937, in Varre-e-Sai, Brazil **Died** 2000

An outstanding virtuoso on the nylon-string acoustic guitar, Baden Powell established a modern style of Brazilian playing that incorporated elements from classical, jazz, and African music.

Growing up within the rich environment of Brazilian music and studying classical guitar, Baden Powell was influenced by the approach of guitarists such as Garoto and Paulinho Noguiera. He built his own vocabulary by mastering jazz harmonies blended with samba, bossa nova, and native rhythmic traditions. His fingerstyle approach is characterized by a strong tone and physicality, technical flair, and rhythmic verve. He wrote classics such as "Samba Triste" (1959), and worked with Tom Jobim. His personality can be heard in the early 1960s on "The Girl From Ipanema," where he plays rolling chords, rhythms, and flowing inventive arpeggios. His standard "Berimbau" (1964) features a powerfully hypnotic, rhythmic modal figure, and a catchy melody. Powell continued to create beautiful and varied material on the album *Poema On Guitar* (1967), where "Feitinha Pro Poeta" contrasts dissonant chords, and a light, dancing melody. His unique approach to jazz can be heard on Jerome Kern's "All The Things You Are."

Brazilian passion
Powell's intensity and musicality enlarged the repertoire of the nylon-string guitar and inspired players throughout the world.

Nylon-string legend
During his long career, Powell created a large body of work both as a player and a composer and made many recordings.

CAREER HIGHLIGHTS

1959 Has hit with his composition "Samba Triste." Releases first album *Apresentando Baden Powell e Seu Violão.*

1962 Meets lyricist and poet Vinicius de Moraes and works with him on compositions.

1967 Plays at the Berlin Jazz Days festival. Releases solo album *Tristeza On Guitar.*

Django Reinhardt

Born January 4, 1910, in Liverchies, Belgium   **Died** 1953

The legendary genius of jazz guitar, Django Reinhardt emerged with a unique swing style and a flamboyant virtuosity that put him far ahead of his contemporaries.

A Manouche gypsy brought up on the outskirts of Paris, Django Reinhardt was surrounded by gypsy music and absorbed musical ideas from jazz recordings and classical music. At the age of 18, his left hand was severely maimed in a fire and he was forced to reinvent his technique mainly using two fingers.

Gypsy genius
Django's legacy is immortal and will always be an inspiration to all guitarists.

In early recordings with the Hot Club, his playing can be heard on "Tiger Rag," which has fast unison guitar with violin, razor-sharp lines, staccato phrases, and ringing notes. On "Dinah" he weaves and embroiders the melody and takes a solo with imaginative delicate lines, surging passages with fast scales, and cutting octaves. Django's composition "Djangology" (1937) has a lively melody, and soloing full of detail and finely controlled invention, and "Swanee River" (1937) has a snappy solo full of mesmerizing turns of invention. He plays a fizzing solo, catchy discords, and fast bursts of strumming on *Limehouse Blues* (1937).

Django played propulsive backing rhythms in the group, and recorded solo pieces such as the rapturous "Improvisation" (1937). One of his most famous and romantic compositions, "Nuages" (1940), has a haunting, sentimental melody, and a solo with artificial harmonics and sumptuous phrases. After the end of World War II, he used an electric pickup. Late recordings from 1949 to 1953 show Django continuing to play stunningly on pieces such as "Boogie Woogie."

CAREER HIGHLIGHTS

1934 Formed the Quintette du Hot Club de France. The group starts recording.

1935 The group plays at the Salle Pleyel in Paris.

1936 They play in Spain, Netherlands, and England. Django records with Coleman Hawkins and Benny Carter.

1938 Hot Club tops the bill at the Cambridge Theatre, London.

1946 Has a reunion with Stephane Grappelli. Visits the US and tours with pianist and composer Duke Ellington.

The Quintette du Hot Club de France
Appearing in France and Europe in the 1930s, the group featured Stephane Grappelli and Django Reinhardt exchanging wonderful solos.

David Russell

Born June 1, 1953, in Glasgow, Scotland

A marvelous interpreter of classical repertoire, David Russell is able to perform different types of music and convey moods that range from forceful and rhythmic to gentle and lyrical.

CAREER HIGHLIGHTS

1995 Releases *Music of Barrios* album.

1997 Made a Fellow of The Royal Academy of Music.

2001 Releases *David Russell Plays Baroque Music*.

Brought up on the island of Menorca, David Russell was inspired by the recordings of Andrès Segovia and largely taught himself by ear. His sublime tone and range, and depth of musicalty on technically difficult material can be heard on his recording *The Music Of Barrios* (1995), featuring music such as "La Catedral." Russell is a master at drawing tone from the guitar, and creates notes that have a luminous and resonant quality. Today, Russell is critically acclaimed worldwide.

Joe Satriani

Born July 15, 1956, in Long Island, New York

A modern instrumental rock virtuoso, Joe Satriani plays fast, soaring solos and utilizes a range of techniques. His tour de force approach has made him an icon for guitarists.

Influenced by rock and blues as well as jazz rock fusion and classical music, Joe Satriani developed a strong command of theory and musical structure, and worked at mastering electric guitar techniques. On the album *Surfing with the Alien* (1987), the title track opens with crunching rock riffs and a muted wah-wah melody sound. Satriani solos over tonal centers, using screaming high-register playing and trills, finely controlled tremolo bar movements, harmonics, flamboyant bending, double stopping, and tapping. Typical of his work is "Crushing Day," where chopped rock supports violinlike sustained notes playing the melody. "Satch Boogie" has exciting riffs, soaring notes, and advanced rock phrasing taken to the extreme.

CAREER HIGHLIGHTS

1986 Records his debut instrumental album *Not Of This Earth*.

1987 Releases *Surfing with the Alien*, which reaches No.29 in the US charts.

1989 Releases the album *Flying in a Blue Dream*.

1990 Voted Best Overall Guitarist in *Guitar Player* magazine poll.

1993 Releases double album *Time Machine* with both new and live material and his unavailable 1984 EP *Joe Satriani*.

Electric maestro
Satriani has extended rock guitar with altered scales and unusual chords, and his approach has made him one of the most influential of guitarists.

Andrès Segovia

Born February 21, 1893, in Linares, Granada, Spain   **Died** 1987

A legend of the classical guitar in the 20th century, Andrès Segovia gave the instrument new stature. He was the guardian of tradition, and worked to establish the guitar within the mainstream in classical music.

Segovia mastered a large repertoire, and transcribed and adapted J. S. Bach for the guitar. His interpretation can be heard on recordings from 1927, including a "Gavotte" and "Rondeau" from Bach's Partita in E major and a "Courante" from a Cello Suite. His playing of Bach has a strong, characterful musicality and accenting, with emphasized tempos, rubatos, and dynamics. Through his advocacy, many composers wrote new works for the guitar. The Spaniards Joaquin Turina and Federico Moreno Torroba wrote works with Spanish flavors, including elements from flamenco.

Segovia also encouraged the Mexican composer Manuel Ponce to write music in the style of earlier eras, and Italian Mario Castelnuevo-Tedesco wrote a guitar concerto for him in 1939. After the war, Segovia continued to make important recordings of Albeniz and Granados and continued to contribute at many levels.

Concert artist
Segovia performed in the Alhambra in Granada, Spain. He maintained his concert career for more than 70 years.

Maestro
Segovia was a self-taught player with a charismatic presence.

CAREER HIGHLIGHTS

1909	Makes his debut at the Centro Artistico in Granada.
1912	Plays at the Ateneo in Madrid for the first time.
1916	Tours South America.
1927	Makes his first recordings of Bach and Sor.
1935	Performs his adaptation of the "Chaconne" from Bach's *Second Partita* for solo violin in Paris.
1947	Persuades Albert Augustine to start making nylon strings.
1958	Gives the first performance of Joaquin Rodrigo's *Fantasia para un Gentilhombre*.

Richard Thompson

Born April 3, 1949, in London, England

A pivotal figure in the history of folk rock, Richard Thompson is an outstanding guitarist and singer-songwriter, whose incisive tone and originality have created new forms of modern crossover music.

As a young man, Richard Thompson was interested in a wide range of music and developed an original sound and touch on the electric guitar, projecting motifs and solos with a powerful tremolo and adding a rocky edge. He has absorbed melodic ideas from British folk music and transmuted them into fascinating guitar parts. This can be heard on Fairport Convention's folk rock album *Liege & Lief* (1969). He adds expressive searing touches to "Matty Groves" and "Tam Lin," and on "Medley" he plays traditional jigs and reels. On *Rumour and Sigh* (1991), one of his popular solos is "Mother Knows Best," and an acoustic highlight is "1952 Vincent Black Lightning."

CAREER HIGHLIGHTS

1967 Forms Fairport Convention with Ashley Hutchings on bass, Simon Nicol on guitar, Martin Lamble on drums, and Judy Dyble on vocals.

1969 Releases *Liege and Lief* with Fairport Convention.

1974 Records debut album with Linda Thompson *I Want to See the Bright Lights Tonight.*

1982 Releases *Shoot Out The Lights.*

Ralph Towner

Born March 1, 1940, in Chehalis, Washington

An individualist in crossover jazz, Ralph Towner plays nylon-string classical and 12-string guitar. His compositions are a blend of classical techniques and jazz, with imaginative textures.

Ralph Towner studied classical guitar and was inspired by jazz and Brazilian music. On his album *Solstice*, he creates magical soundscapes such as "Oceanus" and "Nimbus" using sparkling textures. On his live album *Solo Concert* (1980), the astonishing "Train Of Thought" has a variety of textures, with Japanese kotolike sounds, interwoven dissonant harmonies, harmonics, tapped notes, and catchy, low bass figures. Towner's visionary playing and writing have broken down barriers and opened new vistas.

CAREER HIGHLIGHTS

1970 Joins the group Oregon, and they release *Our First Record.*

1975 Releases album *Solstice* with Jan Garbarek, Eberhard Weber, and Jon Christensen.

Steve Vai

Born June 6, 1960, in Long Island, New York

A guitar player who has built up a style of virtuosic force and great projection, Steve Vai has a tremendous command of the instrument and plays with confidence.

Steve Vai was inspired by players such as Jimi Hendrix and Eddie Van Halen and studied with Joe Satriani. He worked with Frank Zappa and released a solo instrumental debut album *Flex-Able* (1984), which featured fast soloing and unusual arrangements. His playing is powerful, assured, and virtuosic with solos that use scales, patterns, and motifs. He plays dense concentrations of notes with telling, long sustain, and often builds his solos to a a high point with screaming, linear pyrotechnics. On his album *Passion and Warfare* (1990), "Erotic Nightmares" uses modern techniques to convey the strange and bizarre. "For

The Love Of God" has a contemplative sustained melody and a tour de force solo. Vai is as an influential rock soloist, and his differing moods and humor give his music a refreshing dimension.

CAREER HIGHLIGHTS

1981 Plays and tours with Frank Zappa and appears on the live album *Tinseltown Rebellion* (1981).

1990 Releases album *Passion and Warfare*, which reaches No.18 in the US charts and No.8 in the UK charts.

1996 Releases the album *Fire Garden*, which is split into Phase I with instrumental music and Phase II mainly with vocal tracks.

Stevie Ray Vaughan

Born October 3, 1954, in Dallas, Texas **Died** 1990

A guitarist who reforged electric blues soloing, Stevie Ray Vaughan produced a strong, rich-textured tone and played with verve and commitment. His wide command of the traditional blues vocabulary of licks and phrases, and his intensity, gave his roots style great appeal.

Brought up in a musical family, Stevie Ray Vaughan was inspired and molded by guitarists of the 1950s and 1960s, including Albert King and Jimi Hendrix. Vaughan brings an authentic touch to the blues, and his timing, feel, and ability to juxtapose combinations of motifs and ideas can be heard on his album *Texas Flood* (1983). The title track has inspired soloing with sustaining notes and tension release phrasing. Vaughan infused blues and rock guitar with vitality and meaning.

CAREER HIGHLIGHTS

1962 Starts playing the guitar at the age of seven.

1983 Releases solo debut album *Texas Flood*, which is critically acclaimed and reaches No.38 in the US charts.

1984 Releases album *Couldn't Stand The Weather* featuring heavy rock approaches.

1985 Awarded a Grammy for his contribution to *Blues Explosion* anthology.

Eddie Van Halen

Born January 26, 1957, in Nijmegen, Netherlands

An innovator who revolutionized electric guitar techniques, Eddie Van Halen absorbed ideas from classical music to create an entirely new linear vocabulary of arpeggios and motifs.

Eddie Van Halen came from a musical family and played the piano as a child. He took up the guitar after being inspired by rock guitar and eventually worked out his own way of playing the instrument, so that he could play lines and arpeggios with a seamless, flowing virtuosity. He taps upper notes on the fingerboard to conjure effortless speed, and he often groups notes into fast patterns that swirl and cascade in a breathtaking torrent. His playing can be heard on the album *Van Halen* (1978), where his astonishing solo on "Eruption" has a ferocious edge and a torrent of keyboard-style lines, which then sounded almost impossible to play on a guitar. His velocity and wild dive-bombing tremolo bar sounds injected a new type of physical excitement and shifted the gears in rock soloing. His playing on nylon-string guitar can be heard on "Spanish Fly" (1979), as well as electric solos with a challenging edge such as "Hot For Teacher" (1984). Van Halen's explosive metallic attack brought about a sea change in rock and heavy metal guitar-playing.

Guitar virtuoso
Van Halen's style of technically incisive soloing brought about a revolution in guitar-playing.

Tapping
Van Halen astounded the guitar world with his technique of tapping upper fingerboard notes to create surging virtuosic lines.

CAREER HIGHLIGHTS

1965 Moves with his family to the United States.

1975 Forms the group Van Halen with his brother Alex on drums.

1978 Makes his debut on the seminal album *Van Halen*.

1979 Releases *Van Halen II*, which goes to No.6 in the UK charts. Wins the Best Rock Guitarist poll in *Guitar Player* magazine.

1984 Releases the album *1984*, which incorporates the use of synthesizers.

Doc Watson

Born March 2, 1923, in Deep Gap, North Carolina

An exceptional acoustic folk and bluegrass guitarist, Doc Watson plays intricate instrumentals, and his flatpicking style is a model of melodic, harmonic, and rhythmic control.

CAREER HIGHLIGHTS

1963 Debut album with *The Doc Watson Family*. Plays at the Newport Folk Festival.

1964 Releases his solo album *Doc Watson*.

1966 Records the album *Southbound* with his son Merle on guitar.

1967 Records *Ballads from Deep Gap*, an album of traditional material from around his home.

Doc Watson developed a style that was based on instrumental folk music. He was influenced by figures ranging from Blind Lemon Jefferson to Merle Travis. Watson's fine, beautifully controlled technique flows with chordal harmonies and melodic ideas, and he plays improvised breaks. His emergence from the backwoods stunned folk purists and had a great impact on acoustic guitar-playing. His lively, dancing style, that mixes single lines with strumming, can be heard to great effect on his album *Doc Watson* (1964). "Sitting On Top Of The World" has rolling bass and inventive arpeggiation, and his infectious flatpicking virtuosity can be heard on "Black Mountain Rag." Later, Watson played for a number of years in an outstanding duo with his son Merle.

John Williams

Born April 24, 1941, in Melbourne, Australia

A classical guitarist possessed of a seemingly effortless technical accuracy, clarity, and articulation, John Williams has become one of the world's greatest players.

John Williams was taught by his father, Len Williams, and subsequently studied with Andrés Segovia. Early concerts featured works by Sanz, Bach, Scarlatti, and Sor. His abilities with European and South American composers display clinical technical mastery and fine interpretation. He has also had a great deal of music written for him, including works by Stephen Dodgson and Peter Sculthorpe. Among recording highlights is Paganini's Capriccio No.1 (1965). The album *John Williams Plays Spanish Music* (1970) has a definitive reading of the music of Granados, and at the beginning of the 1970s, his arrangements of the Bach Lute Suites were outstanding. Williams is also a pioneer of crossover music, and his album *Changes* (1971) includes the famous "Cavatina" by Stanley Myers, and Bach with a rock backing.

He continued to play classical music and during the 1970s he rediscovered the music of Barrios. He formed the group Sky in 1979, fusing classical with rock and jazz, and introducing the use of a microphone to amplify the guitar. Williams has maintained his popularity and he continues to experiment with innovative world music ideas.

CAREER HIGHLIGHTS

1958 Plays a recital in Siena, Italy, and at the Wigmore Hall, London, to great acclaim.

1977 Releases the album *John Williams Plays The Music Of Agustin Barrios*.

1979 Has a hit with "Cavatina," which goes to No.5 in the UK singles chart. Forms the group Sky.

1990 Records the album *Spirit of the Guitar— Music of the Americas*.

Frank Zappa

Born December 21, 1940, in Baltimore, Maryland   **Died** 1993

A brilliant visionary whose work reflects advanced compositional methods and inspirational writing, Frank Zappa was one of the most original and creative electric guitarists in rock.

Growing up with rock 'n' roll and blues, Frank Zappa took up the guitar and became interested in modern and avant-garde jazz and classical music. His guitar technique with its legato articulation had an array of detail with slides, slurs, hammer ons and pull offs, bends, and trills. His reedy sustaining sound, with wah wah and sophisticated studio effects and procedures, had a speech-inflected intensity and has affinities with the violin and saxophone. Zappa used blues, jazz lines, Indian, and Arabic flavors and modes to create exclamatory melodic phrases, and intervals and complex rhythmic passages. An intense singing guitar tone with distortion and wah wah is used on the outstanding album *Hot Rats* (1969), where he played theme and variations style guitar solos on "Son Of Mr. Green Genes."

A genius with humor
Zappa's humor and imagination have inspired guitarists and broadened and enriched music. He produced an unparalleled body of material.

Guitarist and composer
Zappa's writing was highly original, and his guitar playing, with its rich, idiosyncratic vocabulary, was often central to his work and conveyed a challenging outlook and philosophy.

CAREER HIGHLIGHTS

1966	Releases first album *Freak Out* with the Mothers Of Invention.
1969	Releases double album *Uncle Meat* as well as *Hot Rats* with Captain Beefheart on vocals.
1974	Records album *Apostrophe*, which reaches No.10 in the US charts.
1975	Releases album *One Size Fits All*, which features the solo "Inca Roads."
1982	Compilation album *Shut Up 'N Play Yer Guitar* features guitar highlights from the late 1970s.
1987	Wins a Grammy for *Jazz From Hell*.

CLASSIC
GUITARS

History of the guitar

The earliest surviving guitars from Europe in the 16th and 17th centuries have a body with incurved sides and gut strings played with the fingers or a quill plectrum. Ancestors of the guitar may be very ancient: Hittite stone reliefs dating from 1350BC found in central Turkey show a stringed instrument bearing a striking resemblance to depictions of similar European instruments dating from the 9th to the 15th century AD.

EVOLUTION OF THE GUITAR

When the guitar first emerged during the 16th century, it was a small instrument with four or five courses of strings set in pairs. During the 17th and 18th centuries, the body increased in size and tunings evolved. A milestone in the development of the modern guitar was the establishment of six single strings tuned to EADGBE, which can be seen from the 1780s onward in the work of the Neapolitan maker Giovanni Fabricatore. The large, modern classical guitar of today was first designed by the Spanish maker Antonio de Torres in the mid-19th century. Around the same time in North America, C. F. Martin established X bracing, and toward the end of the 19th century, Orville Gibson carved arched tops for guitars, paving the way for the modern instrument in the 20th century.

1581 Belchior Dias
This small instrument made in Lisbon by Dias has a vaulted back and is the earliest dated guitar.

The lute
With its pear-shaped body and curved back, the lute is related to the Arabic instrument, the 'Ud. In the Middle Ages, the guitar was called the *guitarra latina* and the lute the *guitarra moresca*.

1500

1500s Vihuela
Made in the 1500s, this instrument has six courses of strings and originally had 10 gut frets tied to the neck. In effect, the vihuela is a large guitar with its own repertoire.

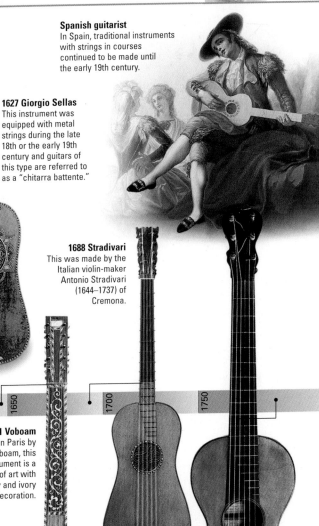

Spanish guitarist
In Spain, traditional instruments with strings in courses continued to be made until the early 19th century.

1627 Giorgio Sellas
This instrument was equipped with metal strings during the late 18th or the early 19th century and guitars of this type are referred to as a "chitarra battente."

1688 Stradivari
This was made by the Italian violin-maker Antonio Stradivari (1644–1737) of Cremona.

1641 Voboam
Made in Paris by René Voboam, this instrument is a work of art with ebony and ivory decoration.

1614 Matteo Sellas
Guitars by Sellas were made in Venice, and his labels often stated that he was based at the "sign of the star."

1785 Fabricatore
Giovanni Battista Fabricatore was based in Naples and is considered to be one of the first makers to build guitars with six strings. This instrument is one of the earliest six-string guitars.

1600 1650 1700 1750

1836 Panormo
Louis Panormo (1784–1854) came from a family of instrument makers. Born in Paris, he was based in London. He used a form of fan bracing and his instruments have finely carved slotted headstocks. They were advertised as "guitars in the Spanish style."

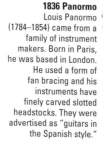

The Giulianiad
This 1833 English guitar magazine was named after guitar virtuoso Mauro Giuliani (1781–1829).

1835 Lacôte
The French maker René-François Lacôte (1785–1855) was born in Mirecourt and worked in Paris. The frets are set into the top of his guitars.

Dionisio Aguado
The Spanish virtuoso Dionisio Aguado (1784–1849) performed and wrote extensively for the guitar. His *Method for Guitar* (1825) contains a wide range of studies to help in developing right-hand technique.

1838 Martin
The German maker C. F. Martin (1796–1873) worked with Johann Staufer in Vienna before emigrating to the US in 1833. This asymmetric headstock shows Staufer's influence.

1800   1825   1850

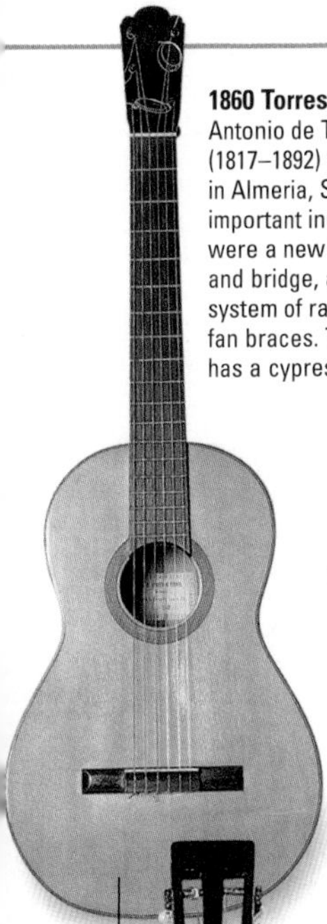

1860 Torres
Antonio de Torres (1817–1892) was born in Almeria, Spain. His important innovations were a new body shape and bridge, and a system of radiating fan braces. This guitar has a cypress body.

Miguel Llobet
The Spanish guitarist Llobet (1878–1938) studied with Tarrega and paved the way for modern playing.

1882 Torres
This guitar has a Brazilian rosewood body. Inside, it is labeled as being made during Torres's second epoch of guitar making— from 1875–92.

1908 Gibson Style 0
This type of radical design, with its arched top, was pioneered by Orville Gibson. It features a sharp cutaway and a scroll-shaped upper bout.

1875

1900

1870s Martin
During the 19th century, C. F. Martin established X bracing inside his guitars. This guitar, with its size 2 body, has the new slotted headstock with a straight top edge and can be compared to the earlier Martin (left).

Orville Gibson
Gibson (1856–1918) introduced arched carved tops at the end of the 19th century.

Hauser

Based in Munich, the legendary German guitar-maker Herman Hauser (1882–1952) originally made guitars that followed 19th-century central European traditions. In the 1920s, he took a dramatic change in direction after meeting Segovia (*see* p.50) and seeing his Santos Hernandez guitar.

Andrès Segovia
Segovia used an instrument built by Santos Hernandez, who had worked with Ramirez. Segovia's guitar inspired Hauser and he copied it.

Fleta

Ignaçio Fleta (1897–1977) made many different types of instrument in his workshop in Barcelona, Spain, before being inspired by Segovia in the 1950s to concentrate on making guitars. One of the great 20th-century guitar-makers, Fleta was joined in the 1960s by his nephews Francisco and Gabriel.

Cedar top

NORTHERN EUROPEAN MAKING

In the 1920s and 1930s, Herman Hauser studied Spanish guitar-building and was influenced by the system of the 19th-century guitar-maker Antonio de Torres. The guitars Hauser made in the 1930s were a brilliant synthesis of the best traditions. He created his own individual style of guitar with an attractive character. They use the Torres system of radiating fan braces. They are sometimes slightly smaller than Spanish instruments, and often feature a highly sympathetic tonal blend between the top and the body, which helps to create a sound that is both clear and full as well as lyrical. Hauser started a northern European tradition of guitar-making and his work has been carried on by his son, Herman Hauser II, and grandson, Herman Hauser III. A Hauser instrument was used for a number of years by Julian Bream (*see* p.24) in the early part of his career.

Rosette with inlays

Spruce top

1941 HAUSER I

Body Rosewood with spruce top	**Scale length** 25⁹⁄₁₆in (650mm)
Neck Mahogany	**Nut width** 2in (50mm)
	Lower bout width 14³⁄₈in (365mm)
Fingerboard 19-fret ebony	**Feature** Seven fan braces

CEDAR TOPS

Ignaçio Fleta's early guitars have spruce tops, but in the early 1960s he started using cedar, which adds a warm mellow sound and a vibrant immediacy to the notes. Fleta used nine struts in a standard Torres-pattern bracing system, and added an element of asymmetry by incorporating a diagonal strut below the soundhole. This gave an extra edge to the treble strings by stiffening the top on the lower side of the body. Fleta guitars have a strong wood sound, considerable volume, and good projection. They were used by John Williams (*see* p.54).

1976 FLETA

Body Rosewood with cedar top
Neck Cedar
Fingerboard Ebony
Scale length 25⁹⁄₁₆in (650mm)
Nut width 2in (50mm)
Lower bout width 14³⁄₈in (365mm)
Feature Transverse bar

Ebony fingerboard   Machinehead   Headstock

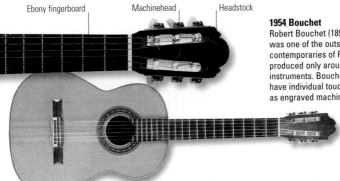

1954 Bouchet
Robert Bouchet (1898–1986) was one of the outstanding contemporaries of Fleta. He produced only around 100 instruments. Bouchet guitars have individual touches such as engraved machineheads.

Smallman

One of the most important innovators of the 20th century, the Australian guitar-maker Greg Smallman (b.1948) pioneered the use of carbon fiber and bracing in 1980 to create a revolutionary type of classical guitar in which the top works on new acoustic principles. His guitars have a different tone and character to that of a standard classical guitar.

John Williams
After using a Fleta for a number of years, Williams (*see* p.54) adopted a Smallman in the 1980s. He particularly likes the sustain produced by the instrument.

Ramirez

Ramirez, based in Madrid, Spain, is the world's oldest classical guitar company. It was founded by José Ramirez I (1858–1923) in the 1880s. His younger brother, Manuel Ramirez (1864–1916), joined him and they made outstanding classical and flamenco guitars that evolved directly from the work of Antonio de Torres.

Neck to body junction

Spruce top

Binding

Golpeador plate

CARBON-FIBER INNOVATION

The Smallman guitar has a heavy body and strong construction with a pronounced arched back. The thin cedar top is reinforced with a latticework pattern of braces that incorporate carbon fiber and balsa wood. This makes the top very lively and sensitive. Carbon-fiber material gives the guitar extra resonance and volume, and a slightly artificial, even sound where some of the colors normally created by wood are missing. When a note is plucked it sustains for longer, and on the Smallman high bass string notes are astonishingly responsive. These guitars are ideal for live performing as they give more projection. They have been championed by John Williams and their radical tonal characteristics have broken with tradition.

Cedar top

Metal fret

Ebony fingerboard

Headstock

Slot

1987 SMALLMAN

Body Laminated rosewood with cedar top

Neck Cedar

Fingerboard Ebony

Scale length 25⅝in (650mm)

Nut width 2¹⁄₁₆in (52mm)

Lower bout width 14⅜in (364mm)

LIGHTER CONSTRUCTION

The outline body shape of flamenco guitars is the same as that of classical guitars, but their construction is different in a number of important ways. Many flamenco guitars have pale-colored cypress bodies, a light construction, and lower string action. This gives them their own type of warm tone as well as good attack with an audible string sound. Flamenco guitars have a golpeador plate fixed to the top to protect them from fierce, highly energized strumming and tapping techniques. Some guitars have a longer string scale length between the nut and the bridge, which gives it a higher string tension and extra power.

1913 RAMIREZ

Body Cypress with spruce top

Neck Cedar

Fingerboard 19-fret ebony

Scale length 26in (660mm)

Nut width 2in (50mm)

Lower bout width 14³⁄₁₆in (360mm)

Features Slotted headstock (many guitars of this period have solid headstocks); thin, light internal braces

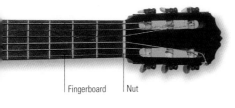

Fingerboard

Nut

Ramirez label
Classical guitars have a paper label with the maker's details glued to the back of the body. Makers are called luthiers.

Whiteman

An exceptional maker with a great knowledge of construction combined with outstanding touch and intuition, David Whiteman produces guitars that have both traditional form and modern concepts. Whiteman guitars have an individual character, often with skilled carving and attractive bindings.

Sitka spruce top

Cutaway heel
This guitar has a beautifully carved heel with an incurved shape and a pointed end.

Wide lower bout

Dean

Classical guitars by Christopher Dean are noted for their aesthetic beauty. They have an attractive outline, outstanding craftsmanship, and superb tonal qualities. Drawing on European traditions and the philosophy behind English guitar-making, Dean guitars represent the classical sound at its best.

Rosette   Spruce top

CUTAWAY

Instruments by David Whiteman (b.1965) combine influences from both Hauser and Fleta, and embody classical guitar-building at its finest. The innovative guitar featured here was commissioned by the author and is a unique collaboration between a player and a maker. To reach higher registers, the guitar has a 14-fret neck-to-body junction, a dropped shoulder cutaway giving access to the 16th fret, and an extension that reaches C♯. The guitar has a slightly wider body than a normal classical guitar and a North American sitka spruce top, which gives it a warm, rich musicality.

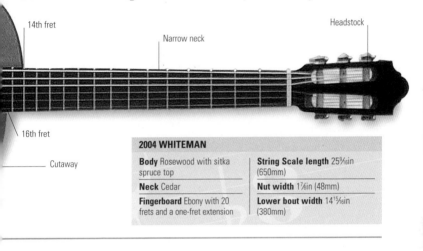

14th fret

Narrow neck

Headstock

16th fret

Cutaway

2004 WHITEMAN

Body Rosewood with sitka spruce top	**String Scale length** 25⁹⁄₁₆in (650mm)
Neck Cedar	**Nut width** 1⅞in (48mm)
Fingerboard Ebony with 20 frets and a one-fret extension	**Lower bout width** 14¹⁵⁄₁₆in (380mm)

MODERN CLASSIC

Christopher Dean (b.1958) is one of the world's leading makers and has been building guitars professionally for more than 20 years. His instruments are made using standard woods and methods of construction. Dean has continued to refine and develop his guitars, and manages to evolve continually in his search for quality of sound and projection. His instruments have a fine, crisp response and the added dimension of shining resonance. They are widely used today.

2003 DEAN

Body Rosewood with spruce top

Neck Mahogany

Fingerboard 19-fret ebony

Scale length 25⁹⁄₁₆in (650mm)

Nut width 2¹⁄₁₆in (52mm)

Lower bout width 14⅜in (365mm)

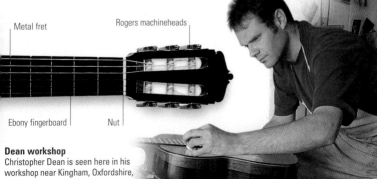

Metal fret

Rogers machineheads

Ebony fingerboard

Nut

Dean workshop
Christopher Dean is seen here in his workshop near Kingham, Oxfordshire, England, finishing a guitar with a Brazilian rosewood body.

Martin 000-18

C. F. Martin & Co. is the world's most famous steel string guitar-maker.
The classic "000" body size was introduced in 1902. The 18 refers to the
choice of woods and bindings and dates from 1857. The 000-18 guitar has
continued to be popular and its appearance
today is the result of a gradual evolution.

Square
shoulders

Spruce top

Black pickguard

Martin D-18

Martin brought in guitars with a large body and square shoulders as part of
their standard range in 1931. These guitars were termed "D" models which
stands for "Dreadnought." The D-18, which was at first called the D-1, and
the related rosewood-body D-28 are well-known
and very popular in most types of music.

Joni Mitchell
The outstanding singer-songwriter Joni
Mitchell used a rosewood-bodied Martin
D-28 in the early part of her career.

Tortoiseshell-
effect pickguard

MAHOGANY BODY

Early 000-18 models from 1911 have gut strings, rosewood bodies, ebony fingerboards, and a cedar neck that joins the body at the 12th fret. From 1917, the guitar was made with a mahogany body, steel strings were added in the 1920s, a 14-fret neck-to-body junction and solid headstock came in during 1934, and a rosewood fingerboard in 1940. The modern 000-18 featured here has a metallic, springy sound with a cutting clarity. The model has been popular with folk guitarists.

Martin Carthy
The traditional English folk guitarist and singer Martin Carthy has used a Martin 000-18 throughout his career.

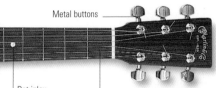

Metal buttons

Dot inlay

Rosewood fingerboard

2003 MARTIN 000-18

Body Mahogany with spruce top	**Nut width** 1¹¹⁄₁₆in (43mm)
Neck Mahogany	**Lower bout width** 15in (381mm)
Fingerboard 20-fret rosewood with dot inlays	**Features** Internal X bracing and solid headstock
Scale length 24⅞in (633mm)	

DREADNOUGHTS

The first D-18 model with an ebony fingerboard came out in 1931. During the 1930s the guitar underwent a number of small refinements. This guitar, made in 1942, was bought by Elvis Presley in 1953. It was used by him for performing and recording until 1956, and he played it on his first single "That's All Right Mama." The D-18 model was given a rosewood fingerboard and bridge in 1947. The guitar has a full sound with depth and character and bright, tonal colors. The D-18 and its more expensive relatives, the D-28 and the D-45, have been used by countless players in country, folk, rock, and pop for many decades.

1942 MARTIN D-18

Body Mahogany with spruce top

Neck Mahogany

Fingerboard 20-fret ebony with dot inlays

Scale length 25⅜in (645mm)

Nut width 1¹¹⁄₁₆in (43mm)

Lower bout width 15⅝in (397mm)

Features Internal X bracing and solid headstock

HD-28
Martin introduced the HD-28 model in 1976. This has the D-28 rosewood body with herringbone purfling and scalloped bracing.

Martin D12-28

Guitars have used doubled courses of strings for centuries, and in the 1930s, blues players often used 12-string models with metal strings. In the 1960s, their shimmering tone became popular and Martin introduced a 12-string model in 1964. In 1970, the company produced a 12-string version of their classic D-28 called the D12-28.

Square shoulders

14th fret

Large bridge with 12 pins

Collings D3

Bill Collings (b.1948) started making guitars in 1975 and is based in Austin, Texas. His instruments are among the finest steel string acoustics made today. They draw on tradition and the D3 model is seen as a reinterpretation of the 1930s Martin D-28.

Bridge
The ebony bridge has six individual pins holding the strings, and a separate saddle.

Tortoiseshell-effect pickguard

TWELVE STRINGS

The D12-28 has a heavy construction with extra bracing to take the higher tension created by 12 strings. It has a long headstock for the 12 tuners, a large ebony bridge to accommodate the extra pins, and a wide neck to give adequate string spacing. The strings are arranged in six pairs—the top two strings are doubled at the same pitch and the four lower strings have an upper octave string that sits above the normally pitched string. The guitar has a majestic, full sound which gives the sensation of continual ringing. The Martin D12-28 is used in recordings to give sparkling layering.

Leo Kottke
The American folk and blues instrumentalist Leo Kottke used a 12-string guitar for his early recordings in the 1960s.

Dot inlays

Long headstock

1970s MARTIN D12-28

Body Rosewood with spruce top	**Nut width** 1⅞in (48mm)
Neck Mahogany	**Lower bout width** 15⅝in (397mm)
Fingerboard 20-fret ebony with dot inlays	**Features** Heavily built body with large bridge and headstock
Scale length 24⅞in (633mm)	

AMERICAN TRADITIONS

The Collings D3 is built to a very high standard, with outstanding craftsmanship, fine woods, and an almost mirrorlike clear finish. Internally, it uses a fine type of scalloped bracing to enhance the tone, which has come to be termed prewar bracing. During the 1930s, Martin guitars were considered to be at their apogee, and Collings guitars are built with similar specifications. They have a tortoiseshell-effect pickguard and fine touches, such as pearl eyes in the bridge pins and an abalone soundhole ring, to give them added character. The guitar has a sparkling tone, a fine balance, and a good response in all registers. Collings guitars represent the American steel string tradition at its best. They are used by many players today, including North American guitarists Lyle Lovett and Joni Mitchell. Collings also make an OM model and a small-bodied C model series.

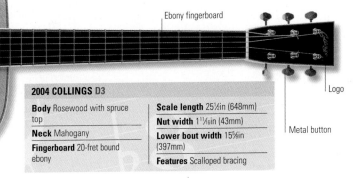

Ebony fingerboard

Logo

Metal button

2004 COLLINGS D3

Body Rosewood with spruce top	**Scale length** 25½in (648mm)
Neck Mahogany	**Nut width** 1¹¹⁄₁₆in (43mm)
Fingerboard 20-fret bound ebony	**Lower bout width** 15⅝in (397mm)
	Features Scalloped bracing

Gibson J-45

The J-45 was introduced in 1942 as an economy round-shouldered dreadnought to replace the previous J-35 model, which was discontinued. A variant, called the Southerner Jumbo, was brought out at the same time. This was a more expensive model with double parallelogram inlays. A natural finish J-45, called the J-50, came out in 1947.

Round shoulders

Cream binding

Pickguard

Bridge

Gibson J-200

The premier Gibson flattop acoustic guitar, the J-200, first appeared as the Super Jumbo in 1937. The guitar was made to a high standard and features a large body with a distinctive "moustache" bridge, a floral pickguard, multiple bindings, and decorative fingerboard inlays.

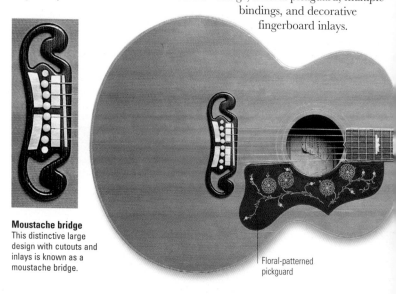

Moustache bridge
This distinctive large design with cutouts and inlays is known as a moustache bridge.

Floral-patterned pickguard

ROUND-SHOULDERED DREADNOUGHT

The first J-45 models have a sunburst finish, and a "banner" headstock logo with the words "Only a Gibson is Good Enough." The guitar has a pin bridge and a "firestripe" pattern pickguard. With its mahogany body, the guitar has a lively response and a bright sound suitable for backing the voice. The J-45 and J-50 have been used by Buddy Holly, Davey Graham, Jorma Kaukonen, and Gillian Welch. In 1969, the guitar underwent various modifications, including the change to a square-shouldered body. In 1984, the guitar regained its original shape.

Dot inlay

1940s GIBSON J-45

Body Mahogany with spruce top	**Nut width** 1¹¹⁄₁₆in (43mm)
Neck Mahogany	**Lower bout width** 16⅛in (410mm)
Fingerboard 19-fret rosewood with dot inlays	**Features** Sunburst finish and oval button machineheads
Scale length 24¾in (619mm)	

Hank Williams
American country legend Hank Williams often used a Southerner Jumbo guitar.

THE JUMBO

The first models from the 1930s have a rosewood body and an ebony fingerboard. In its long history, the guitar has undergone a number of modifications. It was given a rosewood fingerboard from 1941 and a maple body from 1946. An ebony fingerboard was reintroduced at the beginning of the 1970s. The J-200 has a superb range of balanced sounds, with a rich bass and a clear detailed treble. It has been used by Elvis Presley, Emmylou Harris, and Albert Lee.

Bound fingerboard

Crest inlays

Reverend Gary Davis
US blues and gospel finger-style player, the Reverend Gary Davis has played a J-200 during his career.

1952 GIBSON J-200

Body Maple with spruce top	**Nut width** 1¹¹⁄₁₆in (43mm)
Neck Maple	**Lower bout width** 17in (432mm)
Fingerboard 20-fret bound rosewood with crest inlays	**Features** Ornate decoration with multiple bindings
Scale length 25½in (648mm)	

Gibson J-160E

With the success of electric archtops and solid body guitars, Gibson decided to produce electric flattop acoustic guitars with pickups. In 1954, there was the launch of the J-160E, which was a round-shouldered dreadnought with a fitted single-coil pickup and controls, and a 15-fret neck-to-body junction for improved fingerboard access.

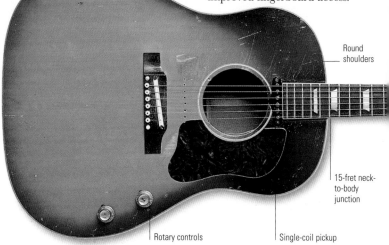

Round shoulders

15-fret neck-to-body junction

Rotary controls

Single-coil pickup

Selmer Maccaferri

The Maccaferri guitar was launched in 1932. It was a revolutionary concept—an acoustic guitar with a new body shape that incorporated a slightly arched top, a cutaway, an internal sound chamber to enhance volume and sustain, and a long, 24-fret fingerboard. It was adopted by Django Reinhardt.

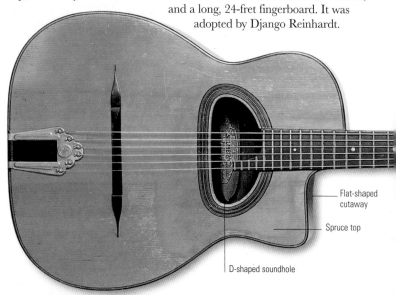

Flat-shaped cutaway

Spruce top

D-shaped soundhole

AMPLIFIED ACCOUSTIC

The J-160E has a full-size acoustic body based on Gibson's J-45 model (*see* p.72). It has a single-coil pickup fitted between the edge of the soundhole and the fingerboard, controlled by rotary volume and tone controls. It has a pin bridge and a height-adjustable saddle. The model has a strong, clear tone and is particularly associated with The Beatles. This guitar was bought in 1962, and was owned and used by both John Lennon and George Harrison. It had an extra pickup introduced at one time. The J-160E was discontinued in 1979 and reintroduced in 1991.

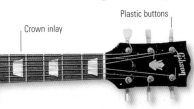

Crown inlay

Plastic buttons

1962 GIBSON J-160E

Body Mahogany with laminated spruce top	**Scale length** 24¾in (619mm)
Neck Mahogany	**Nut width** 1¹¹⁄₁₆in (43mm)
Fingerboard 20-fret bound rosewood with crown inlays	**Lower bout width** 16¼in (413mm)

John Lennon
The J-160E is versatile and was often used by John Lennon and George Harrison for songwriting, recording, and performing.

INDIVIDUAL VISION

With its distinctive flat cutaway and D-shaped soundhole, the Maccaferri guitar was invented and developed by the visionary Italian guitarist and maker Mario Maccaferri (1900–93) and built by the Selmer company in Paris. It has a fingerboard extension and the internal sound chamber gives the guitar projection and its own distinctive penetrating sound and sustain. The guitar was adopted by the jazz guitarist Django Reinhardt and helped him to play virtuoso solos acoustically and use notes in a high register. The original series was discontinued in the 1930s.

1932 MACCAFERRI

Body Laminated with spruce top

Neck Walnut

Fingerboard 24-fret ebony with dot inlays

Scale length 25³⁄₈in (640mm)

Nut width 1⅞in (48mm)

Lower bout width 15¾in (400mm)

Zero fret

14-fret neck-to-body junction

Rob Aylward guitar
This guitar was built by the talented British maker Rob Aylward. It has a small, oval soundhole and a 14-fret neck-to-body junction that is better suited for soloing.

Taylor 714CE

First set up in the 1980s, Taylor produces good-quality, modern acoustic guitars that have an attractive appearance and proportions. The company has specialized in a range of electroacoustic models with cutaways, which are suitable for both acoustic and amplified playing and performing.

James Dean Bradfield
The Manic Street Preachers singer and guitarist James Dean Bradfield has recently performed solo using a Taylor.

Ovation Custom Legend

The revolutionary Ovation guitars, first built in the late 1960s, brought in the use of new synthetic materials coupled with a bowl-shaped back. The company pioneered electroacoustic guitars with transducers, and their unique tonal characteristics and playability helped them to become popular.

Abalone purfling   Large soundhole

ELECTROACOUSTIC GUITARS

The Taylor 714CE electroacoustic guitar has abalone and koa wood inlays. The pickguard has been shaped to follow the waist of the body. The cutaway gives comfortable access to the upper register, and the neck profile and action makes it easy to play. The guitar is equipped with both a transducer and an internal microphone to give an added natural-sounding depth. The combination of transducer and microphone can be controlled proportionally to give a different range of sounds. A range of easily accessible controls governing tone sit on the side of the body on the upper shoulder. The guitar has a good overall balance with a bright tone, and a midrange sound without a strong bass response. These guitars have been popular with both amateur and professional singers in a wide range of music.

Abalone inlay

Truss rod cover

Dot inlays

Cutaway

1992 TAYLOR 714CE

Body Rosewood with cedar top	**Nut width** 1¾in (44mm)
Neck Mahogany	**Lower bout width** 15¾in (400mm)
Fingerboard 20-fret ebony with dot inlays	**Features** Internal microphone as well as Fishman transducer pickup under the saddle with sophisticated range of controls
Scale length 25¼in (648mm)	

BOWL BACKS

The Custom Legend model was first introduced in 1974 as a highly decorative version of the Balladeer. The guitar has a large soundhole with a foliate soundhole ring, dot- and diamond-shaped abalone fingerboard inlays with abalone purfling around the rims and a distinctive modern headstock shape. The bridge is equipped with a transducer with individual piezoelectric elements governed by a rotary control on the upper shoulder of the body. It has a clean, even response and a distinctive sound of its own. The Custom Legend has been used by players ranging in style, from Glen Campbell to Adrian Legg. Ovation went on to introduce further models including the Adamas.

Paul McCartney and Wings
In the 1970s, Paul McCartney performed with Ovation six- and 12-string models.

Abalone inlays | Ebony fingerboard

1976 OVATION

Body Lyrachord body with spruce top

Neck Mahogany and maple

Fingerboard 20-fret ebony with diamond and dot inlays

Scale length 25¼in (641mm)

Nut width 1¹¹⁄₁₆in (43mm)

Lower bout width 15¾in (400mm)

Ovation rounded back
Lyrachord is used to mold a distinctive bowl-shaped back.

Dobro

Dobro resonator instruments were made from 1928 by John Dopyera, and the company was merged with National in 1932. Today, the term "Dobro" normally refers to a wooden-bodied resonator guitar. Most have a single cone, and their own particular type of sound and character that is often associated with country and bluegrass music.

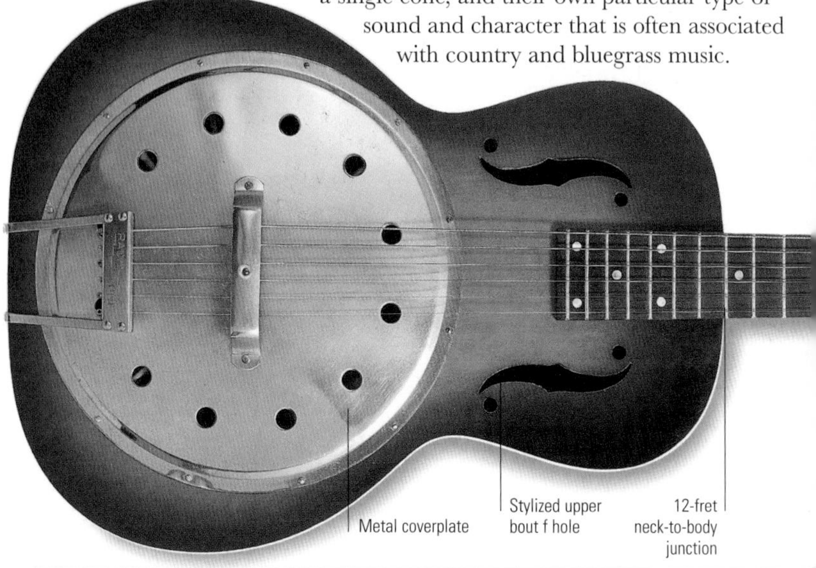

Metal coverplate

Stylized upper bout f hole

12-fret neck-to-body junction

National Style 3

Resonator guitars were developed by the Dopyera brothers, who founded the National company in 1926. The guitars were introduced to meet the demand for louder instruments that could project for performing. The first metal-bodied resonators, with their entirely new principles of construction, are among the most radical designs in the history of the guitar.

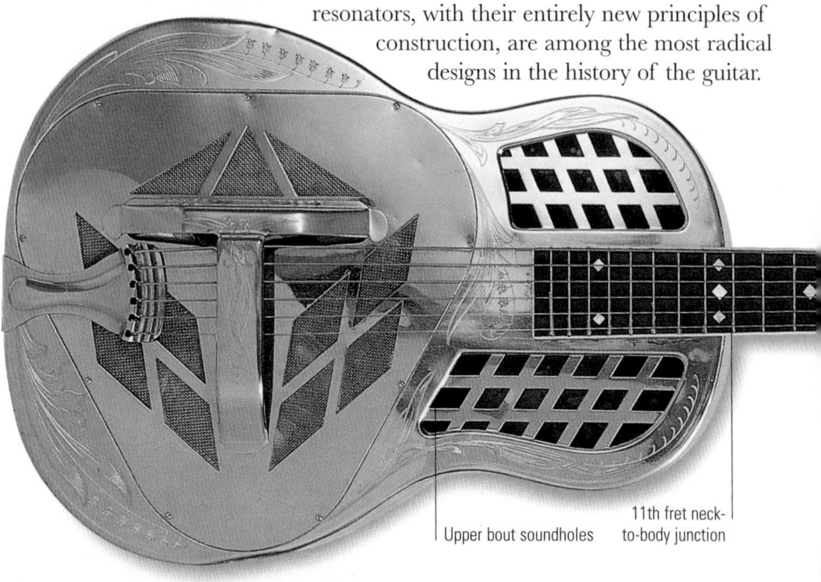

Upper bout soundholes

11th fret neck-to-body junction

WOODEN BODIES

Dobros are wooden-bodied resonators. The body has a single, large, aluminium resonating cone set under a slightly domed metal coverplate with patterned cutouts and a simple handrest. By comparison to metal-bodied resonators, wooden-bodied resonators have a more natural sound, with less attack on the notes. There is a tradition of Dobro playing with both plucked and slide styles of music. A Dobro was used by Bashful Brother Oswald with Roy Acuff's band in the late 1930s and early 1940s. More recently Jerry Douglas has become a well-known Dobro specialist.

Resonating mechanism
The metal coverplate has a handrest with a wooden bridge underneath connected to the resonating cone internally with an eight-legged metal "spider".

Nut

Dot inlays

Metal fret

1930s DOBRO

Body Laminated woods

Neck Mahogany

Fingerboard 19-fret rosewood with dot inlays

Scale length 629mm (24¾in)

Nut width 44mm (1¾in)

Lower bout width 362mm (14¼in)

Features Single internal resonator cone

METAL BODIES

National Style 3 guitars have all-metal bodies, upper bout soundholes with latticework inserts, and an attractive triangular-shaped coverplate with geometrical cutouts and a T-shaped handrest. The Style 3 tricone was built between 1928 and 1941 and has lily-of-the-valley engraving. A range of tricones was manufactured, including the plain Style 1 and the highly decorated Style 4. The guitar has a percussive, metallic, banjolike attack and tremendous sustain, and is particularly effective with slide as well as standard techniques. These guitars are used in blues and Hawaiian music.

1928 NATIONAL STYLE 3

Body German silver nickel alloy with nickel plating

Neck Mahogany

Fingerboard 19-fret ebony with diamond inlays

Scale length 25¼in (641mm)

Nut width 1¾in (44mm)

Lower bout width 14¼in (362mm)

Features Three internal cones

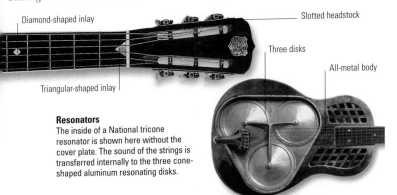

Diamond-shaped inlay

Triangular-shaped inlay

Slotted headstock

Three disks

All-metal body

Resonators
The inside of a National tricone resonator is shown here without the cover plate. The sound of the strings is transferred internally to the three cone-shaped aluminum resonating disks.

Monteleone Radio City

One of the world's great guitar-makers, John Monteleone (b.1947) is following in the tradition of D'Angelico and D'Aquisto. His guitars have an outstanding sound, and his exceptional craftsmanship features sublime touches of art deco design. Monteleone's instruments are works of art.

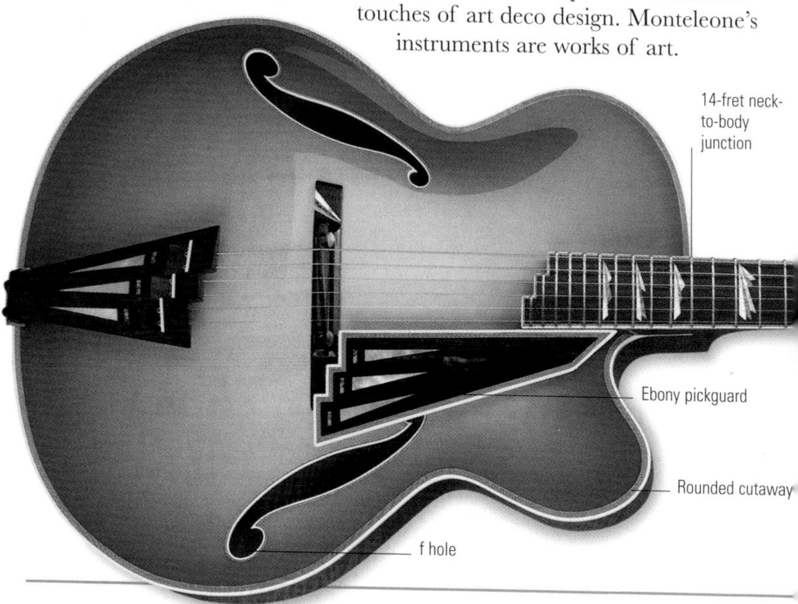

14-fret neck-to-body junction

Ebony pickguard

Rounded cutaway

f hole

D'Angelico Excel

The legendary archtop guitar-maker John D'Angelico (1905–64) was based in New York and his early models were initially based on the Gibson L-5. D'Angelico developed his own distinctive art deco features in the 1930s, and his instruments became famous for their exceptional tonal qualities.

Bound f hole

Johnny Smith
The great American jazz guitarist Johnny Smith often used a D'Angelico Excel model.

VIRTUOSO CRAFTSMANSHIP

John Monteleone builds his range of guitars and mandolins in his workshop on Long Island, New York, and the Radio City is one of his top models. It was inspired by the type of art deco styling that can be seen inside the Radio City music hall in New York City. The guitar has superb woods with a curly maple body and a carved top made with European spruce, supported internally by an asymmetric X brace and tone bar

system. The guitar has flowing body lines, a rounded cutaway, and distinctive f holes. It features brass fittings and an ebony pickguard and tailpiece, with subtle features such as fine inlays and matching steps on the end of the fingerboard and the pickguard. The instrument featured here has a striking blue finish in contrast to the normal natural or sunburst finishes. The guitars are highly sought after today.

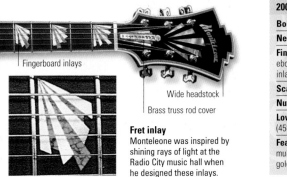

Fingerboard inlays

Wide headstock

Brass truss rod cover

Fret inlay
Monteleone was inspired by shining rays of light at the Radio City music hall when he designed these inlays.

2003 MONTELEONE

Body Maple with spruce top

Neck One-piece maple

Fingerboard 24-fret bound ebony with "ray of light" inlays

Scale length 25½in (648mm)

Nut width 1¹¹⁄₁₆in (43mm)

Lower bout width 18in (458mm)

Features Decorative multiple bindings and gold-plated fittings

ARCHTOP MASTERY

The first Excel models were produced in 1936. In 1947, D'Angelico started offering models with cutaways. The guitars have a finely carved top with bound f holes, a large headstock design, and engraved tailpieces with a stairstep pattern. This guitar has an added floating pickup that rests on top of the body, with the controls attached to the pickguard. D'Angelicos have been used by jazz guitarist Chuck Wayne and country player Chet Atkins. The guitars have a smooth sound with a luminous tone and tremendous sustain.

1950 D'ANGELICO EXCEL

Body Maple with spruce top

Neck Maple

Fingerboard 22-fret bound ebony with block inlays

Scale length 24¾in (629mm)

Nut width From 1⅝in (42mm) to 1¹¹⁄₁₆in (43mm)

Lower bout width 17in (432mm)

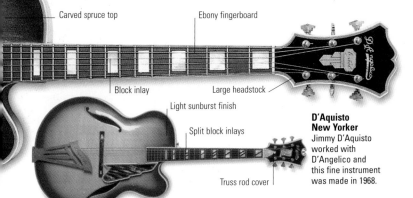

Carved spruce top

Ebony fingerboard

Block inlay

Large headstock

Light sunburst finish

Split block inlays

Truss rod cover

D'Aquisto New Yorker
Jimmy D'Aquisto worked with D'Angelico and this fine instrument was made in 1968.

Fender Telecaster

This model has become one of the most popular, versatile, and widely used electric solid-body guitars. Shortly after the introduction of the Esquire in 1950, Fender brought out the Broadcaster, which was effectively the same guitar with an added pickup near the fingerboard. The name was already in use and so was changed to the Telecaster in 1951.

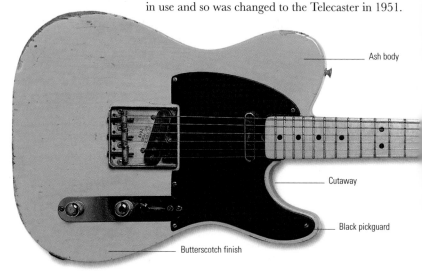

Ash body

Cutaway

Black pickguard

Butterscotch finish

Fender Esquire

The world's first production-line solid-body guitar, the Fender Esquire came out in 1950 just before its more famous partner, the Telecaster. It was an incredibly simple and revolutionary design, which was set to change the world of guitars. The body is a slab of wood with a single cutaway. It has a one-piece maple neck.

Flat slab body

Single-coil pickup

Rotary controls

Leo Fender
A visionary engineer and designer, Leo Fender (1909–91) developed the solid-body electric guitar and the electric bass.

TWO PICKUPS

This is an early Telecaster from 1952. It has two pickups and the three-way selector switch gives a combination of pickup sounds. During the 1950s, the guitar acquired a white pickguard. In 1959, a rosewood fingerboard was introduced. A Custom model also came out in 1959, with a sunburst finish and binding. The guitar has a bright, metallic cutting tone and a plangent, twangy string sound that makes it ideal for solos, fills, and rhythm playing in many styles of music.

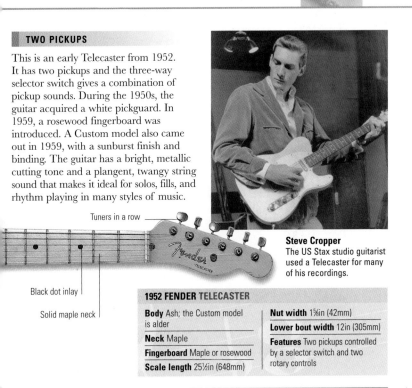

Tuners in a row

Black dot inlay

Solid maple neck

Steve Cropper
The US Stax studio guitarist used a Telecaster for many of his recordings.

1952 FENDER TELECASTER

Body Ash; the Custom model is alder

Neck Maple

Fingerboard Maple or rosewood

Scale length 25½in (648mm)

Nut width 1⅝in (42mm)

Lower bout width 12in (305mm)

Features Two pickups controlled by a selector switch and two rotary controls

SINGLE PICKUP

Early Esquires, such as the one featured here from the early 1950s, have a body made of ash with a blonde finish and a single-coil pickup set into a metal tray, which also holds three brass saddles. The strings run through to the back of the body where they are held by ferrules. There is a volume and tone control, a tone selector switch, and a bakelite pickguard. The solid maple neck is attached to the body with a metal neckplate, and the 21 frets and black dot markers are set directly into the top. There is no separate fingerboard. The headstock is asymmetric, with the tuners set in a line on the upper edge for ease of access. It was discontinued in 1970.

1950s FENDER ESQUIRE

Body Ash

Neck Maple

Fingerboard Maple or rosewood

Scale length 25½in (648mm)

Nut width 1⅝in (42mm)

Lower bout width 12in (305mm)

Features Single pickup with two rotary controls and selector switch

Solid maple neck   Dot inlays   Nut

Asymmetric headstock

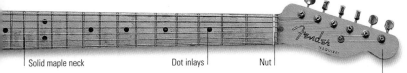

Side view
The Fender Esquire and Telecaster have a simple flat body, and the neck is attached with a four-bolt metal neckplate. The body is routed for the pickups.

Fender Stratocaster

The world's most famous electric guitar, the Fender Stratocaster, came out in 1954. A brilliant double cutaway design with attractive curves and body contouring, it has become a true icon of the 20th century. With three pickups and a new built-in tremolo system, the guitar was ahead of its time.

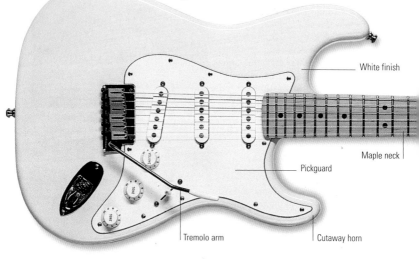

White finish

Maple neck

Pickguard

Tremolo arm

Cutaway horn

Fender Stratocaster

In 1959 the Fender Stratocaster was given a rosewood fingerboard, which not only changed the appearance of the guitar but altered the sound and feel as well. Maple necks added an extra sparkle to the sound. Rosewood, in contrast, has a slightly warmer, smoother effect.

Dave Gilmour
The Pink Floyd guitarist used both rosewood and maple fingerboard Stratocasters.

Fiesta red finish

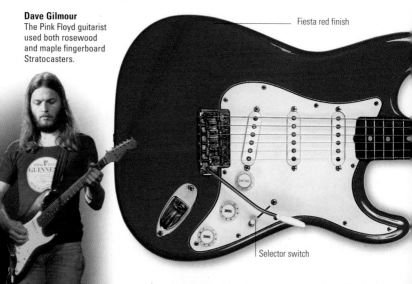

Selector switch

MAPLE FINGERBOARD

Early Fender Stratocasters have a sunburst finish, bakelite pickguards, and a solid 21-fret maple neck. The body is ash or alder, with three single-coil pickups controlled by two volume controls and one tone control with a three-way selector switch. The guitar has a bright tone and ringing sustain, with a lively string sound in all registers that has tremendous clarity. The pickup combinations give a range of different sounds. This model from 2003 has a five-way selector switch and a 22-fret fingerboard. Maple-neck Strats were adopted by Buddy Holly and Jimi Hendrix, and are used by Eric Clapton.

Buddy Guy
The great US blues guitarist Buddy Guy was one of the first prominent figures to use a 1950s maple fingerboard Stratocaster.

Dot inlay   Metal fret

2003 FENDER STRATOCASTER

Body Ash or alder	**Nut width** 1⅝in (42mm)
Neck Maple	**Lower bout width** 12¾in (324mm)
Fingerboard 21-fret maple with dot inlays	**Features** Three pickups with controls and tremolo system
Scale length 25½in (648mm)	

ROSEWOOD FINGERBOARD

A choice of custom colors came in during the 1950s, in addition to the standard sunburst finish. Rosewood fingerboards were seen by Fender as an improvement on the original Stratocaster. They made the guitar appear sophisticated, and similar to other standard instruments. For a number of years, rosewood fingerboards were fitted to all Stratocasters. Maple fingerboards did not come back as an option until late 1967, when there was an increased demand. Most Stratocaster players, including Jimi Hendrix, use both maple and rosewood fingerboard guitars. Guitars with rosewood fingerboards have been used by Jeff Beck and Stevie Ray Vaughan.

1962 STRATOCASTER

Body Ash or alder

Neck Maple

Fingerboard 22-fret rosewood with dot inlays

Scale length 25½in (648mm)

Nut width 1⅝in (42mm)

Lower bout width 12¾in (324mm)

Features Three pickups with controls and tremolo system; custom color finish

Rosewood fingerboard

Slim side view
From the side, this maple fingerboard Stratocaster can be seen to have comfort contouring on the upper bout.

Fender Jaguar

The Jaguar model was launched in 1962. It is a close relative of the Jazzmaster and has the same body with a short-scale neck and an extra fret. With this guitar, Fender further developed the concept of multiple controls with individual slider switches for the pickups.

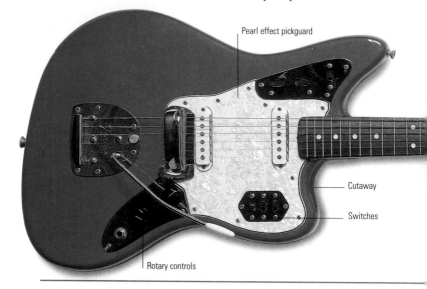

Pearl effect pickguard

Cutaway

Switches

Rotary controls

Fender Jazzmaster

Fender expanded their range in 1958 with the addition of the Jazzmaster. This was developed to provide a sophisticated top-of-the-line guitar with new pickups and controls that give different tone combinations. The design marks the introduction of rosewood fingerboards.

Tom Verlaine
The guitarist with innovative American band Television, Tom Verlaine used a Jazzmaster in the 1970s.

Metal bridge

SOPHISTICATED CONTROLS

The Jaguar has narrow, single-coil pickups, a floating tremolo system, a string mute, and the controls are set on metal plates to give the guitar a more expensive look. There are standard rotary tone and volume controls, three on/off switches controlling the pickups, and a switch with roller controls. The Jaguar has its own range of bright sounds and feels easy to play with its short-scale neck.

Although it was developed as Fender's new top instrument, the guitar never caught on and was discontinued in 1974. Old models started to become fashionable in the 1980s and 1990s and the guitar was relaunched in 2000.

Kurt Cobain
Nirvana guitarist Cobain used the Mustang with Jaguar controls and a Jagstang.

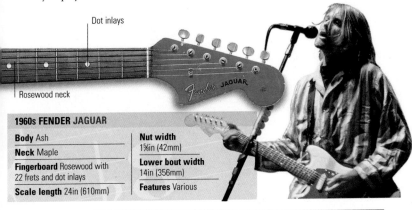

Dot inlays

Rosewood neck

1960s FENDER JAGUAR

Body Ash	**Nut width** 1⅝in (42mm)
Neck Maple	
Fingerboard Rosewood with 22 frets and dot inlays	**Lower bout width** 14in (356mm)
Scale length 24in (610mm)	**Features** Various

NEW BODY DESIGN

The Jazzmaster model was brought out with a new Fender-style body design. This has a pronounced offset waist and a swept-back, rounded, lower cutaway horn. It has a new type of floating tremolo system and the strings run over a separate metal bridge. The guitar has very wide, single-coil pickups, which have their own type of sound. In addition to the standard rotary tone and volume controls and a

selector switch, there is an upper bout slider switch. This provides two different wiring circuits to give further tone and volume settings for individual pickups. The Jazzmaster has a warm, diffused range of sounds. Although moderately successful, it was overshadowed by the classic Stratocaster and Telecaster models and discontinued in 1982. The guitar was rediscovered in the 1990s and brought back into production in 2000.

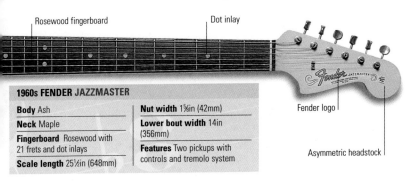

Rosewood fingerboard

Dot inlay

Fender logo

Asymmetric headstock

1960s FENDER JAZZMASTER

Body Ash	**Nut width** 1⅝in (42mm)
Neck Maple	**Lower bout width** 14in (356mm)
Fingerboard Rosewood with 21 frets and dot inlays	**Features** Two pickups with controls and tremolo system
Scale length 25½in (648mm)	

Gibson Les Paul Custom

After the launch of the Les Paul in 1952, Gibson decided
to introduce a range of Les Paul models in 1954, including
a Junior, a TV, and Custom. The new top-of-the-line
Custom model acquired gold plating, multiple bindings,
an ornate headstock, and a black finish.

All-mahogany body

Keith Richards
Rolling Stones guitarist Keith
Richards used a black Les
Paul Custom in the late 1960s.

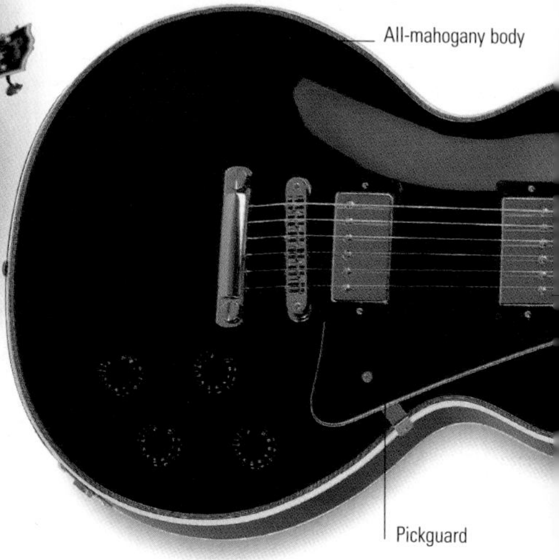

Pickguard

Gibson Les Paul Standard

One of the classic electric guitar icons, the Les Paul was originally launched
in 1952. With endorsement from the guitarist Les Paul, the new model was
Gibson's first electric solid-body guitar. Its design was traditional, with a body
shape that was in effect a scaled-down version
of their recent electric archtop models.

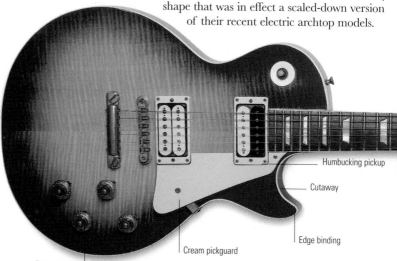

Humbucking pickup

Cutaway

Edge binding

Cream pickguard

Rotary control

LES PAUL CUSTOM

The Les Paul Custom was the new top-of-the-line Les
Paul. It was first brought out with an Alnico pickup in
the rhythm position, and with its block inlays and black
finish, it became known as the "black beauty." The
ebony fingerboard and mahogany body help to give the
guitar a mellow, jazzy sound. It was given three
humbucking pickups in 1957, was discontinued in
1960, and then reintroduced in 1968. New models have
two humbucking pickups. Robert Fripp (*see* p.29)
is among those who have used the guitar.

2004 LES PAUL CUSTOM

Body Mahogany

Neck Mahogany

Fingerboard 22-fret ebony with
block inlays

Scale length 24¾in (629mm)

Nut width 1¹¹⁄₁₆in (43mm)

Lower bout width 12¾in
(324mm)

Features Gold-plated parts

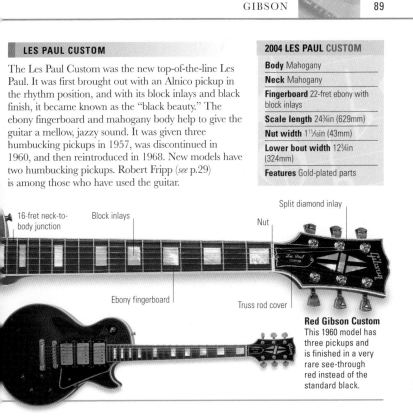

16-fret neck-to-body junction · Block inlays · Nut · Split diamond inlay · Ebony fingerboard · Truss rod cover

Red Gibson Custom
This 1960 model has
three pickups and
is finished in a very
rare see-through
red instead of the
standard black.

NEW SOLID BODY

The first Les Paul models had a gold
sparkle finish, two P-90 single-coil
pickups, and a trapeze tailpiece. The
guitar evolved during the 1950s with
the addition of a stud tailpiece, a Tune-
O-Matic bridge, humbucking pickups,
and a sunburst finish. Despite all these
developments, it was out of step with the
times and was discontinued in 1960, and

replaced by the SG model. It was
resurrected by Keith Richards and Eric
Clapton, and later used by Jeff Beck and
Jimmy Page. A new version of the guitar
was introduced in 1968. The Les Paul
has tremendous sustain and a distinctive
smooth tone, with high output from the
pickups that makes it ideal for overdriven
and distorted guitar solos and riffs.

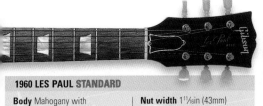

1960 LES PAUL STANDARD

Body Mahogany with
maple top

Neck Mahogany

Fingerboard 22-fret rosewood
with crown inlays

Scale length 24¾in (629mm)

Nut width 1¹¹⁄₁₆in (43mm)

Lower bout width 12¾in
(324mm)

Features Two humbucking
pickups with rotary controls and
selector switch; flamed maple top
with sunburst finish

Duanne Allman
One of the outstanding US blues
rock guitarists, Duane Allman
used a Les Paul with the Allman
Brothers in the 1960s.

Gibson ES-335

Launched in 1958, the ES-335 model was designed as a new type of thinline electric guitar. It combines the characteristics of a solid body with elements from archtop instruments, such as f holes and acoustic cavities. It is one of a family of guitars, including the ES-330, ES-345, and ES-355, which have different specifications and appointments.

f hole

Double
cutaways

Rotary controls

Binding

Gibson Flying V

This radical design was launched in 1958 by Gibson as a "modernistic" guitar. The Flying V was created on a drawing board. It has two wings of wood, giving it an aerodynamic shape. It is equipped with standard Gibson pickups and controls.

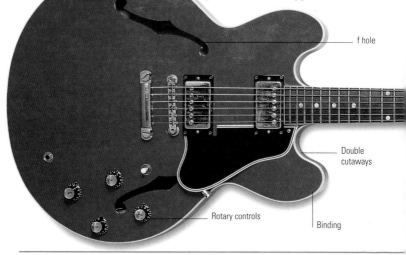

Albert King
Blues legend Albert
King used a Flying V
during the 1960s.

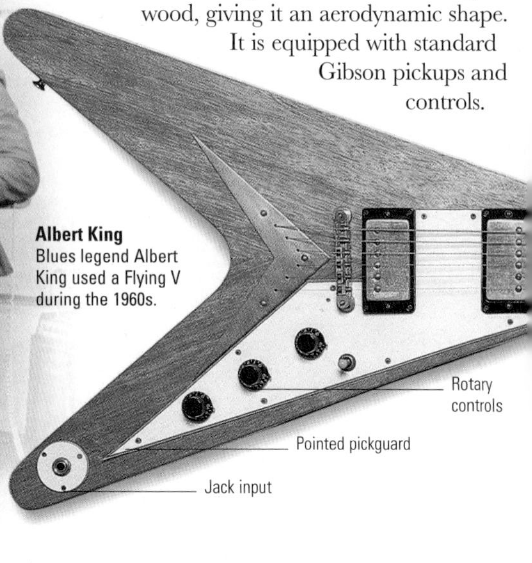

Rotary
controls

Pointed pickguard

Jack input

DOUBLE CUTAWAY BODY

With its symmetrical double cutaways and laminated body with arched top and back, the ES-335 is one of the most beautiful of the electric guitars. When launched, it had either a sunburst or natural finish. In 1960, the natural finish was replaced with cherry red. From 1962, small block inlays replaced dots on the ES-335, and an ES-335 DOT with dot inlays was added to the range in 1982. The guitar has a solid internal central block that helps to eliminate feedback. It has a rich, reedy sound and good sustain, and is highly versatile. This model and its close relatives, such as the more elaborate ES-355, have been used by blues artists such as Freddie King, rock 'n' roll legend Chuck Berry, and jazz fusion guitarists Larry Carlton and John Scofield. This guitar continues to be popular today with players in blues, rock, and jazz.

Rosewood fingerboard — Plastic tuner buttons —

Truss rod cover

1961 GIBSON ES-335

Body Laminated maple	**Nut width** 43mm (1¹¹⁄₁₆in)
Neck Mahogany	**Lower bout width** 407mm (16in)
Fingerboard 22-fret rosewood with dot inlays	**Features** Two humbucking pickups with controls
Scale length 629mm (24¾in)	

Electric blues
BB King has used both ES-335 and ES-345 guitars. Here he is using a ES-345 with double parallelogram inlays.

FUTURISTIC DESIGN

The Flying V was way ahead of its time, produced in small quantities, and quickly discontinued. New modified versions were reintroduced from 1965 onwards in a climate that was open to way out ideas. The second version had a smaller headstock, a large pickguard surrounding the pickups, controls grouped in a triangle, and a cherry red or sunburst finish. This version was the one painted with a psychedelic pattern and played by Jimi Hendrix. The guitar has a bright tone, and can be used to create a range of rock and blues sounds.

1958 GIBSON FLYING V

Body Korina
Neck Korina
Fingerboard 22-fret rosewood with dot inlays
Scale length 629mm (24¾in)
Nut width 43mm (1¹¹⁄₁₆in)
Lower bout width 426mm (16¾in)
Features Two humbucking pickups with controls and natural finish; headstock with amplifier logo

Tuners

Pointed headstock

Dot inlays

Truss rod cover

1980 Gibson Explorer
Gibson made another unusual design in 1958, the Explorer. A new version appeared in 1975.

Upper bout cut away

Extended lower bout

Gibson SG Standard

The SG model came out in 1961 as a fresh design to replace the original 1950s Les Paul series. It has double cutaways with sharp, incurved horns, and a shallow body. In addition to the Standard model, a range of SGs, including the Junior, Special, and Custom, were brought out with different fittings and decorative features. The SG range was very popular in the 1960s and 1970s and underwent a number of minor structural changes. It became one of the rock icon guitars.

Vibrola tremolo

Cherry red finish

Rotary controls

Metal arm

Gibson Firebird VII

In 1963, Gibson introduced the Firebird series. It incorporated ideas from car designer Ray Dietrich and motifs from North American Indian mythology. It features a highly effective "reverse" body shape, where the guitar is virtually upside down. A series was launched, with I, III, and V models, in addition to the top-of-the-range VII.

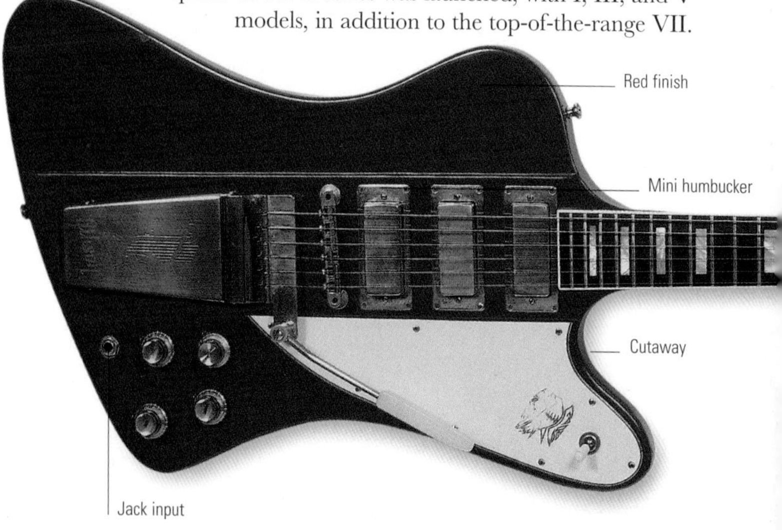

Red finish

Mini humbucker

Cutaway

Jack input

SOLID GUITAR

The SG, short for Solid Guitar, was launched in 1961 and the guitar featured here is from that year. It is fitted with a sideways vibrola unit, which Gibson added to provide a tremolo system to match the Fender Stratocaster. The guitar was replaced with a more efficient plate vibrola unit in 1963. Light and easy to play, with tremendous upper register access, it has a lively yet balanced tonal response, and is ideal as a stage instrument. The model was used by Frank Zappa.

Pete Towshend
Performing with The Who in the early 1970s, Pete Townshend found the SG ideal for rock music.

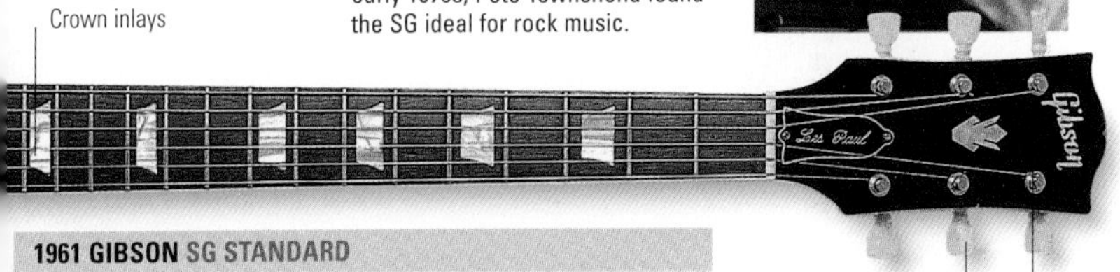

Crown inlays

Tuner

Headstock

1961 GIBSON SG STANDARD

Body Mahogany	**Nut width** 43mm (1¹¹⁄₁₆in)
Neck Mahogany	**Lower bout width** 330mm (13in)
Fingerboard 22-fret rosewood with crown inlays	**Features** Two humbucking pickups and Vibrola tremolo
Scale length 629mm (24¾in)	

REVERSE BODY

An interesting design, the Firebird has a beak-shaped headstock that faces upwards. The lower bout is extended out with the upper bout swept back giving it a revolutionary shape. The guitar also has a "neck through body" construction, where the side wings are glued onto the narrow central area that runs from the headstock to the base of the body. Gibson developed small, new "mini-humbuckers" for the guitar. The Firebird has its own tonal qualities of attack and sustain yet retains the Gibson sound. The "reverse" models were discontinued in 1965. The design was reintroduced in 1990.

1960s FIREBIRD VII

Body Mahogany

Neck Through neck with laminated mahogany and walnut

Fingerboard 22-fret ebony with block inlays

Scale length 629mm (24¾in)

Nut width 43mm (1¹¹⁄₁₆in)

Lower bout width 356mm (14in)

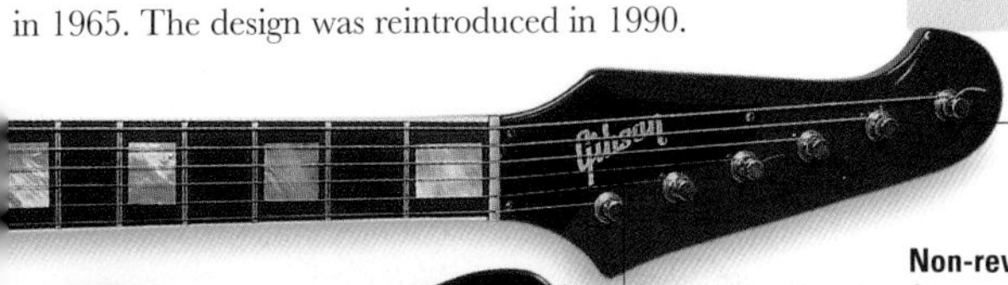

Reverse headstock

Logo

Non-reverse Firebird III
A non-reverse model was made from 1965 until 1969. This guitar was made in 1966.

Rosewood fingerboard

Normal headstock

Gibson L-5CES

Introduced in 1951, the L-5CES was a modified electric version of the archtop acoustic L-5C, with pickups and controls set into the body. A high-level Gibson, it was introduced to meet the growing post-war demand for a quality electric guitar with a carved spruce top.

Carved spruce top

Scotty Moore
The guitarist playing with Elvis Presley when he broke through in the mid-1950s, Scotty Moore often used an L-5CES and found its sound ideal for rock 'n' roll.

Rotary controls

Gibson Super 400CES

The Super 400CES first came out in 1951 at the same time as the L-5CES, and is also a modified electric version of the acoustic Super 400C. It was the top-of-the-range Gibson electric guitar as well as the largest, with a 457mm (18in) wide body, and stands out as a high-quality instrument.

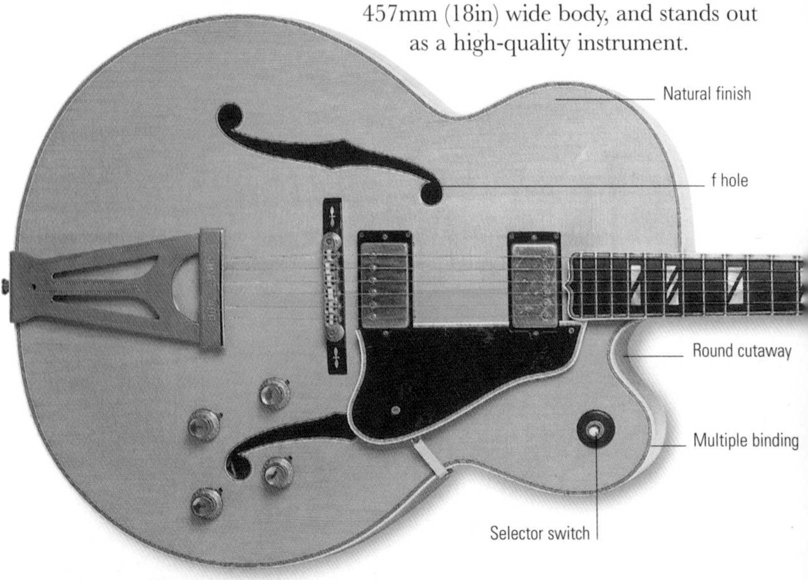

Natural finish

f hole

Round cutaway

Multiple binding

Selector switch

ELECTRIC ARCHTOP

The first L-5CES models were fitted with P-90 pickups and came in either a sunburst or natural finish with attractive maple woods and gold-plated parts, such as the pickup covers and tuners. The body and the fingerboard have multiple black and white bindings. In 1957, they were fitted with humbucking pickups, and from 1960–69 a rounded "Venetian" cutaway replaced the sharp "Florentine" cutaway. The guitar has a sound that has penetrating edge as well as a jazz-flavoured depth. It has been popular in jazz, and a single pickup model was used by Wes Montgomery in the 1960s. The L-5CES was also used in country music, and occasionally by rock musicians in the studio to provide a sound with an additional dimension. This guitar is a 40th Anniversary model from 1991. The L-5CES is still produced as a special order guitar.

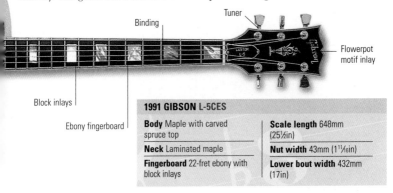

Tuner

Binding

Flowerpot motif inlay

Block inlays

Ebony fingerboard

1991 GIBSON L-5CES

Body Maple with carved spruce top

Neck Laminated maple

Fingerboard 22-fret ebony with block inlays

Scale length 648mm (25½in)

Nut width 43mm (1¹¹⁄₁₆in)

Lower bout width 432mm (17in)

LARGE-BODIED ARCHTOP

The first Super 400CES models came with P-90 pickups and a choice of a sunburst or natural finish with high-quality maple woods. It has decorative split block fingerboard and headstock inlays, and gold-plated fittings. The development of the guitar ran parallel to the L-5CES with humbucking pickups in 1957, and the introduction of the less pleasing rounded "Venetian" cutaway from 1960–69. This model from 1970 has the classic rounded cutaway. The Super 400CES has a deep, full-bodied resonant sound ideal for jazz guitar soloing and chords.

1970 SUPER 400CES

Body Maple with carved spruce top

Neck Laminated maple

Fingerboard 22-fret ebony with split block inlays

Scale length 648mm (25½in)

Nut width 43mm (1¹¹⁄₁₆in)

Lower bout width 457mm (18in)

Features Two pickups

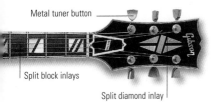

Metal tuner button

Split block inlays

Split diamond inlay

Ornate Headstock
The Gibson Super 400 has a long ornate headstock with inlaid mother-of-pearl effect motifs. Apart from the logo, there is a large split diamond motif, multiple edge-binding, and a fancy truss rod cover.

Gibson ES-175

The ES-175 was Gibson's second dedicated electric guitar design with a cutaway to be launched for the mass market. It was first introduced in 1949 and quickly became established as a widely used instrument in jazz. The arched top with f holes was made from manufactured, pressed, laminated maple instead of carved spruce.

Raised pickguard

Sharp cutaway

Clear natural finish

Rickenbacker 360/12

The guitar shown here is the 360/12 used by George Harrison with The Beatles. It was made by Rickenbacker in 1963. The design was derived from the company's thinline 300 series models introduced in the late 1950s, and its sound became an important part of rock and pop during the 1960s.

21-fret neck-to-body junction

Roger McGuinn
The guitarist with the Byrds was inspired by hearing George Harrison in 1964. He often used the later round-edged body 360/12 with a natural finish.

Two-tiered pickguard

SHARP CUTAWAY ELECTRIC ARCHTOP

The first ES-175 model was launched in 1949 and had a single P-90 pickup with two rotary controls, a wooden bridge, a 19-fret rosewood fingerboard with double parallelogram inlays, and a sunburst finish. Over the next ten years, natural finish models became available. An extra fret was added, as well as a metal Tune-O-Matic bridge. In 1953, a model was introduced that had a second pickup with its own pair of controls and a selector switch, and in 1957, P-90 pickups were replaced with humbuckers.

Jim Hall
Outstanding US jazz guitarist Jim Hall played an ES-175 in the 1950s and 1960s.

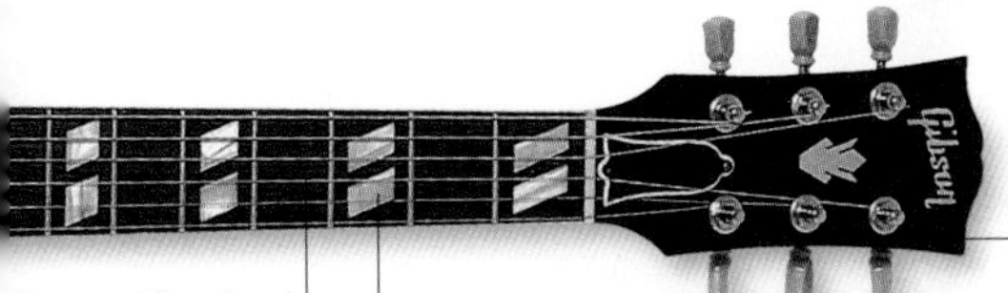

Headstock

Rosewood fingerboard

Double parallelogram inlays

1960 ES-175	
Body Laminated maple	**Nut width** 43mm (1¹¹⁄₁₆in)
Neck Mahogany	**Lower bout width** 413mm (16¼in)
Fingerboard 20-fret rosewood with double parallelogram inlays	**Features** Two humbucking pickups with four rotary controls
Scale length 629mm (24¾in)	

ELECTRIC 12-STRING

The model has 12 strings that are positioned in pairs: the four lower pairs have the standard pitch string on the bottom with a higher octave string above; the upper pairs of strings are in unison. The lower stringing is the reverse of normal acoustic twelve-string guitars. The guitar has a 21-fret rosewood fingerboard with triangular inlays and the double cutaway body is made of maple. It has an extra rotary blender control to mix sounds from the pickups. An alternative model with a rounded-edge body shape was also introduced in late 1964. The 360/12 is still used today for studio recording.

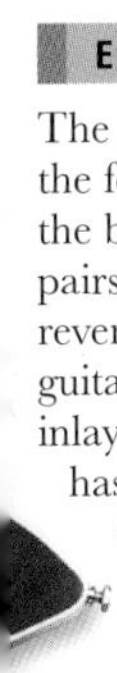

1963 360/12
Body Maple
Neck Laminated maple and walnut
Fingerboard 21-fret African rosewood with triangular inlays
Scale length 629mm (24¾in)
Nut width 42mm (1⅝in)
Lower bout width 381mm (15in)
Features Two "toaster top" pickups with controls

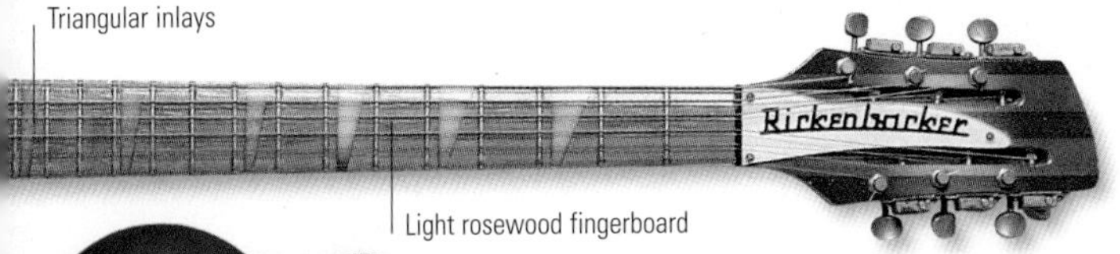

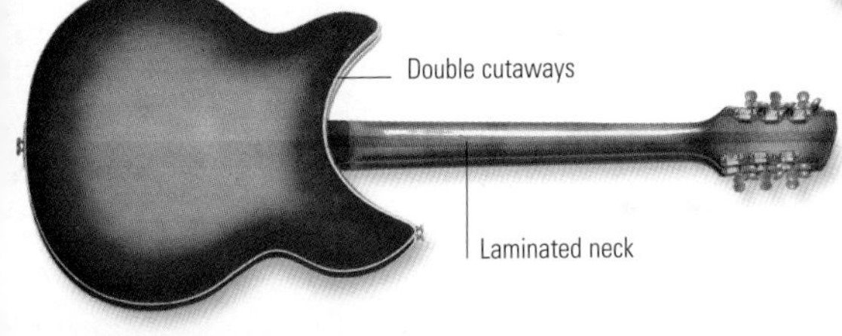

Triangular inlays

Rickenbacker

Light rosewood fingerboard

Double cutaways

Laminated neck

Back view
The Rickenbacker 360/12 can produce textures ranging from a vibrant jangly sound to chiming single notes and arpeggios.

PRS McCarty

Paul Reed Smith started making guitars in 1975, and in the 1980s he developed a new and original, yet instantly classic, modern electric design. PRS guitars are highly attractive and well-made, and they represent the American electric guitar tradition at its best.

Carlos Santana
A surviving 1960s icon, Carlos Santana has started playing PRS guitars in recent years.

Flamed maple top

Sunburst finish

Gretsch 6120

In the 1930s, Gretsch started developing a range of guitars with their own highly distinctive modern styling, and in 1954 they involved the country player Chet Atkins (*see* p.20) in a range of models that included the archtop Chet Atkins Hollow Body, numbered 6120. This has "cowboy" styling.

Rotary control

DeArmond pickups

CLASSIC DESIGN

First launched in 1994, the PRS McCarty model was brought out with the participation of former Gibson engineer and designer Ted McCarty. The guitar has the highly elegant PRS body shape, with beautifully designed double cutaways and a distinctive headstock shape. The McCarty has a simple "wraparound" stop tailpiece, with compensating ridges for intonation held by anchor posts rather like some 1950s Gibson models. It has basic rotary controls and a selector switch, which are recessed into the maple top. The guitar has a smooth feel and can be used to produce a range of traditional rock sounds. Today, PRS are one of the world's top makes, and they produce a wide range of models which have become increasingly popular.

Moon inlays   Rosewood fingerboard   Truss rod cover

Incurved sides

Tuner button

1994 PRS McCARTY

Body Mahogany with maple top

Neck Mahogany

Fingerboard 22-fret rosewood with moon inlays

Scale length 635mm (25in)

Nut width 43mm (1¹¹⁄₁₆in)

Lower bout width 327mm (12⅞in)

Features Two pickups

ROCKABILLY ICON

The first Gretsch 6120 guitars have hollow bodies with a comfortable depth and arched tops with large f holes. The guitar has an amber red finish, and cowboy and western motifs such as a G brand on the body and cactus fingerboard inlays. It has a responsive feel, twangy string sound, and acoustic depth. The guitar underwent radical changes in the 1960s with a shallower body, painted f holes and double cutaways. The model was discontinued in 1979 but reintroduced in 1989.

Cactus inlay

1956 GRETSCH 6120

Body Laminated maple

Neck Maple

Fingerboard 22-fret rosewood with decorated block inlays

Scale length 629mm (24¾in)

Nut width 43mm (1¹¹⁄₁₆in)

Lower bout width 394mm (15½in). This varies.

Features Two pickups and Bigsby vibrato unit

Eddie Cochran
During the 1950s rock 'n' roll boom, players such as Eddie Cochran adopted the new Gretsch 6120 model. Cochran's guitar was fitted with a black Gibson P-90 pickup, which gave it a distinctive tone.

Parker Fly

Launched in 1993, the Parker Fly was a futuristic model designed by
guitar-maker Ken Parker with input from pickup designer Larry Fishman.
Unusually, it is one of the few radical designs to be accepted by guitarists
in recent years. Highly innovative, the Fly uses synthetic materials and
a range of new features,
such as an added piezo
electroacoustic pickup.
The Classic model
was introduced
in 1996.

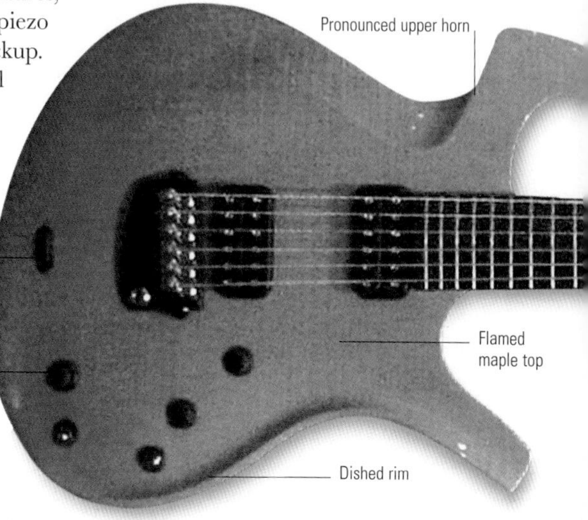

Pronounced upper horn

Tremolo
adjustment

Flamed
maple top

Rotary control

Dished rim

Ibanez Jem

A distinctive "superstrat" design that combines the most practical attributes of
a modern electric guitar, the Ibanez Jem was designed with input from Steve
Vai (*see* p.52) and first made in 1987. With its floral design and "monkey grip"
handle, it became an instantly recognizable classic.

Carrying
handle

High register access

Sharp
cutaway

Floral design

FUTURISTIC DESIGN

The Parker Fly has a light "exoskeleton" body—a synthetic hard carbon and glass fiber outer body shell, with soft woods inside to add resonance. Parker thought of this as being in the tradition of early lutes, which had a hard ebony outer casing. The Parker Fly has an unusual thin, asymmetric headstock shape, almost rectangular, parallel, drooping cutaways and a pronounced dish around the lower rim of the body. This Classic model has a flamed maple top. The Fly has humbucking pickups and an added piezoelectric pickup set in the bridge to give an electroacoustic tone. Both individually and in combination, the pickups give an interesting range of unusual bright sounds. The guitar has been used by players such as Reeves Gabrels accompanying David Bowie.

Steel frets   Resin fingerboard   Tuner

Thin, drooping headstock

2003 PARKER FLY

Body Woods and synthetic fibre

Neck Synthetic fibre

Fingerboard 24-fret phenolic resin

Scale length 25½in (648mm)

Nut width 1⅝in (42mm)

Lower bout width 12¾in (324mm)

Features Two humbucking pickups, piezo pickup

IBANEZ SUPERSTRAT

The Ibanez Jem has three pickups that can be used in straightforward combinations. There are two humbuckers and a single-coil pickup, giving a varied range of tones governed by two simple rotary controls and a selector switch. The 24-fret fingerboard has excellent upper-register access and the tremolo system can be moved in either direction to pull notes up as well as down in pitch. Ibanez guitars have been adopted by a number of modern electric guitar virtuosos, including Joe Satriani (*see* p.49).

1993 IBANEZ RG

Body Basswood

Neck Maple

Fingerboard 24-fret maple with foliate inlays

Scale length 25½in (648mm)

Nut width 1¹¹⁄₁₆in (43mm)

Lower bout width 12¼in (311mm)

Features Three pickups, five-way selector switch, locking nut and tremolo system

Foliate inlay   Locking nut

Ibanex 2620
This 2004 model has a maple top, 24-fret fingerboard, two DiMarzio humbucking pickups, and simple controls.

Deep wide cutaways

Rotary controls

Locking nut

PLAYING THE GUITAR

First steps

Choose the type of guitar that suits the music you want to play, such as steel-string acoustic or electric for pop or folk styles, or nylon-string for classical. Try different techniques before going in one direction with finger styles or a pick. You will need to tune the guitar so that all the strings are at their correct pitch, but at first just strum open strings and pick out single notes.

SOUNDING THE STRINGS

To begin with, play with just the right hand, without pressing down any notes on the fingerboard with the left. Look down at the guitar and place the right hand above the soundhole on an acoustic, or the pickups on an electric. With the thumb, play a downstroke across some or all of the strings. Then pick out a top or bottom string and pluck it on its own. Now try this with the index (first) finger— in this case you have to pluck upward, which requires concentration. Repeat single notes with the thumb or first finger and a group of strings together with the thumb.

Getting used to playing
Try pressing different frets with the fingers of the left hand. Find and hold a note with the first finger of the left hand, then strike the string with the right hand purposefully, but not too hard.

Looking Tilt the guitar slightly inward to see the fingerboard. Bring the neck upward or closer to the body so that the left hand can reach the strings.

Fingerwork The first finger is playing a note on the 3rd fret. The other fingers are lifted away from the strings.

Stabilize the guitar Balance the instrument so that both hands are able to hold it lightly.

Holding the guitar
Practice requires a sitting position. Place the guitar on the right leg close in to the body. For classical playing, place the guitar on the left leg.

STRING ACTION

The end of the fingerboard has a nut where the strings are raised clear so that they do not rattle against the frets. The bridge on the body has the same function. The height of the string, termed its "action," affects how easy a guitar is to play.

ELECTRIC GUITAR
An electric guitar has low string action. Therefore, it is much easier to press the strings down.

CLASSICAL GUITAR
Classical guitars have a higher string action and are harder to play.

LEFT-HAND POSITION

It is essential to cut the fingernails short on the left hand, so that they do not impede the fingertips from playing notes. Place the thumb on the back of the guitar neck, and use the fingers to press the strings down against the frets. Pressure from the thumb stabilizes the fingers and lets them exert muscular power. After the right hand has played the required notes, release the pressure of the left hand's fingers to stop the notes from sounding. Stretching and muscular pressure can be difficult at first. Make sure that you do not strain the left hand.

Thumb position
Place your thumb on the back of the neck, just above its center. Place the first finger on a string and push it down. Pressure should be firm, but the fingers should be flexible.

Finger angle
The finger has to go straight down on to the fret, so that the tip is holding the string—it does not have to be vertical. The fingers are curved as they bend round to play the notes.

Fret position
Hold notes firmly so that the strings do not buzz. Press about two-thirds of the way between any two frets and nearest to the fret where the string is being sounded.

Clearance
While fretting the note, ensure that the fingers are not muting any other strings that need to sound. For mobility, keep the palm of your hand away from the back of the guitar neck.

THE FIRST FOUR NOTES

Try playing a short series of notes on the top string. The "top" string, meaning the thinnest and highest in pitch, is at the bottom of the series of six strings as you look down at the guitar. On a steel-string acoustic or electric guitar, the top string has a bright, thin, metallic sound. On the classical guitar, the string is thicker and made of nylon, producing a softer, warmer, full sound.

Open string

Right hand only
Play the top string by resting the right-hand thumb on the string and then sweeping off it in an arc to make the sound. Try this with the right-hand first finger.

Left hand on 2nd fret
With the left hand, find the 2nd fret. Press just below the 2nd fret with the first finger. Hold it down while you sound the note with your right thumb.

Left hand on 3rd fret
Release the pressure from the left-hand finger on the 2nd fret. Lift the finger above the string and move it up one fret. Play the new note as before.

Left hand on 5th fret
Release the pressure from your finger and move up two frets to play a note on the 5th fret. Repeat, playing all four notes, and try them in a different order.

Fundamentals

To play the guitar, you need to recognize note positions. Standard guitars have six strings running along a fingerboard. Metal frets sit at intervals all along the fingerboard: they divide the smallest degree of pitch between each note. When you press a string against a fret and strike it with the right hand, it vibrates between the fret and the bridge, sounding a note.

NOTES AND SYMBOLS ON THE STAVE

Music is written down using a five-line grid called a stave. Each line and space is used to place a symbol that represents the pitch and time-value of a note. The first seven letters of the alphabet, A to G, are used to name the notes. A stylized letter G (𝄞)—known as a treble clef—fixes the second line of the stave as the note G. Notes that sit above and below

the stave are placed on ledger lines. To make guitar music easy to read, the notes on the fingerboard are written one octave higher than their actual pitch. Middle C occurs on the 1st fret of the 2nd string, not on the 3rd fret of the 5th string. When reading music not written specifically for the guitar, remember to play it one octave higher.

Notes on the treble stave
The notes on the stave lines are, from bottom to top, E-G-B-D-F. Remember them by the first letter in each word of the phrase "Eat Good Bread Dear Father," or "Every Good Boy Does Fine." The notes in between the stave lines are F-A-C-E, spelling the word "FACE."

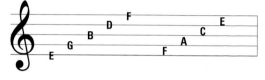

The stave and open strings
The notes of the guitar's six open strings (played using the right hand only) are shown (right) as symbols on the stave. The lowest note, E, corresponds to the open 6th string on the guitar. A is the open 5th string; D the open 4th string; G the open 3rd string; B the open 2nd string; and E is the open 1st string.

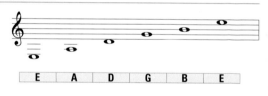

| E | A | D | G | B | E |

Fret The metal fret determines the pitch of the note. The letter shows the note played when the finger sits below it in the correct "fret position."

Open strings	Fret number 1	2	3	4	5
E	F	F♯/G♭	G	G♯/A♭	A
B	C	C♯/D♭	D	D♯/E♭	E
G	G♯/A♭	A	A♯/B♭	B	C
D	D♯/E♭	E	F	F♯/G♭	G
A	A♯/B♭	B	C	C♯/D♭	D
E	F	F♯/G♭	G	G♯/A♭	A

SCALE ON THE 5TH STRING

The interval between any 12 chromatic steps on the fingerboard, such as that between an open 1st string and the 12th fret of the 1st string, is called an octave. Each of these 12 steps is called a semitone. An interval of two frets is called a tone. To name every semitonal step, the letters A to G have intermediate names: they are raised by adding sharps (♯), and lowered by adding flats (♭). The natural sign (♮) is used in written music to "cancel" a sharp or flat. The interval between B and C is a semitone. A tone, such as that between F and G, is twice this interval. Using the 5th string as an example, the order of note names runs from the open string (the note A), through the chromatic series up to the 12th fret, when A is repeated on the octave. It vibrates at twice the frequency of the open string A, giving a higher register of the same pitch.

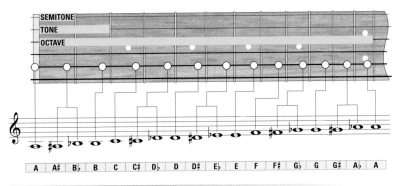

| A | A♯ | B♭ | B | C | C♯ | D♭ | D | D♯ | E♭ | E | F | F♯ | G♭ | G | G♯ | A♭ | A |

NUMBERS AND LETTERS

The diagram below shows a standard guitar fingerboard, with the fret numbers indicated above. Every open string and fret position has its own musical letter name, corresponding to the 12 chromatic semitones (steps) of an octave on the fingerboard. Every semitone is the musical interval between one fret.

So, each string runs in a series of 12 semitones from its open-string note up to the 12th fret. At this point the series of notes starts again—another octave begins. For example, at the 12th fret of the 1st string, the note E reoccurs one octave higher than the note E of the open 1st string. The series of notes begin again with F from the 13th fret upward. Playing these notes is one way to ascend through a series of semitones on the guitar. The same notes also occur at other points on the fingerboard, and in higher and lower octaves.

12th fret The series of notes, played from the open strings, repeat themselves one octave higher here

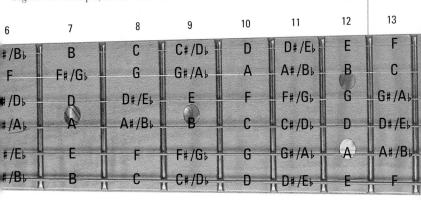

	6	7	8	9	10	11	12	13
	♯/B♭	B	C	C♯/D♭	D	D♯/E♭	E	F
	F	F♯/G♭	G	G♯/A♭	A	A♯/B♭	B	C
	♯/D♭	D	D♯/E♭	E	F	F♯/G♭	G	G♯/A♭
	♯/A♭	A	A♯/B♭	B	C	C♯/D♭	D	D♯/E♭
	♯/E♭	E	F	F♯/G♭	G	G♯/A♭	A	A♯/B♭
	♯/B♭	B	C	C♯/D♭	D	D♯/E♭	E	F

Tuning the guitar

Accurate tuning of the guitar is vitally important. Each of the open strings should be adjusted so that it is in tune with all the others. When the open strings are not perfectly in tune, the guitar produces an unpleasantly discordant and unmusical effect: chords and scales sound wrong, and this can often deter the beginner from playing the instrument altogether. If the strings are tuned to concert pitch (*see below*), the guitar can be played with other instruments.

THE TEMPERED SCALE

The scale length and fret positions on a guitar are constructed to produce a chromatic series of "tempered" intervals. The chromatic scale was tempered during the middle of the 18th century in order to balance the spatial relationships between notes, allowing accurate tuning. The notes of a guitar's open strings, like all musical notes, have a letter name from the series A to G. The intervals between notes are described by their numeric relationship to each other within a scale—the number of notes that separate them—such as a third, a fourth, or a fifth, for example.

OPEN-STRING INTERVALS

The strings of a guitar are tuned to a fixed series of notes, in a fixed series of musical intervals, from the bottom string up to the top. The 6th string (E) and the 5th string (A) are separated by an interval of a fourth—there are four tones running from the notes E to A (E-F-G-A). The remaining strings are also tuned in intervals of fourths, except the 3rd (G) and 2nd (B) strings, where there is an interval of a third—the three notes G, A, and B—between them.

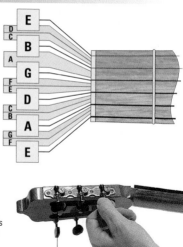

How to use the machine heads

Each string on the guitar is wound onto a machine head. By turning a machine head, string tension can be adjusted until a string is in tune. Turning a machine head counterclockwise increases a string's tension and raises its pitch; turning a machine head clockwise reduces a string's tension and lowers its pitch. Guitar strings may go out of tune as a result of age, string slippage, changes in temperature, or simply because of the movement of playing.

Machine head

TUNING TO A REFERENCE POINT

The guitar is frequently tuned by selecting a single note as a reference point, and tuning one string to that note. That string can then be used as the reference for tuning all of the other strings in turn. A string is tuned by playing the appropriate open-string or fretted note, then turning the machine head until its pitch matches the reference note exactly. For example, a standard tuning fork that provides the concert pitch note A at 440 Hz can be used as a reference for tuning the guitar's 1st string by playing an A on the string's 5th fret. Equally, any musical instrument playing the note E can be used as a source for tuning an open 1st string. For the beginner, tuning an open string is by far the most straightforward approach. Another approach to tuning the guitar is to use a keyboard. Play E-A-D-G-B-E and tune each string individually.

Tuning forks
When struck, a tuning fork vibrates at a specific frequency and sounds a specific note to tune to. Its sound can be amplified by placing the base of the fork against the surface of the guitar. The tuning fork shown above emits an A note at a frequency of 440 Hz. Playing the note A on the 5th fret of the 1st string of the guitar should produce the same pitch if the 1st string is in tune.

Electronic tuners
An electronic tuner monitors the frequency of each of the six strings in turn. It has a display to indicate whether the string you are tuning is sharp or flat. The machine heads are adjusted until the correct reading is given. An electric guitar can be plugged into the tuner, while many also have a built-in microphone that can pick up sound; this allows acoustic guitars to be tuned.

BASIC TUNING METHOD

Once the 1st string is in tune, it can be used as the base for tuning the 2nd string. Play the note E on the 2nd string's 5th fret, and leave the note to ring. Sound E on the open 1st string so that it rings at the same time, then adjust the 2nd-string machine head until the two strings are in tune. This technique of matching adjacent strings can be used right across the fingerboard.

1. Play E on the 5th fret of the 2nd string, then play the open 1st string, E. Compare both pitches and adjust the 2nd string until it is in tune with the 1st.

2. Play the note B on the 4th fret of the 3rd string, closely followed by the open 2nd string, B. Adjust the 3rd string until it is in tune.

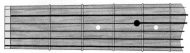

3. Play the note G on the 5th fret of the 4th string of the guitar, then play the open 3rd string, G. Adjust the 4th string until it is in tune.

4. Play the note D on the 5th fret of the 5th string, then play D by sounding the open 4th string. Adjust the 5th string until it is in tune.

5. Play the note A on the 5th fret of the 6th string, followed by A from the open 5th string. Adjust the 6th string until it is in tune.

Playing positions

When playing the guitar, it is essential to adopt a relaxed and comfortable position. For beginners, the sitting positions are easiest. Most guitarists rest the instrument in their lap, supporting it with either the left or right leg for stability and control. Some prefer to play standing up. Nearly all guitar music requires left-hand stretching, and this initially causes difficulties. As a warm-up exercise, to prepare the hands for playing, open out the fingers of the left hand wide, stretching them gently.

ACOUSTIC GUITAR POSITION

A popular and natural sitting position for playing acoustic guitars is with the instrument resting on the right leg. The inside of the right arm keeps the guitar in place and prevents it from tipping forward or sideways. The right arm is drawn back, resting against the guitar with the forearm diagonal to the strings. The neck is close in to the player's body. This gives a comfortable left-arm position for playing any guitar.

CLASSICAL GUITAR POSTURE

When sitting down, classical players rest the waist of the guitar's body on the left leg. The neck is angled upward so that the left arm can easily reach the fingerboard. The right arm rests on the edge of the upper rim of the body. The left foot is placed on a small stool to bring the left leg up to a higher position. In this standard posture, the weight of the instrument is well supported. Some players of other styles prefer this position.

Right arm Pressure from the right arm holds the guitar steady.

Head Beginners need to look down at the strings.

Shoulders These must be relaxed.

Legs Keep legs parallel and feet flat on the floor.

Right arm The forearm should be parallel to the floor.

Head Look ahead or at the strings, whichever is most practical.

Footstool Use an adjustable footstool

Acoustic posture
The standard posture for playing an acoustic guitar while sitting down is to rest the guitar on the right leg. This allows the guitarist to sit in a comfortable and relaxed position.

Classical posture
The waist of the guitar should rest on the left leg. To get the correct neck angle, raise your left foot on a footstool, raising the height of the guitar, helping the left arm position and your overall posture.

STANDING UP

Many live performers play standing up, with the guitar supported by a strap. To an experienced electric guitarist this can become the most natural way to play. But, with the support of a strap, any type of guitar can be played in a standing position. It is important to let the instrument hang from the strap, with its weight against the body and a good center of gravity. This leaves the hands and arms free for easy access and comfortable movement. For many rock guitarists, it is fashionable to place the guitar in a low position. Although this may look good, it makes the instrument harder to play and is not recommended for beginners.

PLAYING LEFT HANDED

For the many left-handed musicians, it is entirely acceptable simply to play the guitar the other way around. But you should try playing the guitar both ways, because some left handers prefer to play right handed. It is a matter of which way feels instinctively correct, and which gives easier control and hand coordination. If you play a symmetrical acoustic guitar or a right-handed electric guitar upside down, change the strings. The thinnest, high-pitch strings must be at the bottom. Of course, there are guitars designed specially for left-handed people. They are made and strung so that they are mirror images of right-handed guitars.

Arm The right arm is crooked to form a triangle.

Thumb You can place the thumb near or on the upper edge of the neck for some playing positions.

Strap support Standing up should feel comfortable when the guitar is supported by a strap.

Legs Keep the weight on both feet when standing still.

Moving the guitar Tipping the neck upward can make it easier to play notes higher up.

Tremolo arm Use the tremolo arm, or "whammy bar," to move the pitch of notes.

Express yourself Many players find it exciting and inspiring to move around with an electric guitar.

Electric guitar posture
Electric guitars are designed primarily for a standing position. For a practical left-hand position, tilt the neck upward. The posture should feel comfortable when a strap supports the electric guitar.

Standing posture
Whether left or right handed, standing up with the guitar can give a creative feeling of freedom and rhythmic movement. There is nothing wrong with playing "air guitar" with the real thing.

Starting to play

When two or more notes are played at the same time, a chord is produced. One of the simplest ways to begin playing is to construct basic chord shapes on open-string positions. The left-hand fingers press strings against the fingerboard to create fretted notes (this makes the fingertips sore at first, but they will soon toughen up) while the right-hand fingers brush or pluck the strings.

INTRODUCTION TO FINGERING

The fingers on the left hand are given numbers from one to four, starting with the index finger. In diagrams, these show the fingerings of single notes or chords. Chords are formed by using one or more fingers to press the strings down on a fretted position. With open-string chords, the fretted notes are combined with open strings. The open-string E minor chord is one of the simplest.

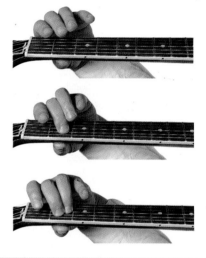

1. Play the open 5th string, A, either with an upstroke of the first or second finger of the right hand, or with a downstroke of the thumb. Then, put the second finger on the 2nd fret of the 5th string and play the note B.

2. Add the third finger. Keep holding the second finger on the note B on the 5th string. Now add the third finger next to it to play the note E on the second fret of the 4th string. The position of the two fingers may feel tight at first.

3. Hold the two notes down firmly, and strum across all six strings with the first or second finger of the right hand. With practice, you will be able to place the fingers of your left hand on a chord position as one movement.

TABLATURE

The tablature system shows the positions for playing notes and chords, as well as the order in which they are to be played. The guitar strings are depicted as six horizontal lines running from left to right. Numbers placed on the lines show the fret positions. Numbers running along the lines indicate notes to be played one after the other.

Chords in tablature
The lines shown on a tablature diagram correspond to the strings, and the numbers to the frets. When the numbers are shown in a vertical line, play all the notes indicated as a chord.

Arpeggios in tablature
If numbers in tablature are written from left to right, play the notes one after the other, in sequence. This way of playing a chord (the one below being E minor) is termed an "arpeggio."

Single note movements
These are also indicated in tablature by writing the numbers from left to right. Start the scale below by playing an open A, followed by B on the 2nd fret, C on the 3rd fret and an open D.

Chords Tablature in one vertical line indicates that the notes are played together.

Arpeggio Staggered tablature indicates that the notes in the chord are played separately.

Single notes These positions indicate a four-note scale played on the 5th and 4th strings.

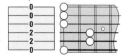

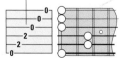

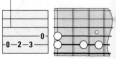

INTRODUCING CHORDS

Each of these chords should be learned, both visually and by name. To begin with, build up a chord one note at a time. Eventually the chord should be formed by placing the fingers accurately in position all at the same time. Every note should ring clearly and not buzz against the frets, and open strings must not be muffled by adjacent fingers. Remember to play the chord evenly. Strum or pluck from the lowest string through to the top string.

E minor
The E minor chord shape consists of the notes E, B, E, G, B, and E. All six strings should be played at the same time.

E major
The E major chord shape consists of the notes E, B, E, G♯, B, and E. All six strings should be played at the same time.

A minor
The A minor chord shape consists of the five notes A, E, A, C, and E. Only the 5th to the 1st strings should be played.

D major
The D major chord shape consists of the four notes D, A, D, and F♯. The 4th to the 1st strings should be played.

PLAYING A MAJOR CHORD SEQUENCE

To begin with, chord changes should be practised slowly, and speed built up gradually. The final chord change, from A minor to D major, requires the biggest jump in technique, and should be practiced separately. Remember to play the A and D notes and avoid the bottom string on the third and fourth chords.

E minor
Place the second finger on the 5th string 2nd fret, and the third finger on the 4th string 2nd fret. Strum the chord gently downward.

E major
While still holding down the E minor chord, change it to E major by adding the first finger to the 1st fret of the 3rd string.

A minor
Move the E major shape across from the 3rd, 4th, and 5th strings and onto the 2nd, 3rd, and 4th strings, to form the A minor chord.

D major
Place the first finger on the 3rd string 2nd fret, the second on the 1st string 2nd fret, and the third on the 2nd string 3rd fret.

Scales and timing

Having linked together a series of chords, the next step is to pick out individual notes and play them as scales. To play any sort of scale structure, it is important to develop the ability to play notes evenly and to build up timing control. The left hand must be able to pick out each individual note clearly, and the right hand must be coordinated with the left. These skills are vital in laying the foundations for playing correctly.

FINGERING ON ONE STRING

A good first step toward developing single-note technique is to play a five-note chromatic scale (a scale composed of semitone intervals) on the top string of the guitar. Start the scale with the open top E string and use a finger for each consecutive fret, up to the G♯/A♭ on the 4th fret, before coming back down again. The notes are E-F-F♯-G-G♯-G-F♯-F-E. As a new note is played, any previous note held should be released. This will help to build up an equal facility with each finger of the left hand. You can break the scale down and practice the one-note movement between each of the fingers.

THE MAJOR SCALE

Most scales in Western classical music are made up of seven different notes, with fixed intervals, within an octave. Each note of a scale is termed a degree of the scale, the first note being the first degree, or key note. The major scale always has the following ascending order of tones and semitones: tone-tone-semitone-tone-tone-tone-semitone. This sequence of intervals can be repeated in any octave, and a major scale pattern can be built from any note on the fingerboard. The guitar is constructed in such a way that the same notes can be played in different positions on the fingerboard. The same scale can be played by moving up just one string, or by moving across different strings.

The C major scale
To play the C major scale shown on the right, the guitar's lowest C—the 3rd fret of the 5th string—must be located. The scale ascends from this point. The notes in the C major scale have letter names without sharps (♯) or flats (♭)—they are the same as the white notes on a piano keyboard.

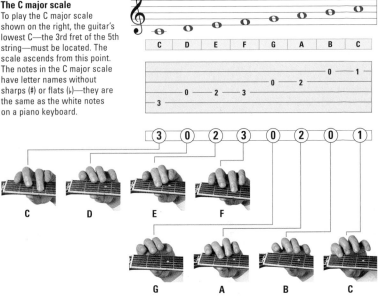

RHYTHM, TIMING, AND TEMPO

So far, chords and scales have been played as a sequence of movements without any sort of strict time value. However, virtually all music is played or written down using an ordered system defining the duration and position of musical notes. Once the left hand has become reasonably comfortable at forming the E major and A minor chord shapes, the next step is to start playing chord changes to a rhythm, in a set period of time. The speed of a piece of music—the amount of time between each beat—is referred to as the tempo.

CROTCHETS

The crotchet is often used as a reference point for tempo. This bar contains four crotchets. It represents the note A played four times, with an equal lapse of time between each note.

Playing in time
A crotchet (also called a quarter note) written down with a number next to it indicates how many are played during each minute. For example, if a crotchet is marked as ♩ = 60, the rate of movement in the music is one crotchet beat per second. Play the eight crotchet beats shown on the right slowly and evenly, counting four seconds between each chord. While still counting at the same speed, play a chord every two seconds—this doubles the tempo. Working up to playing a chord every second requires practice. Playing along with a metronome or drum machine will ensure accuracy.

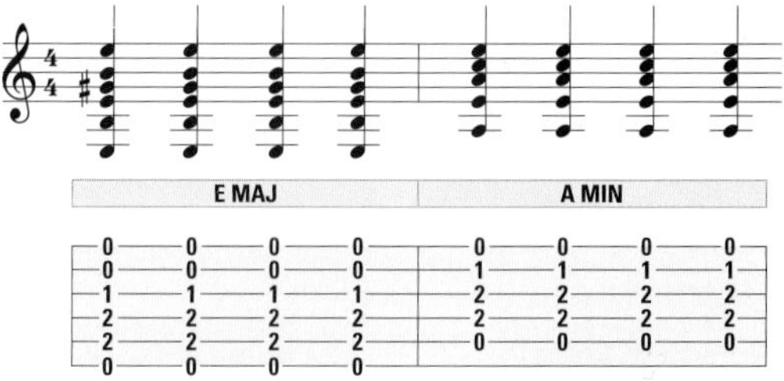

E MAJ   A MIN

```
0----0----0----0        0----0----0----0
0----0----0----0        1----1----1----1
1----1----1----1        2----2----2----2
2----2----2----2        2----2----2----2
2----2----2----2        0----0----0----0
0----0----0----0
```

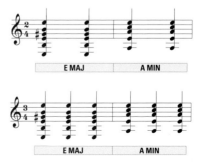

BAR LINES

Repeating the eight chords above and playing the first downstroke on each chord change with a greater volume, gives an accent to each group of four beats. In the diagrams below, each of the accented groups is separated by a bar line—bars group together notes, defining their overall rhythmic length and structure. The two numbers at the beginning of a bar show the time signature—a grouping of four crotchet beats is 4/4 (four-four) time. Groups of three notes (3/4), and two notes (2/4) can also be played.

Time signature of 2/4
The top figure (2) represents the number of beats in the bar, and the bottom figure (4) represents crotchets, or quarter notes. Play E major with an accent, and repeat it. Play A minor with an accent and repeat it.

E MAJ   A MIN

Time signature of 3/4
There are three crotchets per bar. This time signature is termed "waltz" or "triple" time. Play E major with an accent and repeat it twice. Play A minor with an accent and repeat it twice. Strum the chords evenly, and try using a metronome.

E MAJ   A MIN

Pick technique

The majority of electric and many steel string acoustic guitarists use a pick—a flat, triangular piece of plastic held between the thumb and first finger. Playing with a pick, or plectrum, produces a strong, clear, and even tone. The key to a good pick technique is mastering the upstroke and downstroke. The symbol "⊓" represents a downstroke, and "∨" represents an upstroke.

HOLDING THE PICK

Accurate pick movement with a relaxed position is essential for playing with control. Your grip should be firm enough to stop the pick from moving out of position as it strikes the strings. Guitarists tend to play by swiveling the wrist and forearm and moving the joints of the thumb and fingers. For extra stability, rest the side of your hand or fingers on the body, pickguard or the bridge.

Pick position
The pick should be pointed directly down, toward the body of the guitar. Do not allow it to turn around as you use it to pick strings. Keep it in line with the string, to ensure control.

Gripping
Hold the pick between the side of the top joint of the first finger and the bottom of the first joint of the thumb. The second, third, and fourth fingers should be curved inward.

Striking
Play the top E string with a downstroke. The tip of the pick should touch the strings evenly and make just enough contact with the string to produce a full tone.

PICK DIRECTION

Fast passages of notes are played more economically by using alternate strokes—an upstroke after a downstroke as a single movement. The exercises below will develop a grounding in pick control, essential for speed and fluency in soloing. At this stage, simple downstrokes, upstrokes, and then more advanced combinations of both are played on an open string.

Downstrokes
Play four downstrokes, using similar volume and attack for each one. As you position the pick to play the repeat downstroke, take care not to hit the string.

Upstrokes
Play four upstrokes with a similar level of volume and attack. The upstroke movement is important for balancing the overall control of the pick.

Alternating
Pick a downstroke, then an upstroke. Repeat, using an even motion. Passages are usually played with alternating strokes for economy of movement.

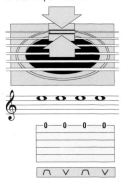

PLAYING A SCALE

To master pick technique, it is important to be able to play a series of single notes using all types of directional movement. The ability to play repeated downstrokes or upstrokes is necessary for controlling tone, rhythmic phrasing, and other techniques. A short succession of notes, such as part of a scale or a melody, can be played using a combination of alternate pick movements on a single string. When moving from one string to another, it is helpful if the pick is on the correct side of the string just played, ready to play the adjacent string.

Picking C major
Play C and D as downstrokes, then E and F using alternate picking. Play the open G as a downstroke followed by A as an upstroke. Play the open B as a downstroke, and complete the movement with an upstroke on C.

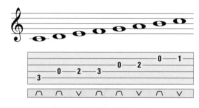

CHORD STRUMMING TECHNIQUE

Some of the basic principles of movement for playing single notes with a pick apply equally to strumming. The pick should be parallel to the strings, and the arc of movement should not take the hand too far away when a stroke has been played. The hand should not rest against the face of the guitar. The inside of the forearm can rest on the edge of the body, but the hand and forearm must be free to make a sweeping movement across the strings.

Downstrokes
Play E major as a series of four downstrokes.

The downstroke
Downstroke technique is important for strumming chords: a fast downward sweep, playing every note is the main method. Play a full downstroke across the open strings at first. Now form the chord of E major and hold it firmly while strumming a down stroke. Try not to go in too steeply as you hit the bass strings.

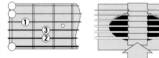

Upstrokes
Play E major as a series of four upstrokes.

The upstroke
Play an upstroke, with a movement similar to the downstroke. This is a much more difficult technique at first. When you play an upstroke sometimes the pick gets caught under the top string. Start by strumming without forming a chord, and try to get an even sweep of movement across all six strings. Now add the E major chord and play upstrokes.

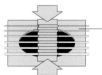

Alternating
Play E major as a downstroke then as an upstroke.

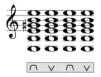

Alternating strokes
To develop an alternating strumming technique start by playing four downstrokes, followed by four upstrokes. Reduce this to two movements in each direction. Now move to alternate strumming by playing a downstroke followed by an upstroke slowly. Try to play with a metronome or even a recording with the strings dampened at first.

Basic chords

Chords can use any combination of positions on the guitar. Every chord has a letter name and a short definition of its harmonic structure. Most guitar chords are built from, and named after, the root, which is usually the lowest pitched note. The open-string position forms an initial area for playing where basic chord types can be formed, using fretted notes and open strings.

CHORD PATTERNS

The following group of 12 chords should be added to the four shown on page 113, giving a total vocabulary of 16 chords. Memorizing the available string positions provides a framework for a large number of sequences. Four chord types are used here: major, minor, dominant seventh, and diminished. These include three that do not use open strings: F major, B major, and B diminished.

C major
Built from the notes C, E, G, C, and E, this chord uses three fretted and two open strings. Only the top five strings are played.

0
1
0
2
3

D minor
This consists of the notes D, A, D, and F, using three fretted notes and one open string. Only the top four strings are played.

1
3
2
0

D dominant 7th
Formed from the notes D, A, C, and F♯, this uses three fretted notes with one open string. Only the top four strings are played.

2
1
2
0

E dominant 7th
The notes for this chord are E, B, D, G♯, B, and E, played on two fretted and four open strings. All six strings are used.

0
0
1
0
2
0

F major
This chord is formed from the notes F, A, C, and F. All of these notes are fretted. The first finger holds the 1st and 2nd strings.

1
1
2
3

G major
The notes G, B, D, G, B, and G make up this chord. All the strings are used; three of them are fretted, and three are open.

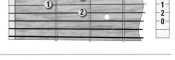

3
0
0
0
2
3

G dominant 7th
This chord consists of the notes G, B, D, G, B, and F, using three fretted and three open strings. All six strings are played.

1
0
0
0
2
3

A major

With the notes A, E, A, C♯, and E, this uses three fretted and two open strings. The top five strings are played.

A dominant 7th

This consists of A, E, G, C♯, and E, played on two fretted and three open strings. Only the top five strings are used.

B diminished

This is formed from the notes B, F, B, and D. The four middle strings are played and all of the notes are fretted.

B dominant 7th

The notes B, D♯, A, and B, on the four middle strings, are used. Three of the strings are fretted, and the other is open.

B major

This is made up of the notes B, F♯, B, and D♯, using four fretted strings. The four middle strings are played.

MOVING A SHAPE AROUND THE FINGERBOARD

Every chord has a distinctive shape. This shape is formed by the order in which a chord's notes occur, and is known as a "voicing." When a fixed voicing is moved across the fingerboard (across in the sense of crossing the strings, as opposed to moving up or down the fingerboard) then its shape must alter. The first diagram below illustrates this: the three chords E, A and D all have the same voicing, but in moving across

the fingerboard, from a 6th-string to a 5th-string, and then to a 4th-string root, the note on the 2nd string of each chord must move up one fret each time. In the second example, there is a similar process. G major with the root on the 6th string is voiced root, third, fifth, root. It has a similar voicing to C major, which starts on the 5th string, and F major, which starts on the 4th string. Compare the three shapes.

E major, A major, D major

The E major chord built from the 6th string has the same type of voicing as A major on the 5th string and D major on the 4th string.

G major, C major, F major

The chord shapes for G major, C major, and F major have the same type of basic structure on the fingerboard. Listen and compare the chords.

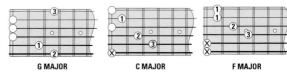

E MAJOR   A MAJOR   D MAJOR

G MAJOR   C MAJOR   F MAJOR

Song sequences

One of the primary roles of the guitar is to accompany songs. Some common chord sequences underlie numerous pieces. The easiest way for the beginner to play chord sequences and understand how they work is to learn a basic vocabulary of related chords in C major. The chords shown here can be used to make songs, and form the basis of simple progressions.

NUMBERING CHORDS

Roman numerals are sometimes used instead of letters of the alphabet to refer to chords in a sequence, for example **I–VII** in relation to the key of a song. So, for a song in the key of C, the numeral **V** would refer to the chord G.

C	D	E	F	G	A	B	C
I	**II**	**III**	**IV**	**V**	**VI**	**VII**	**I**
1	2	3	4	5	6	7	1

BASS NOTES

Learn the names and fingerboard positions for the notes C, D, E, F, G, A, and B. The lowest position of each note is the chord bass note. So, the lowest C is on the 3rd fret of the 5th string and matches the C note in the chord voicing shown below. Use open D for the D minor chord. Drop down to the bottom open string for E minor. Move up through F, G, A, and B for the other bass notes.

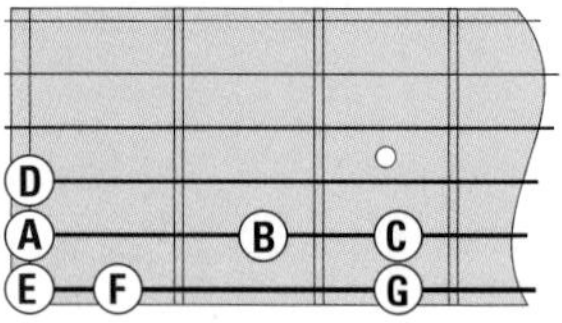

F major
The full F major chord shown at the bottom of this page requires a first finger "barre" (*see* pp.156–9). To begin with, try the simpler version on the right.

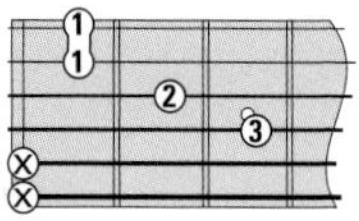

C MAJOR CHORD CHANGES

At first, get used to counting the numbers under the chords and playing them at the same time. You can lightly emphasize **1**, the first beat. Count, play evenly, and rest at the point where it says **1 & HOLD**. If you find these shapes difficult, simply hold as many upper string notes as you can. Later on, try playing the full chord. Simple movements start by just playing pairs of chords.

C major (I) to G major (V)
Start by moving from C major to G major and back to C. Practice this in your own time, without trying to rush the change to the following chord.

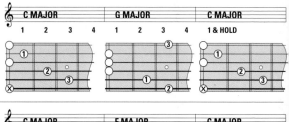

C major (I) to F major (IV)
Now move from C major to F major. Play F on just the top four strings if you find the shape difficult, or start building from the bass note upward.

I-IV-V-I and I-IV-I-V
Combine C, F, and G chords in short sequences, practicing a smooth transition between them. Count and play C, F, G and return to C in the first exercise; then C to F, and C to G in the second exercise. Notice that the G chord sounds unresolved; go back to C so the sequence will sound complete. Play each sequence and then hold the last chord and sustain it at the end. Then try playing each four-bar sequence as a cycle.

4/4

C MAJOR	F MAJOR	G MAJOR	C MAJOR
1 2 3 4	1 2 3 4	1 2 3 4	1 & HOLD

4/4

C MAJOR	F MAJOR	C MAJOR	G MAJOR
1 2 3 4	1 2 3 4	1 2 3 4	1 & HOLD

I-V-IV-I
The sequence below is light and jaunty. It moves around the chords in another direction and is in a time signature of 3/4 (three-four), often known as waltz time. Each bar has three beats, as opposed to the four of 4/4. Strum each chord three times, emphasizing the chord on the number **1**. Try playing both three chords in the bar and just one chord in the bar by strumming the first chord and letting it sustain.

3/4

C MAJOR	G MAJOR	F MAJOR	C MAJOR
1 2 3	1 2 3	1 2 3	1 & HOLD

THREE-CHORD SONGS AND SEQUENCES

With three chords you have the basis for playing a 12-bar blues and simple rock sequences. Many folk and popular songs are also based on combinations of three chords, in various keys, for example Chuck Berry's "Johnny B Goode," James Brown's "I Got You," and the Carter Family's "Wildwood Flower." Listen for the chord changes in songs in order to develop an ear for basic chord movements. The three **I**, **IV,** and **V** chords occur in all 12 keys. In G major, one of the most common keys for guitar music, they are G major (**I**), C major (**IV**), and D major (**V**). All three full chords can be played without using a barre (*see* pp.156–9).

Amazing Grace
Written in England in the 18th century, this song can be played with the three basic chords shown. The song has a time signature of 3/4. Try strumming three downbeats in the bar. When you reach the end of the sequence, repeat the entire 16-bar structure. Try singing the song or accompanying somebody else with the chords.

3/4

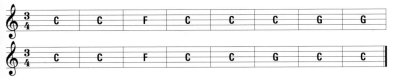

C	C	F	C	C	C	G	G
C	C	F	C	C	G	C	C

Blues in C
The sequences below are three of the basic versions of the blues running over 12 bars. They are all "12-bar blues." At first, just get used to the rate of change between the three chords, before trying for a more rhythmic feel. Play four beats in the bar, and then listen to blues and rock music and copy the rhythm and feel.

4/4

C	C	C	C	F	F	C	C	G	G	C	C
C	C	C	C	F	F	C	C	G	F	C	C
C	F	C	C	F	F	C	C	G	F	C	G

INTRODUCING MINOR CHORDS

Having mastered the three major chords of C, F, and G, it is time to add the three minor chords in C major (that is, the minor chords built up from the notes in the C major scale). These are A minor on the sixth (**VI**) degree of the scale, D minor on the second (**II**), and E minor on the third (**III**). This practical group of chords widens your palette of color and mood, and lets you play more sequences. When playing the strings, either pluck them with the fingers or strum them with the thumb. If playing with a pick, play downstrokes.

C major to A minor
Hold the C major chord and strum it. Now take the third finger off the fifth string and place it on the third string. Notice the change in the harmonic flavor.

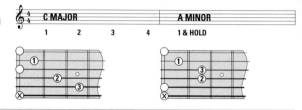

Adding D minor
Move from C major (**I**) to D minor (**II**), and down to G major (**V**). Resolve the sequence by moving back to C major (**I**). The movement from D minor (**II**) to G major (**V**) back to C major (**I**) is a common chord movement.

With D minor, G major, and C major, repeat them as a cycle. Try combining the three chords over a longer number of bars.

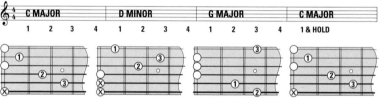

Adding E minor
Move from C major (**I**) to A minor (**VI**). Drop down to the low six-string E minor (**III**) chord and rest on it. Notice how it has a dark, sad quality.

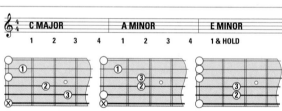

Major with minor chords
Here, the three major chords already encountered, together with the three new minor chords, are combined in some common four-bar sequences that form the introduction, or a part of, many songs. The first sequence, **I-VI-IV-V**, and the variant **I-VI-II-V** are sometimes referred to as "turnarounds," due to the fact that they are often used as endings that lead back to the beginning of a song. The third sequence, **I-VI-III-V**, has a more somber sound to it, while the last sequence, **I-V-VI-IV**, is, by contrast, uplifting.

Two-chord vamp

Sequences can start on any chord in C major (that is, in the group of chords derived from the notes of the C major scale) and can function without the C major chord. D minor (**II**) to G major (**V**) is repeated as a rhythmic "vamp" that can go round and round behind a solo. Build fast strumming patterns with the two chords.

D MINOR	G MAJOR	D MINOR	G MAJOR
1 2 3 4	1 2 3 4	1 2 3 4	1 2 3 4

Step movements

Without strumming all four beats in the bar, move up the scale with chords. Go from C major to D minor. Then, rather than going up to an E, drop an octave for the E minor and up to an F major. In the second example, move in scale steps from C major up through D minor, E minor, F major, and G major and resolve to C major.

C MAJOR	D MINOR	E MINOR	F MAJOR

C MAJOR	D MINOR	E MINOR	F MAJOR	G MAJOR	C MAJOR

Cycle movements

Natural chord cycles, moving in fourths up or fifths down, can be used for all six chords. Count the bass notes as four notes up or five notes down (see the two examples below). The first example uses four chords. Play A minor up to D minor and down to G major, then up to C major. The second example uses six chords.

A MINOR	D MINOR	G MAJOR	C MAJOR

E MINOR	A MINOR	D MINOR	G MAJOR	C MAJOR	F MAJOR

USING THE B BASS NOTE

The seventh degree in the C major scale, B (**VII**), has a diminished chord with the notes B, D, and F. As a simple chord voicing this can sound dissonant, and so has been left out until now. However, it is a highly important chord and it is fundamental in jazz. Simple pop song sequences often use one of the existing C major chords with a B in the bass. This is called an inversion – the root note of a chord is no longer the bass note, and hence the chord has been inverted. It is written as a "/" chord – for instance, G major/B or G/B.

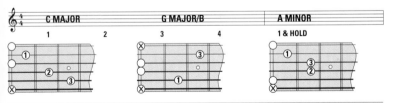

B in the bass: two inversions
The example above uses an inversion of G major with B in the bass to link C major with A minor in a descending chord sequence. The one below shows C major moving down to E minor with B in the bass, which acts as another link to A minor. Play both sequences the other way round as well – A minor going up to C major via the two inversions.

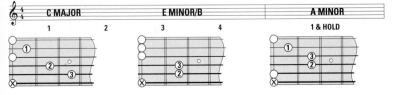

THE MINOR SYSTEM

The notes or chords from one A up to another A, in C major, are also a harmonic system that can be represented with Roman numerals. A minor, the 6th chord (**VI**) of the key of C, is the pivotal home note one (**I**) chord. Powerful chord sequences can be put together using a combination of minor and major chords.

A	B	C	D	E	F	G	A
I	**II**	**III**	**IV**	**V**	**VI**	**VII**	**I**
1	2	3	4	5	6	7	1

A minor to D minor
In the example below, the A minor (**I**) chord moves to the D minor (**IV**) chord. Practice the chords until the transition is smooth. Try strumming different rhythms with these chords and also play them in 3/4 by counting three in the bar.

A MINOR	D MINOR	A MINOR

A minor to E minor
Practice moving smoothly from the A minor (**I**) chord to the E minor (**V**) chord. Again, try strumming different rhythms, and picking out the notes in the chords as arpeggios by picking from the lowest note to the highest note of each chord.

A MINOR	E MINOR	A MINOR

A minor to E major
To give the sequence above a feeling of greater energy and resolution, E minor can be converted to an E major. The E minor (**V**) chord can be easily transformed by simply adding a G♯ to make it an E major (**V**) chord, giving a **V-I** release.

A MINOR	E MAJOR	A MINOR

Three minor chords
Play A minor (**I**), move up to D minor (**IV**), and play two bars of E minor (**V**). Try to move smoothly from one chord to the next. Also try playing E major in the last bar and notice that the chord resolves to A minor. Play the sequence as a cycle.

A MINOR	D MINOR	E MINOR	E MINOR

MINOR BLUES

Blues is essentially a minor-scale music. The minor chord system has its own 12-bar blues sequences based around **I**, **IV**, and **V**. When you have played the two examples below, try this alternative sequence with a different order of minor chords, but retaining the distinctive blues feeling: A-A-E-E-A-A-D-D-A-E-A-A.

A MIN	A MIN	A MIN	A MIN	D MIN	D MIN	A MIN	A MIN	E MIN	D MIN	A MIN	A MIN

A MIN	A MIN	A MIN	A MIN	D MIN	D MIN	A MIN	A MIN	E MAJ	E MAJ	A MIN	A MIN

Mixing minor and major chords
The three majors C, G, and F function as chords that revolve around A minor, forming a system with its own harmonic flavor.

A MINOR	G MAJOR	A MINOR

A MINOR	C MAJOR	G MAJOR	A MINOR

A MINOR	G MAJOR	F MAJOR	G MAJOR

A MINOR	G MAJOR	F MAJOR	E MAJOR

F MAJOR	E MINOR	A MINOR	A MINOR

PENTATONIC ROCK SYSTEM

Rock, blues, and pop often use a hybrid minor system with major chords. Both major and minor chords, in various mixtures, can follow pentatonic basslines—basslines that follow the blues-style pentatonic (five-note) scale. In the key of A, a pentatonic scale has the notes A, C, D, E, and G (see p.126).

A MINOR	C MAJOR	D MINOR	E MINOR	G MAJOR	A MINOR
I	**III**	**IV**	**V**	**VII**	**I**
1	3	4	5	7	1
A MAJOR	C MAJOR	D MAJOR	E MAJOR	G MAJOR	A MAJOR

CHORD AND MELODY RELATIONSHIPS

The pentatonic scale can be a framework for movements, using a mixture of minor and major chords in three-chord or "pentatonic-type" rock sequences. The scale derives from the notes of the Aeolian mode (which, in A minor, is A, B, C, D, E, F, G, A—with no sharps or flats). In blues, pentatonic scales are usually combined with what is known as the Dorian mode. For example, changing the F of the A minor Aeolian mode to an F♯ turns it into the Dorian mode.

ROCK MOVEMENTS

Powerful chord sequences can be put together using the combination of minor and major chords with an outline pentatonic framework. The sequences below show a number of common rock movements. All the examples have an instantly recognizable blues-rock sound. Try chords with just two notes, using the root and fifth notes as chords—they are neither major nor minor.

Three chord moves
Run up and down three major chords: A (**I**), C (**III**), and D (**IV**). The 2/4 beat helps the rhythm. Play one chord in the bar and sustain it; then play two in the bar with a heavy accent and drive. Now try playing it as a cycle using just four bars.

A MAJOR	C MAJOR	D MAJOR	C MAJOR	A MAJOR
1 2	1 2	1 2	1 2	1 & HOLD

Three chord I-IV-III-I
In 4/4, go from A major (**I**) up to D major (**IV**), and down through C major (**III**) to A major (**I**). Play A major and hold it. Try D major and C major holding each chord for half a bar before returning to A major. Try playing this very slowly and then build up speed.

A MAJOR	D MAJOR	C MAJOR	A MAJOR
1 2 3 4	1 2	3 4	1 & HOLD

Four chord IV-III-I-VII-I
From the D major (**IV**) chord, go down to C (**III**), pause on A (**I**), then go down to G (**VII**). Emphasize the final A major (**I**) chord. Try these chords both as two beats in the bar and vary the speed. Try a fast movement from G major to A major to end.

D MAJOR	C MAJOR	A MAJOR	G MAJOR	A MAJOR
1	2	1 2	1	2

Three chord I-VII-IV-I
This is catchy and memorable. Go from A (**I**) down to G (**VII**), then up to D (**IV**), before returning to A major (**I**). Play this evenly as four beats in the bar, then play the chords as sustained half-bars by holding each chord for two beats.

A MAJOR	G MAJOR	D MAJOR	A MAJOR
1 2	3 4	1 2	3 4

Three chord I-IV-V
Treat this three-chord sequence as a major or minor blues movement. The three-chord combination is seen as the foundation of rock and blues because it consists of strong directional chords. Try making up sequences with them.

A MAJOR	D MAJOR	E MAJOR
1 2 3 4	1 2 3 4	1 & HOLD

Playing riffs

Riffs are catchy motifs, or introductions, that are hugely enjoyable to play on the electric guitar, particularly with distortion and effects. They often recur in breaks to strengthen the music. Short and focused, riffs can run over just two bars. The examples below are in simple downbeat crotchet form.

PENTATONIC SCALES AND RIFFS

Riffs are often based around pentatonic-type scales, rhythmically propelled and emphasized by down- and upbeats.

In the scales below, break the notes into groups of three and four, starting from any note, and try making up riffs.

Pentatonic riffs and blue notes
Move up the pentatonic scale playing A-C-D-E-G-A, then move down it playing A-G-E-D-C-A. Now play the same scale,

adding an E♭ before the E. This is a strong "blue note," sometimes called a flat five (or flattened fifth). Experiment with short phrases using this

new note. Now try to play all of this material starting on A on the 5th fret of the bottom string and staying in the middle of the fingerboard.

Phrases
Play the first ascending phrase as even notes. The fall from the top E to C and A gives it a rock-

blues character. Now try the phrase that answers it. The move from E up to the note G complements the first phrase.

The two work together as a call and response. Give the phrases a strong rhythmic framework, turning them into one long riff.

Double-stopped riffs
Try the A pentatonic scale from the first, top example, with a note a fourth underneath it.

Each note has an additional one, on the same fret, four steps lower. The technique is sometimes called "double

stopping," an expression from violin terminology, which means that two notes are held by the left hand.

Fourths above
Now try a completely different sound—the pentatonic scale with fourths above. This requires an additional note four steps above each note of the scale. The notes are on the same fret position apart from the top two, G with C, and A with D.

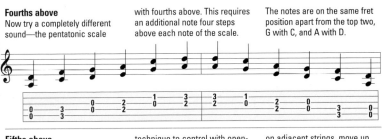

Fifths above
Try the same idea, but playing fifths above. It is a harder technique to control with open-string positions. Once you are used to fretting one pair of fifths on adjacent strings, move up and down the lower strings in a fixed pattern with the left hand.

RIFFS WITH DROPPED TUNING

An effective way to play pairs of double-stopped notes is to tune the bottom string down one tone to D. It is instantly possible to play the entire series of pentatonic double-stopped notes up and down the bottom two strings. These pairs of notes can be made into bigger chords by playing across all three bottom strings to give D5, F5, G5 and others ("5" means the chord is roots and fifths only).

Free movement
In this tuning, try playing up and down, strumming open lower strings and fretting notes on the pentatonic scale with one finger. Instant rock sequences come out. Try other frets, such as the 2nd or 9th, to give different chords and movements.

CHORD RIFFS

Short, pithy chord changes, sometimes with muting and rhythmic emphasis, are termed chord riffs if they are used to give a song a particular flavour. Simple harmonic movements within chords are also sometimes thought of as riffs.

Try experimenting with two- and three-note chords, using the low bass note and the adjacent note, and try two- and three-chord movements. The use of distortion on electric guitars thickens the sound and enhances the effect.

Chord extensions
Hold the A major chord and play an extension with two notes. You can resolve the extension back down to A major.

Suspended notes
Adding a D "suspended note" to A major forms A sus 4, or A sus 11. Its sound suggests a resolution down to C#.

Playing melodies

Songs and melodies are made up of appealing and memorable sequences of notes. When written down as music they should be phrased and interpreted sensitively. The three well-known English folk songs here are sung and played traditionally, and have also been arranged as melodies for orchestra by the British composers Ralph Vaughan Williams and Frederick Delius.

MELODIC TECHNIQUE

Use a new finger for each new fret. Play all 1st fret notes with the first, or index, finger, all 2nd fret notes with the second, or middle, finger and all 3rd fret notes with the third, or ring, finger. The tablature fret numbers coincide with finger numbers. The crotchets in the songs are one beat. Hold the minims for two beats. Hold the dotted crotchets over to the first half of the next beat, and play the quaver note on the upbeat—see the third bar of "Brigg Fair," for example.

"Brigg Fair"
A four-bar phrase opens this 16-bar folk song. "Brigg Fair" uses the notes of C major in 3/4, running throughout a one-octave range—from C to C. It starts on an A and ends on a D, around which it tends to pivot, despite being composed of C major notes. It has a D Dorian modal flavor: the series of notes from D to D within C major acts as a mode (scale). The song has been moved down to an easier position than it is normally played in, and the rhythm has been slightly simplified.

"Lovely Joan"
A lively eight-bar folk song in 4/4, this runs through a range of notes from C to D. As with "Brigg Fair," although it is written with C major notes, C is not the tonal center. It starts on D and ends on a D and it is in the minor mode of D Dorian. At the beginning, a pair of notes lead into the first bar. This lead-in is known as an anacrusis. To play the anacrusis, count four beats. On the fourth beat, play the two notes on the downbeat and upbeat.

"Greensleeves"

This well-known melody is 16 bars long and has been written in 6/4 instead of the standard 6/8 to make it easier to read. "Greensleeves" has notes ranging from E on the 2nd fret of the 4th string to G on the 3rd fret of the 1st string. It uses A minor Dorian, as well as A minor, with its F#, G#, and G natural. It starts on A, with an anacrusis, and it ends on an A. The melody has an F# on the 4th fret of the 4th string, which should be

played with the fourth finger. As in the previous two examples, tablature fret numbers are the same as finger numbers. Chord symbols have been placed underneath so that the melody can be played in a duo, or solo fingerstyle. To learn "Greensleeves" as a piece with chords, start by adding just the bass note under the melody note. Then fill out the chord notes. Where there is one chord in the bar, you should play it twice, on the first and fourth beats.

Fingerstyle

Classical guitar playing is based entirely on a fingerstyle approach, using the thumb and fingers of the right hand. It has been standardized into the **PIMA** system, in which the right-hand's fingers are given letters derived from the initials of their Spanish names. **PIMA** directions are written above the stave.

RIGHT-HAND NAIL TECHNIQUE

Virtually all nylon-string players use their fingernails to play. Some guitarists cut and file their nails in a rounded nail shape, whereas others prefer a straighter edge, where the nail plucks the string. Some guitarists play with their fingertips.

Arm position
Rest the inside of the forearm on the guitar's upper edge, keeping the hand at an angle to the strings. The shoulder and arm should be relaxed, and the hand able to reach all of the strings.

Hand height
The hand should not touch the soundboard or the bridge. The wrist should be about 2½ in (7cm) above the strings. If the hand is too close to them, movement of the fingers is impeded.

Playing action
Move the thumb downward to play the bass strings, and the fingers upward to play the middle and top strings. The fingers should be curved slightly inward.

LEARNING TO PLAY PIMA

The thumb is referred to as **P**, the first finger as **I**, the second as **M**, and the third as **A**. The little finger, when used, is termed **X** (or **E**). In the following exercise, **P** plays the 6th string, and **I**, **M**, and **A** play the 3rd, 2nd, and 1st strings respectively. The fingernails should strike the strings above the soundhole toward the edge closest to the bridge, with a downward movement of the thumb, and an upward movement of the three fingers. After striking the notes, the fingers and thumb should move up and away without hitting or resting on any of the other strings. This action is termed "free stroke movement." Once the exercises have been played on the open strings, they can be repeated using chord shapes.

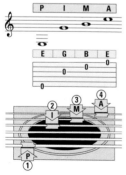

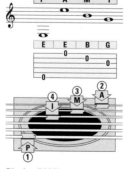

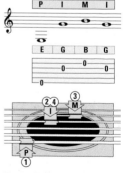

Playing PIMA
Begin by playing the 6th string using the thumb, **P**, followed by the 3rd, 2nd, and 1st strings with the **I**, **M**, and **A** fingers.

Playing PAMI
Play the 6th string with the thumb, the 1st string with the **A** finger, the 2nd with the **M** finger, and the 3rd with the **I** finger.

Playing PIMI
Play the 6th string using **P**, the 3rd string using **I**, the 2nd string using **M**, returning to play the 3rd string with **I**.

PIMA WITH CHORDS

Hold down a simple E major and play the first set of the previous exercises. Then repeat them using an A minor chord, playing the bass note on the 5th string with the thumb. Play these accurately, gradually increasing the tempo.

PIMA using E major
The notes on the 4th and 5th strings should not be played. Just play E major with the 1st finger of the left hand holding G♯, and the 2nd and 3rd fingers removed.

PIMA using A minor
The 1st and 2nd fingers hold down the notes C and A, and the 3rd finger is removed. In these exercises, the note on the 4th string is not played.

PIMA VARIATIONS

The following variations are all based on the E major chord. Play the exercises, and then work on the **IMA** part of each one without the bass note. In these examples, **I** always plays the 3rd string, **M** the 2nd string, and **A** the 1st string.

Exercises
These variations will help to build flexibility of movement and the control of arpeggiation. Hold the G♯ down and make sure that the notes ring and sustain.

Alternatives
Use E major to play more variations, with **P** playing the 6th string, and **I**, **M**, and **A** remaining on the 3rd, 2nd, and 1st strings respectively.

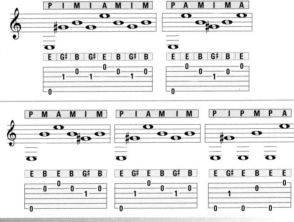

MOVING THE THUMB

Using just **P**, practice moving back and forth across the three lower strings, building up alternate movements between the open 6th and 5th, 5th and 4th, and 6th and 4th strings. Then practice the exercises below, using a standard full E major chord.

PIMA and PIM
In the first bar, play **PIMA** twice, starting first on the 6th string, then on the 5th. In the second bar, play **PIM** three times, starting on the 6th string, then on the 5th, and then on the 4th.

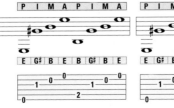

Further thumb movement

The thumb can be used to play more than one note in a five-note arpeggio. Play the first and second notes with the thumb. Complete the arpeggio using the **I**, **M**, and **A** fingers. The thumb can also move across from the bass strings to play notes usually played by the fingers.

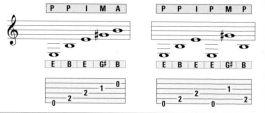

Position during chord changes

It is important to maintain control during chord changes. In this exercise, when E major is changed to A minor, ensure that the thumb hits the correct bass string as the chord changes. Play **P** on the 6th string, followed by **IMA**, then move **P** onto the 5th string as the chord changes, again followed by **IMA**.

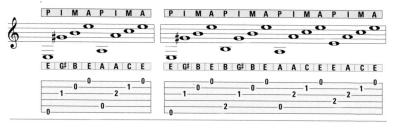

Arpeggio with thumb scale

The thumb can also be used to play scales and melodies below arpeggios. In this exercise the thumb is used to play notes from the G major scale against a pattern on the open top strings. Play IMA on its own before adding the scale that ascends from the 3rd fret of the 6th string. Alternatively, play the scale and add the other notes.

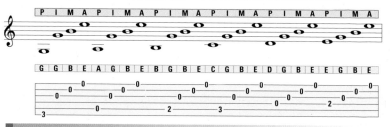

PLAYING BLOCK CHORDS

When a chord of more than four notes is played quickly with the fingers of the right hand, the thumb (**P**) is used to play more than one string. For example, when an E major chord is played on the bottom five strings, **IMA** plays the 4th, 3rd, and 2nd strings, and **P** strikes the 6th and 5th strings at the same time. In a six-string chord, the thumb plays the bottom three strings.

Block chord exercises

In the four variations on the right, chords can be broken up into sections and played with different bottom notes. The thumb can be used to play bass notes and the **I**, **M**, and **A** fingers to play a section of the chord.

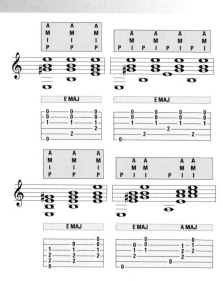

INDEX FINGER STRUMMING

When strumming with the index finger, the movement should be made by the finger itself, rather than by the entire wrist. In the exercises below, when using alternating strokes, care should be taken to prevent the nail from catching the strings and impeding movement on the upstroke. The exercises can also be played with the **M** finger.

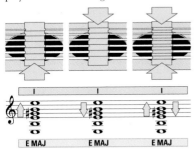

TREMOLO TECHNIQUE

The **I**, **M**, and **A** fingers can be used to play a continually repeating single note. This is known as tremolo, and is widely used in classical and flamenco styles. Try playing tremolo slowly on the top string, while playing the open 6th or 5th string with the thumb, as shown below. When played quickly, the effect should have an even and rippling sound.

AMI movement
Play the open E string, with **A**, **M**, and **I**. Repeat the sequence slowly and evenly. Build up speed, and play it as a continuous pattern, eventually connecting each sequence of **AMI** without stopping between the **I** and the **A** fingers.

RIGHT-HAND SCALE TECHNIQUE

Many players alternate the **I** and **M** fingers. An alternating **IMA** technique may be used as well. Play the scales below with both combinations of fingers. Ascending and descending passages sometimes use different combinations. The use of **IM** and **IMA** depends on the number of notes on a string. For example, in a five-note scale, two notes on a string will be played by **IM** or **MI**, and three notes on an adjacent string will use **IMA** or **AMI**.

IM technique
Play the scale above, alternating the right-hand fingers **I** and **M**. Start on the bottom E with the **I** finger and finish on E on the top string. The scale should then be played starting with the **M** finger, alternating the fingers the other way.

IMA technique
In the scale shown above, use the **A**, **M**, and **I** fingers to play groups of three notes on the 6th, 5th, and 4th strings. Then strike the notes in reverse in an **IMA** sequence. Playing **IMA** or **AMI** on the lowest strings may be difficult to begin with.

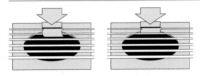

Rest stroke using IMA
The rest stroke is used to play notes with greater volume and a fuller tone. When a note is struck, the finger plays down toward the body of the instrument and completes its movement by resting on an adjacent string.

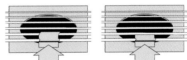

Rest stroke using the thumb
The thumb can also be used to play rest strokes. Play with a downward movement, resting on the adjacent string after the completion of the stroke. Rest strokes can be played with considerable volume.

LIGADO

The ligado technique is used to give the impression of smooth, flowing movement. After a note has been struck, the left hand plays further notes by hammering on and pulling off strings. Play an ascending ligado line from the open E string: strike the open string,

and quickly place the first finger on the 1st fret, causing the note F to ring. Similarly, move from F to G by striking F, and hammering on G. Play a descending ligado by striking F on the first fret and, as you take the finger away, pull it down slightly to sound the open E.

The following note
Play ligado between the pairs of notes E–F, F–G, and G–A. Descend with A–G, G–F, and F–E.

Full-scale position
These two exercises move across the fingerboard, using all the notes to play both ascending and descending ligados. Play three-note variations on both of these exercises by hammering on and pulling off two succeeding notes.

ARPEGGIO EXERCISES

Play the first exercise (far right), placing the thumb (**P**) on the 6th string, and the **IMA** fingers on the 3rd, 2nd, and 1st strings respectively. For the downward-moving arpeggios (right), place the **P** and **A** fingers on the outer voices only.

Prepared arpeggios
A system of setting the hand down into position, touching the notes that are about to be played, is sometimes used to stabilize the right-hand position.

MALAGUENA

A traditional Spanish and flamenco flavoured theme, "Malaguena" is based on the chords E major and A minor. The **M** finger plays the top E string

throughout the piece and the thumb (**P**) plays the melody below. Build the ascending and descending phrase with the thumb with a clear even movement.

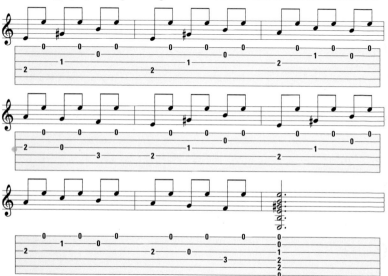

THUMB MOVEMENT

This relatively easy piece, "Study No 1 in A minor", is by Dionisio Aguado (1784–1849), a Spanish virtuoso guitarist. The piece comprises two 16-bar sections. It is helpful for developing thumb movement, and building independence between the thumb and fingers. Play the lowest note of each arpeggio with the thumb, and the upper three notes smoothly and evenly with the index and middle fingers. In the first bar, the thumb plays an open A string, the index finger plays the fretted C note, the middle finger plays

the open E note, and the index finger plays the C note again. Throughout the piece the thumb plays a series of bass notes and melodic links, while the index and middle fingers play simple variations to give harmonic variety.

Work out the easiest and most sensible fingering positions. Practise the movement on the top strings with the index and middle fingers to get an even control for the upper register movements. Separate out the bass note pattern so that the fingering is clearly memorized. Play slowly at first.

Alternative picking

There are various ways to use a pick for playing chords on a steel-string acoustic or electric guitar. Many guitarists, particularly in folk and country, combine pick use with fingers to play bass notes with chords, counterpoint, arpeggios, and chordal variation. Such techniques widen your options.

RIGHT-HAND TECHNIQUES

Nails break easily, so many steel-string guitar players use short nails and the hard flesh on the ends of their fingers.

They play in a loose classical style. Try playing the exercises below with fingers as well as a pick.

Picking G major
With the pick, play the full G major chord shape (see p.118) from its lowest note, on the 6th string, to its highest note, on the 1st. Use downstrokes

on the ascent and upstrokes on the descent. Now try the exercise below, breaking up the chord into groups of three notes. Play the descent with downstrokes as well.

Jumping strings
In the first exercise below, use the pick to play the three lower notes, then the bass note, and then successive pairs of upper notes, by jumping over strings. In the second exercise, jump from the bass note to each string. Pick direction determines down- and upstrokes.

Scales with G notes
In the third exercise, use the pick to play an F next to an open G string and move down the scale. Try ascending—the fourth exercise below— using a G major scale with an F# and ending with two G notes. These exercises will develop speed and control between two adjacent strings.

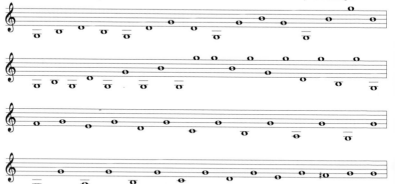

Hybrid picking
This combines a normal pick position and technique with use of the middle and ring fingers. Use the pick for bass notes or even soloing. Use the fingers in an upward picking movement for chords, partial chords, arpeggiation, or fast flourishes and rolls.

Thumbpicking
Putting a thumbpick over the thumb gives free movement to all the fingers. Use them in the normal way, similar to classical technique. The extended shape of the thumbpick lends itself to scalar passages as well as to strumming.

HYBRID PICKING EXERCISES

In the first exercise below, use just the pick to play the G chord bass note and alternate it with other parts of the chord as three notes, and two pairs of notes. Now, for comparison, play the same notes using the pick together with the middle and ring fingers, in hybrid picking technique. In the second exercise, fill out a three-note chord into a four-note chord, by using the middle finger to play a pair of notes or, alternatively, the little finger to play the top note. In the third exercise, play a series of ascending three-note arpeggios quickly, like banjo rolls.

THUMBPICKING VARIATIONS

The thumbpick can give you a wide variety of chordal control. Follow the examples shown below. First, block chords: play the bass note with the thumb and the other three notes with the index, middle, and ring fingers. Then, separate the bass note from the other chord notes and break them into pairs. Once you get used to this, it is an easy technique. In the second exercise, play simple arpeggios with the thumbpick and fingers. Try to play all the notes very evenly.

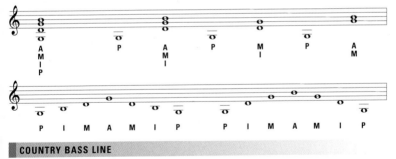

COUNTRY BASS LINE

This country-style approach, which has been simplified here by removing bar lines, uses a thumbpick to play a linking bass line between chords. The bass line goes up to C major, and alternates with G and the upper chord notes. It moves to the G major chord with G and D in the bass. To get the feel for this exercise, play the first three notes, G-A-B, and the accent the note C as the beginning of the piece. Each bar goes root to fifth, C-G and G-D, on each of the chords.

Tunings and slide

The open strings can be altered from the EADGBE tuning to create
alternative tunings that give interesting voicings and chord progressions as
well as drone effects. Using slide guitar technique, it is possible to move the
pitch of notes and chords freely. Many of the tunings shown below are
useful for both playing slide guitar, and for fretting and extending chords.

DETUNED STRINGS

Most alternative tunings use detuned
notes, lower than standard open strings,
which makes the strings looser. With
loose tension, strings can be pushed out
of position, and even rattle. This can
add a certain atmosphere.

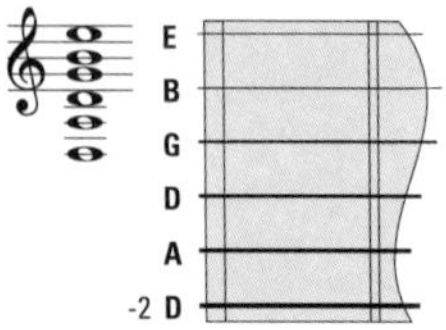

E B G D A -2 D

DADGBE
Tune the bottom 6th string down two
semitones (a tone) to a low D—an
octave below the open 4th string, D.

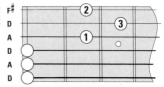

DADGBE—D major chord
Low D can act as a drone note underpinning
chords and melodies. It can also create a bigger
sound for a chord, such as this D major voicing.

-2D -2A G D A -2D

DADGAD
Tune the top two strings down two semitones,
creating an attractive open tuning for fresh
chords, used in folk and crossover styles.

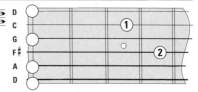

DADGAD—D 11 chord
This D11 chord, with its bass with fifths, and two
pairs of close-voiced notes, is a shape that can
only be played easily using an open tuning.

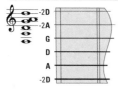

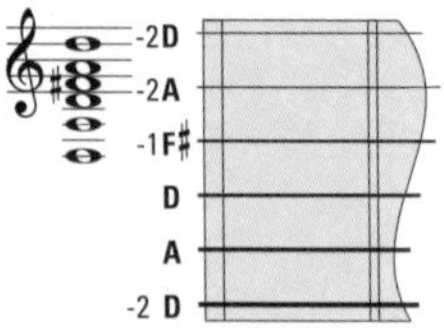

DADF#AD—open D major
Tune the 3rd G string down a semitone. The
resulting D major voicing is the same shape
as an open E major chord. Use for slide.

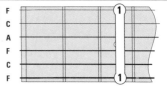

DADF#AD—F major chord
Place the first finger across the 3rd fret to form
an F major shape. This tuning is good for fretting
simple barre chords and chord extensions in rock.

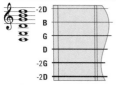

DGDGBD—open G major
From DADGBE, tune the 5th and 1st string down
two semitones to a G major chord, the same
shape as open A major. Use for slide.

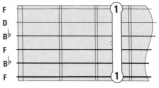

DGDGBD—B♭ major chord
Place the finger across the fret to form a B♭ major
chord with F in the bass. Sometimes the bottom
string is removed for this tuning to give it focus.

USING A CAPO

Short for *capo d'astro*, the capo is a device that raises the pitch of the open strings. It has various mechanisms to lock it over any fret. Its function is similar to that of the nut or a first-finger barre (*see* pp.156–7). Here, it is fitted to the third fret giving the notes G-C-F-Bb-D-G. If you play an E major shape, it forms the chord of G major.

USING A SLIDE FOR BLUES

Slides are tubular cylinders made of metal or glass that are used to move the pitch of notes expressively. They fit over the ring or little finger. The index or middle finger can be placed behind the slide to stop unwanted string noise. The slide itself needs to be lightly placed across the strings and vertically in line with the frets so that the strings are in tune with each other.

GLASS SLIDE ON RING FINGER

METAL SLIDE ON LITTLE FINGER

Open D and G tunings
In the first exercise, play the open D major tuning. Place the slide at the 3rd, 5th, 7th, 10th, and 12th frets to play a pentatonic D scale in chords. Try playing single lines and pairs of notes. The pairs of notes on the two top strings and the 4th and 5th strings can be used to play the same phrases an octave apart. Hold the slide on the string, sustaining the note, and move it up and down. In the second example, try the G major tuning with the same positions.

SLIDE VARIATIONS

The slide technique is often called bottleneck because it is derived from the use of an actual bottleneck. Glass, in various shapes, has a warm sound, while brass or chrome-plated metal is brighter and metallic. Try moving the slide up from the 3rd fret (*right*) or down from the 4th fret to play a flattened third blue note that sits between the frets. Now try playing a scale on the top string using notes on other frets, such as the 2nd, 6th, and 9th. This creates a fuller blues scale of open string, 2, 3, 5, 6, 7, 9, 10, and 12.

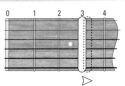

Single-note slide
With slide, it is possible to achieve microtonal nuances between notes. Experiment with single-note slide using both standard tuning and alternatives.

The major scale

The major scale is formed from a series of fixed intervals. Every note in the scale is assigned a name that denotes its relationship to the first note, known as the tonic. These names label the seven notes in the major scale system, both as individual tones and as roots for chords. There are also names denoting the number of tones and semitones between two points. For example, an interval of three tones and a semitone from a note is referred to as a perfect fifth.

NAMING MAJOR SCALE NOTES

The formal name of a note on the major scale describes its relationship to the tonic (the root, or first note of the scale) and to the dominant (fifth). The supertonic is the note above the tonic, or the second note of the scale. It is followed by the mediant (midway between the tonic and the dominant), sub-dominant, dominant, sub-mediant, and the leading note.

The sol-fah system
Each note of the major scale has a sol-fa series of note names. They are doh, ray, me, fah, soh, lah, te, doh. These one-syllable words can help the player to memorize the sound of intervals.

A useful exercise is to sing each note as it is played on the guitar. This helps the ear to recognize notes and melodies. The diagram below shows each note of the C major scale, giving both its sol-fah name and its formal name.

DOH	RAY	ME	FAH	SOH	LAH	TE	DOH
C	D	E	F	G	A	B	C
TONIC	SUPERTONIC	MEDIANT	SUB-DOMINANT	DOMINANT	SUB-MEDIANT	LEADING NOTE	TONIC

INTERVALS ON A MAJOR SCALE

The series of tone and semitone steps on the major scale are termed major seconds and minor seconds. For example, C to D is a tone, or a major second, and E to F is a semitone, or a minor second. Larger steps between notes of the major scale also have an interval name to identify the number of scale notes and the size of the space between them. Compare the names used to describe intervals between individual notes within a scale and the root note of the scale. For example, C to E is a major third, and C to F is a perfect fourth.

THE SCALE OF C MAJOR

There are several ways to play a scale from its root to its octave note. The C major scale is usually played by crossing strings. To illustrate the intervals from the root, the C major scale shown below is played entirely on the 5th string. The scale consists of a mixture of tones over two frets and semitones over one fret.

C major shape
Compare the arrangement of the notes in C major, both on the 5th string and in the standard position. The scale on the 5th string shows the relationship of the notes as a series of tone and semitone steps. They are exactly the same notes using the four middle strings.

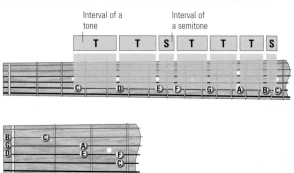

Interval of a tone

Interval of a semitone

FURTHER SCALE POSITIONS

The C major scale has already been played from the 5th string to the 2nd using a combination of open strings and fretted notes. However, it can also be played from several other positions. One of the most widely used standard patterns starts on the 3rd fret of the 5th string and moves across the fingerboard to the higher octave C on the 5th fret of the 3rd string. This pattern is played using the fourth finger to fret notes. The fingering pattern can also be moved, to start the scale on the 8th fret of the 6th string, and extended across the fingerboard to an upper octave. Compare the eight notes of C major running from the third fret of the 5th string to the eight notes of C major running from the eighth fret of the 6th string. They are exactly the same notes in different positions. The upper two octave position has the same fingering and is extended across the fretboard to play the higher octave.

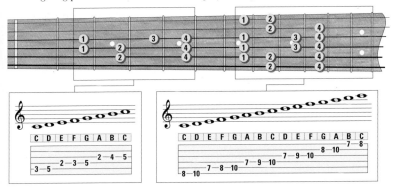

INTERVAL NAMES

The diagram below uses the note C as a fixed point, and shows a one-octave chromatic scale that includes all seven notes of the major scale, as well as the five remaining notes unused in the C major scale. The notes are shown on the 5th string, from the 3rd fret to the 15th fret, along with the names for all the intervals. There are 12 chromatic intervals before the octave is reached. It should be remembered that an interval may have more than one name.

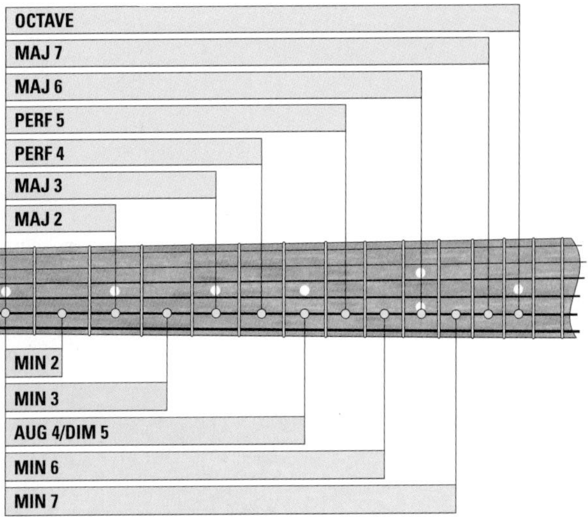

Major scale intervals
The C major scale is shown here ascending the 5th string. The intervals, labelled with their relationship to the root, are found on the 5th, 7th, 8th, 10th, 12th, 14th, and 15th frets.

| OCTAVE |
| MAJ 7 |
| MAJ 6 |
| PERF 5 |
| PERF 4 |
| MAJ 3 |
| MAJ 2 |

Other intervals
These five notes, which are not in C major, are the remaining intervals in the octave. They occur on the 4th, 6th, 9th, 11th, and 13th frets.

| MIN 2 |
| MIN 3 |
| AUG 4/DIM 5 |
| MIN 6 |
| MIN 7 |

CHORD THEORY

Major, minor, and other triads are chords with a three-note structure: a root (from which the chord takes its name), a third (three notes above the root), and a fifth (five notes above the root). Each note on the C major scale can be used as a root from which a triad can be built. Triads can be either major, minor, or diminished.

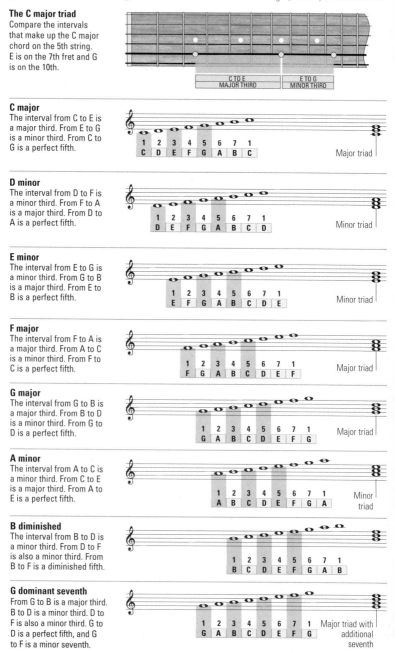

The C major triad
Compare the intervals that make up the C major chord on the 5th string. E is on the 7th fret and G is on the 10th.

C TO E
MAJOR THIRD

E TO G
MINOR THIRD

C major
The interval from C to E is a major third. From E to G is a minor third. From C to G is a perfect fifth.

1	2	3	4	5	6	7	1
C	D	E	F	G	A	B	C

Major triad

D minor
The interval from D to F is a minor third. From F to A is a major third. From D to A is a perfect fifth.

1	2	3	4	5	6	7	1
D	E	F	G	A	B	C	D

Minor triad

E minor
The interval from E to G is a minor third. From G to B is a major third. From E to B is a perfect fifth.

1	2	3	4	5	6	7	1
E	F	G	A	B	C	D	E

Minor triad

F major
The interval from F to A is a major third. From A to C is a minor third. From F to C is a perfect fifth.

1	2	3	4	5	6	7	1
F	G	A	B	C	D	E	F

Major triad

G major
The interval from G to B is a major third. From B to D is a minor third. From G to D is a perfect fifth.

1	2	3	4	5	6	7	1
G	A	B	C	D	E	F	G

Major triad

A minor
The interval from A to C is a minor third. From C to E is a major third. From A to E is a perfect fifth.

1	2	3	4	5	6	7	1
A	B	C	D	E	F	G	A

Minor triad

B diminished
The interval from B to D is a minor third. From D to F is also a minor third. From B to F is a diminished fifth.

1	2	3	4	5	6	7	1
B	C	D	E	F	G	A	B

G dominant seventh
From G to B is a major third. B to D is a minor third. D to F is also a minor third. G to D is a perfect fifth, and G to F is a minor seventh.

1	2	3	4	5	6	7	1
G	A	B	C	D	E	F	G

Major triad with additional seventh

C major chord voicing

The root, third, and fifth can all be doubled by adding extra octave tones. This enlarges the basic triad and gives a fuller-sounding chord. The standard C major triad – C, E, and G – is shown below with an additional C and E in a higher octave. The illustration below shows the five notes that are used to make up the C major voicing in position over a 10-note scale running from C to E. The root, C, on the 5th string, has E above on the 4th string, then G above that on the 3rd string, and then the doubled root on the 2nd string, and finally the doubled third on the top string.

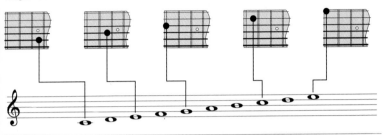

A minor chord voicing

The root, third, and fifth can all be doubled by adding extra octave tones. In this voicing of the chord, an extra octave root (A) and fifth (E) have been added. The third (C) only appears in the higher octave. The illustration below shows the five notes used to make up the A minor voicing in position over a 12-note scale. The root A on the 5th string has E above it on the 4th string, doubled root A on the 3rd string, the third C on the 2nd string, and finally the doubled fifth on the open top string.

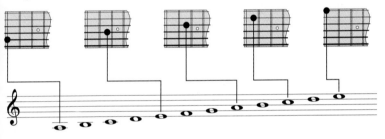

THE DOMINANT SEVENTH CHORD

The fifth chord on a major scale is termed the "dominant" chord. In the scale of C major this chord is G major. The standard G major chord, built from the notes of the triad G, B, and D, is often extended into a G dominant seventh chord – the seventh note (in this case, F) from the root is added to the chord. From the root (G), the scale from which the chord derives has the following notes: G-A-B-C-D-E-F. On the guitar, the seventh note often replaces an existing note in a basic chord. In this instance, the high G on the 3rd fret of the 1st string is replaced with an F on the 1st fret of the 1st string.

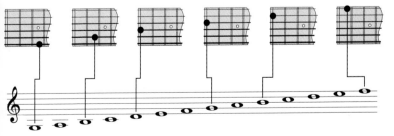

G dominant seventh

This dominant seventh voicing has the root (G), the third (B), the fifth (D), an additional doubled root note (G) and doubled third (B), and a seventh (F). The voicing uses notes from G to F of the major scale in the key of C.

Time values

Rhythmic effects are created by playing combinations and patterns of beats and accents, with spaces of differing lengths. When playing in any time signature, louder or implied accents are often related to bar lengths. Musical phrases also relate to bars of music in this way. Groups of beats are put together to create a number of different types of time signature.

TIME VALUE SYMBOLS

Symbols are used to denote the duration and position of musical sounds in relation to a beat. A note or a chord can be written for it to be held for different lengths of time. For example, in a bar of 4/4, a chord sounded on the first beat and left to ring over the remaining beats (taking up the entire bar) is written down using a specific symbol (ο), known as a semibreve – a semibreve is the length of four crotchets.

Subdivisions of time
In 4/4, a chord or note can be played evenly 8 times within a bar – ie twice on each beat. These subdivisions of the crotchet beat are called quavers (♪). The bars (*right*) show different time value subdivisions that are possible over a bar of 4/4. The three bars (*far right*) show time values in 3/4. A hemidemi-semiquaver is double the maximum subdivision shown. However, it rarely occurs in guitar music.

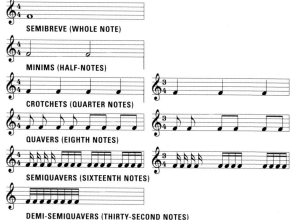

SEMIBREVE (WHOLE NOTE)

MINIMS (HALF-NOTES)

CROTCHETS (QUARTER NOTES)

QUAVERS (EIGHTH NOTES)

SEMIQUAVERS (SIXTEENTH NOTES)

DEMI-SEMIQUAVERS (THIRTY-SECOND NOTES)

TIME SIGNATURES WITH CROTCHETS

In these examples, the 12 crotchet beats are played over the same length of time, but each one's different accent and bar line gives it a different time signature – 4/4, 3/4, and 2/4 respectively.

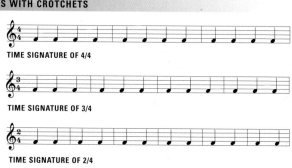

TIME SIGNATURE OF 4/4

TIME SIGNATURE OF 3/4

TIME SIGNATURE OF 2/4

TIME SYMBOLS

These symbols represent the seven different time values for notes, and are accompanied by the symbols for their equivalent rests.

ο	Semibreve	♪	Demi-semiquaver	Ɩ ξ	Crotchet rests
♩	Minim		Hemidemi-semiquaver	૭	Quaver rest
♩	Crotchet			૭	Semiquaver rest
♪	Quaver	▬	Semibreve rest	૭	Demi-semiquaver rest
♪	Semiquaver	▬	Minim rest	૭	Hemidemi-semiquaver rest

RESTS

Whenever silence or a space are required, a rest symbol is written to signify its length. For example, in a time signature of 4/4, if nothing is to be played on the fourth crotchet beat, that note is replaced by a crotchet rest symbol. Rest symbols with a greater value can be used to replace more than one beat, and rests with shorter time values can subdivide notes or beats. Rests can also be used to mark out entire bars.

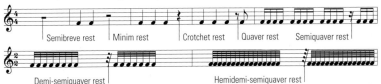

| Semibreve rest | Minim rest | Crotchet rest | Quaver rest | Semiquaver rest |

| Demi-semiquaver rest | Hemidemi-semiquaver rest |

TIES AND DOTTED NOTES

The length of time for which a note is played can be altered in notation by the addition of ties and dots. A note is sustained when a tie is used to link it with succeeding notes – it is sustained for the value of the note it is tied to. A dot placed after a note adds half the note's value, and a second dot adds half the value of the first dot. The same musical phrase can be written using either dots or ties.

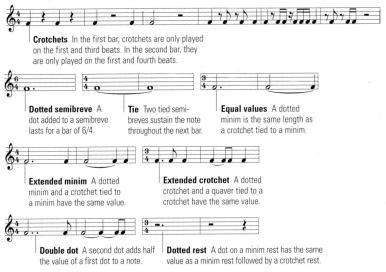

Crotchets In the first bar, crotchets are only played on the first and third beats. In the second bar, they are only played on the first and fourth beats.

Dotted semibreve A dot added to a semibreve lasts for a bar of 6/4.

Tie Two tied semibreves sustain the note throughout the next bar.

Equal values A dotted minim is the same length as a crotchet tied to a minim.

Extended minim A dotted minim and a crotchet tied to a minim have the same value.

Extended crotchet A dotted crotchet and a quaver tied to a crotchet have the same value.

Double dot A second dot adds half the value of a first dot to a note.

Dotted rest A dot on a minim rest has the same value as a minim rest followed by a crotchet rest.

UNDERSTANDING TRIPLETS

A beat can be divided into three, creating a triplet. Any note with a time value can be made into a triplet, although minims, crotchets, and quavers are the most common. Triplets can easily be understood by comparing a bar of 3/4 or 4/4, containing quaver triplets under the crotchet beats, with bars of 9/8 and 12/8. Try playing the middle bars below in the same duration as the 3/4 and 4/4 bars.

Quaver time signatures
The 8 in the time signature indicates that the bar consists of quavers. With two quavers making up a crotchet, each bar is one and a half times as long as the others.

Playing a rhythm

Developing the ability to play time and rhythm accurately is essential in order to play chord sequences, arpeggios, melodies, and solos. The exercises below should first be played as shown, using only one note. When the right hand is moving accurately, the exercises can then be applied to chord sequences or scales. The grey shading on the staves indicates the length of a note within a beat and acts as a guide to timing and note duration.

COUNTING BARS

Counting groups of bars is an important skill. Being able to think of the position of beats in groups of bars is partly a matter of acquiring a musical feel from listening to recordings, and partly an awareness of accents and timing patterns. Stabilizing right-hand technique and thinking in time leads to faster overall development, enabling the player to concentrate on left-hand vocabulary. The examples below show four time signatures – 4/4, 3/4, 2/4, and 6/8. Play them while counting the beats and bars. Note that the duration of a beat in each time signature can be of any time length.

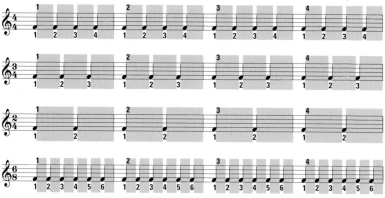

DAMPING THE STRINGS

The hands are often used to dampen the strings during silent passages, or to control rests. When a fast chordal rhythm requires short rests, the fingers on the left hand can quickly release pressure from the strings in order to mute them when pick strokes (*see* pp.116–17) are used. For certain styles of music – rock in particular – a plectrum stroke played on deadened strings is often used as part of the guitar sound. The right hand may also be used to mute the strings.

Left hand damping
The first finger of the left hand can be used to mute the strings. A chord can be muted by leaving the fingers in place but with no pressure on the strings.

Right hand damping
Placing the right hand across the strings is an effective mute. Resting the hand on the bridge allows control over the amount of muting.

CROTCHET SUBDIVISIONS

Each one of the four crotchet beats in a 4/4 bar can be subdivided by playing two quaver notes of equal value. For example, when a crotchet beat is counted as "one" on the first beat of a bar, that same crotchet beat, when subdivided into two quavers, can be played evenly as "one, two" over the same length of time. The quavers can be further divided into semiquavers.

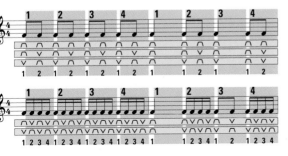

Playing quavers
Begin by using downstrokes. When playing at a faster tempo, practise using alternate strokes.

Playing semiquavers
Play the semiquavers by doubling quavers and subdividing the beat into four even notes.

SYNCOPATED RHYTHM

When a downbeat is not played, and the rhythm is mainly on an accented subdivision of a beat, it is referred to as syncopation. This is extremely important in virtually all areas of music. Play a pattern of alternate strumming on an even quaver beat. Count in crotchets on top of it as "one, two". Start leaving out each "one" beat and just play the "two" – the upbeat. Try this with semiquavers.

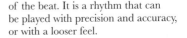

Syncopated playing
On the first bar, count each beat as "one, two", but only play on the off-beat ("two"), shown by the grey shading.

DOTTED QUAVER RHYTHM

This rhythm is widely used in all types of music. The dotted quaver is played and held over until the last semiquaver of the beat. It is a rhythm that can be played with precision and accuracy, or with a looser feel.

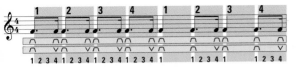

Dotted quavers
Play this slowly. In each bar, sustain the downbeat for half the time of the off-beat.

TRIPLET RHYTHM

When the crotchet beat is subdivided into a triplet (see p.145), it is written as three quavers, beneath a triplet symbol. This can be thought of most simply as three notes of equal value played over one beat. When triplets are played using an alternating strumming technique, the downbeat on every group of three switches from a downstroke to an upstroke on every other beat.

Playing triplets
Play the triplet rhythm as 12 even strokes in the bar. Use both downstrokes as well as upstrokes.

Playing the blues

Blues music originated in the South. It evolved from a heritage of African folk music that was introduced to North America in the 18th century via the slave trade. Vocal chants, rhythms, and work songs merged with European influences and church gospel to forge a highly expressive musical form that still underlies much of today's popular music.

THREE BLUES CHORDS

Blues harmony revolves around the use of three primary chords. These may be major or minor, and are built on the first (**I**), fourth (**IV**), and fifth (**V**) degrees of any named key. The root note of the first chord is equivalent to the first degree of the corresponding pentatonic scale and key. The harmony moves in a **I-IV-V** pattern. With a key note of E, the chords E major, A major, and B major provide a structure for development and variation. Dominant seventh and minor chords are also frequently used to play the blues.

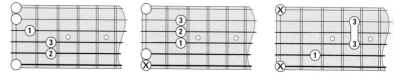

TWELVE-BAR STRUCTURE

The three blues chords above can be played as a chord progression within a repeating 12-bar cycle that follows a set series of movements. The sequence shown below is commonly referred to as the 12-bar format.

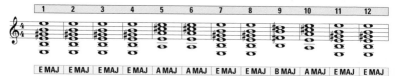

| E MAJ | E MAJ | E MAJ | E MAJ | A MAJ | A MAJ | E MAJ | E MAJ | B MAJ | A MAJ | E MAJ | E MAJ |

BLUES RHYTHMS

A number of different rhythms can be used for playing blues. The top two staves below show a complete 12-bar cycle played in 4/4 time. Practice this cycle, accenting the first beat of each bar. Play the sequence with the other two examples below it—still in 4/4, but using tied triplets and dotted quavers. Then try slowly strumming in 12/8, playing three even chords on every beat.

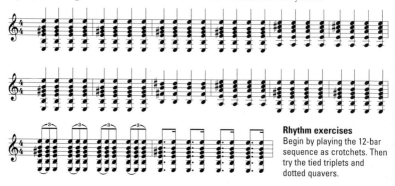

Rhythm exercises
Begin by playing the 12-bar sequence as crotchets. Then try the tied triplets and dotted quavers.

MINOR PENTATONIC SCALE

The starting-point for learning to play the blues is a familiarization with the minor pentatonic scale. This structure contains five notes that are constructed using both minor and perfect intervals. The example below shows two octaves.

E minor pentatonic
The notes in the scale are E, G, A, B, and D. Play them slowly, both ascending and descending.

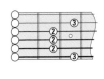

ADDING EXTRA NOTES

Further notes can be added to the scale for melodic flavour and contrast. The most important is the flattened fifth, which creates the classic "blue note" sound. The addition of a major third combines major harmony with the minor scale. A major second and a major sixth can be added to play melodies and solos, with a wide range of colour over twelve-bar blues. Major, dominant seventh, and minor chords can also be altered with the selective addition of extra notes.

Major third
Major thirds from the major chord can be added to the scale. The scale positions are marked by black dots.

E PENTATONIC SCALE WITH ADDED MAJOR THIRD

Flattened fifth
The flattened fifth is added between the perfect fourth and the perfect fifth. It adds expression and feeling.

E PENTATONIC SCALE WITH ADDED FLATTENED FIFTH

Major second/sixth
Adding a major second and a major sixth creates a full seven-note scale. This gives melodic variety.

E PENTATONIC SCALE WITH ADDED MAJOR SECOND AND MAJOR SIXTH

E dominant seventh
Add G♮ on the top string. Then try D♮ as a doubled seventh on the 2nd string, and combine this with the G.

| E7 WITH ADDED G♮ | E7 WITH ADDED D | E7 WITH ADDED D AND G♮ |

A dominant seventh
Add a doubled seventh (G♮) on the top string. A fourth or eleventh (D) can be combined with a G♮.

| A7 WITH G♮ | A7 WITH ADDED D | A7 WITH ADDED D AND G♮ |

B dominant seventh
Add a D♮ on the 2nd string. Try adding other melody notes on the fretted positions on the 1st and 2nd strings.

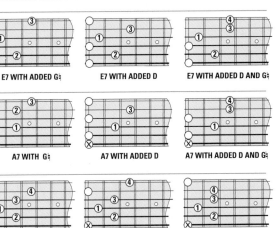

| B7 WITH ADDED D | B7 WITH ADDED G | B7 WITH ADDED C♯ |

The pentatonic scale

The standard pentatonic scale consists of five notes within an octave and is formed from major seconds and minor thirds. A pentatonic scale can be formed from any root note. Here an A minor pentatonic scale has been used. It occurs frequently as a primary scale in all types of music.

TWO-OCTAVE SCALES

The A minor pentatonic scale, running over two octaves, ascends in the sequence A-C-D-E-G-A-C-D-E-G-A, as shown on the stave below. Beginning on the lowest A note, it can be played from either the open 5th string, or from the 5th fret of the 6th string (*see* the fretboard diagram below). When played from the open string, the

scale's notes repeat on the 12th fret, one octave higher. Play both positions, and move between them by shifting the overall left-hand position. The patterns do not cover all the pentatonic notes on the fingerboard. The white circles on the fretboard show the notes of the pentatonic scale not covered by the fingering patterns.

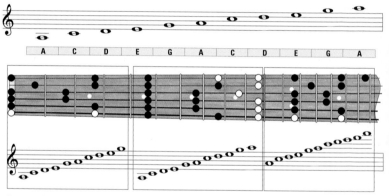

Open position
Play from the open A to the G on the 3rd fret of the 1st string, using standard fingering.

Fifth-fret position
Exactly the same notes can be played starting from the 5th fret of the 6th string.

Upper-octave position
The pentatonic scale in the upper octave is the same as the open-string pattern.

PENTATONIC MODES

The pentatonic scale can be played as a six-note pattern beginning on any one of its constituent notes. This creates five different patterns, referred to as modes of the pentatonic scale. The scales below should be practised as six-note exercises and extended to two octaves.

The five scales
Practise these as a series of separate exercises, starting on a 5th-fret, 6th-string position. Then practise them in the second main pentatonic fingering pattern, which starts on the open 5th string.

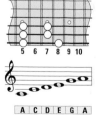

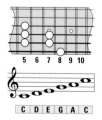

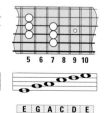

PENTATONIC VARIATION

Standard fingerings, using two notes to a string, are often combined with stretch fingerings, which use three notes to a string. Pentatonic scales may be extended beyond two octaves by either stretching or shifting the overall left-hand position, from every note on each string in one position up to higher pentatonic positions, and two-note patterns. The

minor pentatonic scale can be played in two different patterns beginning on either its 1st or 2nd note. In A minor, on the 6th string, these start from either the 5th or 8th fret. The A minor pentatonic is often related to the Dorian mode. The major pentatonic is formed by starting on the second note of the minor pentatonic scale and is related to the Lydian mode.

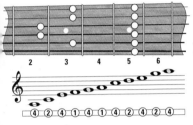

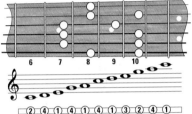

Minor pentatonic
The A minor pentatonic, begun on the 6th string, can be played using the 4th finger on the 5th fret on each string in turn, stretching the first and second fingers to the other notes on other frets. This fingering overlaps a little with that of the A minor pentatonic started on the open 5th-string.

Major pentatonic
This pattern is the second A minor pentatonic mode, but it is often used as a "major" approach to the scale. This is because, in relation to its first note, C, it contains a major third and a major sixth. It can be used in conjunction with the minor pentatonic to cover the fingerboard.

PENTATONIC EXERCISES

These exercises develop skill in playing the minor pentatonic scale freely, and provide basic grounding and control for melody and improvisation. The first exercise is a series of ascending three-note patterns, and should be extended over two octaves. The second is an ascending four-note pattern. The third

combines fourths and thirds, and the final exercise consists of intervals from the root. Move these exercises up to the higher-octave A pentatonic, starting on the 12th fret. Try playing descending three- and four-note patterns and combining all of these exercises in various patterns all over the fingerboard.

Pentatonic to Dorian scale conversion
Five-note pentatonic scales can be converted to seven-note Dorian minor modal scales by

adding a second and a sixth. The natural extensions for the A minor pentatonic are B (the major second) and F# (the major sixth).

Rock and blues

Twelve-bar blues chords and rhythms are the starting point for most types of rock music. Pentatonic and extended blues scales can be used with simple chord structures. Rock and blues music is linked to a reference keynote, which is often both the root of a primary chord and the first note of the related scale. For example, a blues in A can be played with major or minor chords. The riffs, melody or soloing are primarily derived from the minor pentatonic scale, which can be filled out with chord or scale tones. The timing and feel for most 12-bar rock music is derived from blues boogie rhythms.

THE PENTATONIC OVER CHORDS

In traditional rock and blues music, the pentatonic scale is the framework for playing over basic major and minor chords, as well as some extended-note chords. The positions for these chords and pentatonic scales often overlap. A solo using the scale is often played across a chord position, and, as a guitarist changes from single notes to chords, the same area of the fingerboard may be used to play either scales over the chords, or chords in scale positions. In the examples shown below, the circles in black are major thirds and the circles in half-tones indicate notes that are shared by both the chord and scale.

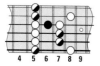

A major (5th fret)
Play A minor pentatonic across A major. The minor third note works perfectly well as a note for melodies or soloing.

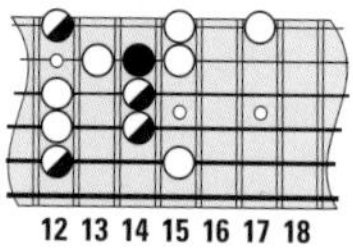

A major (12th fret)
The A minor pentatonic scale should be played from the 12th fret using the minor third.

A7 (5th fret)
Play A minor pentatonic across the A7 chord. The minor third note in the scale is used as a note when playing melodies or solos.

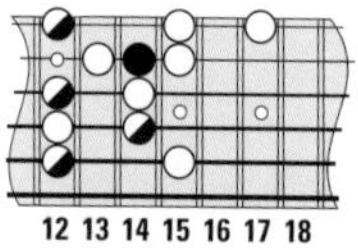

A7 (12th fret)
Play A minor pentatonic across an A7 chord. The minor third note is used when playing melodies or solos.

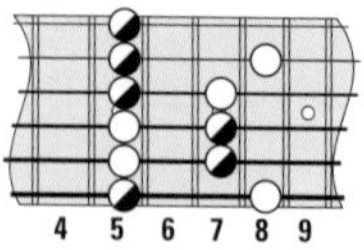

A minor (5th fret)
Play A minor pentatonic over an A minor chord. All the notes in the A minor chord are also part of the A minor pentatonic scale.

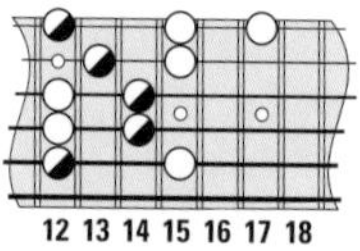

A minor (12th fret)
Play A minor pentatonic over an A minor chord. All the notes in the A minor chord are part of the A minor pentatonic scale.

Twelve-bar sequence
The pentatonic scale, in all registers, can be used to play over the 12-bar structure. Play a twelve-bar sequence in A using either major, minor or dominant seventh chords for A, D, and E. The pentatonic scale fits over most chord types in each sequence. Some notes sound more powerful and melodic than others. Play the A pentatonic across three octaves, up to and beyond the 17th fret. Try playing the exercises and patterns on pages 150–151 and vary them. Also try sustaining notes on the three chords. Try using a metronome to build speed by playing two notes per beat followed by three and four.

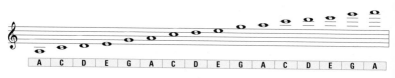

TWELVE-BAR IN ROCK

In rock and blues, major chords are often played with added notes and a boogie style. The blues boogie rhythm is played over a 12-bar sequence by taking each chord and using a dotted-quaver or a triplet rhythm. Strike the chord on a downbeat and hold it over briefly before playing it again before the last element in a triplet quaver. Alternatively, aim for a "modified semiquaver" feel.

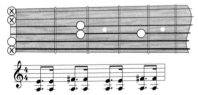

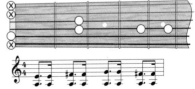

A major with F♯
Play open A, on the 5th string, and E, held with the first finger, on the 2nd fret of the 4th string. Add F♯ with the third finger. The note A on the 3rd string can be added to the A chord.

A major with F♯ and G
Extend the first pattern using the open A string with the note E on the 2nd fret of the 4th string. Add the note F♯ with the third finger, and, after playing F♯, add the fourth finger to play G on the 5th fret.

TWELVE-BAR BLUES IN A

Using the chords A, D, and E major below, the rhythm above is played through a 12-bar sequence in the key of A. Play the chords A-A-A-A-D-D-A-A-E-D-A-A as pairs of notes: root and fifth, root and sixth, and root and seventh. Each pair of notes is struck twice. The finger holding the fifth stays in position. The extra octave note can be played over the basic notes.

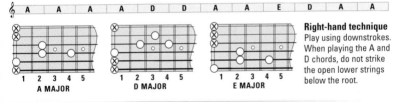

Right-hand technique
Play using downstrokes. When playing the A and D chords, do not strike the open lower strings below the root.

CHORDS ON FRETTED POSITIONS

These rock chords are also played on fretted positions. To play A, place the first finger on the 5th fret of the 6th string (A) and the second finger on the 7th fret of the 5th string (E). The fourth finger stretches to F♯ and G on the 5th string.

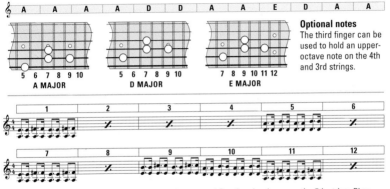

Optional notes
The third finger can be used to hold an upper-octave note on the 4th and 3rd strings.

Fret positions
The root of the A major chord above is on the 5th fret of the 6th string. The roots for the D major and E major chords are on the 5th string. Play the D and E chords by moving the A shape up to the 10th and 12th frets on the 6th string.

The cycle of keys

A major scale can be built on each note of the 12 chromatic degrees. Each scale ascends in a fixed pattern from the note on which it is based – the sequence of intervals is the same for all 12 keys. When major scales start from notes other than C, sharps (♯) and flats (♭) are used to adjust letter names and intervals so that they conform to the major scale pattern. Sharps and flats are shown on the stave at the start of a bar – this is known as a key signature.

SHARP AND FLAT KEYS

Starting from the key of C, the number of sharps or flats in a major key increases by one each time in intervals of fifths (for sharp keys) and fourths (for flat keys). The movement of fifths, using sharps, runs in the following sequence: C-G-D-A-E-B-F♯-C♯. From C to G one sharp is added and from G to D a further sharp is added. A similar pattern, but in intervals of fourths, using flats, runs in the following sequence: C-F-B♭-E♭-A♭-D♭-G♭-C♭. From C to F one flat is added, and from F to B♭ a further flat is added. Each scale can move backwards or forwards through the cycle. A scale can be transposed to any of the other keynotes. Starting on C major the cycle of 12 keys returns to C.

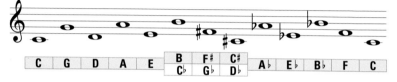

Cycle of fifths
The cycle of keys moving in fifths adds a sharp each time by raising the seventh degree of the new scale. The movement from the key of C, which has no sharps, to G major, which has F♯, is repeated as a mechanism when G is "converted" to D major. Each key progressively adds one sharp until six sharps are reached, with the key of F♯ major. Beyond F♯, it is simpler to write the key of C♯, with seven sharps, as a flat key – D♭ major – with five flats.

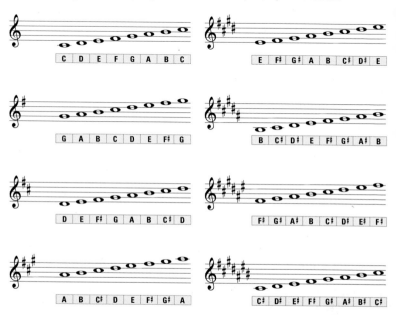

| C | F | B♭ | E♭ | A♭ | D♭ / C# | G♭ / F# | C♭ / B | E | A | D | G | C |

Cycle of fourths

The cycle of keys moving in intervals of fourths adds a flat to each successive key, by flattening the fourth degree of the new key's scale. The movement from the key of C major (which has no flats in its scale), to F major (which has one flat – B♭) repeats as a mechanism when F major is "converted" to B♭ major (which has two flats – B♭ and E♭). Each new key starts from the fourth degree. Each key progressively adds one flat until six flats are reached, with the key of G♭ major. Beyond G♭ major, it is much simpler to write the key of C♭ major, with seven flats, as a sharp key instead – B major – with five sharps.

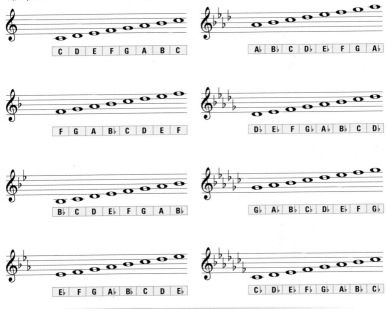

| C | D | E | F | G | A | B | C |

| A♭ | B♭ | C | D♭ | E♭ | F | G | A♭ |

| F | G | A | B♭ | C | D | E | F |

| D♭ | E♭ | F | G♭ | A♭ | B♭ | C | D♭ |

| B♭ | C | D | E♭ | F | G | A | B♭ |

| G♭ | A♭ | B♭ | C♭ | D♭ | E♭ | F | G♭ |

| E♭ | F | G | A♭ | B♭ | C | D | E♭ |

| C♭ | D♭ | E♭ | F♭ | G♭ | A♭ | B♭ | C♭ |

ENHARMONIC RELATIONSHIPS

A note often has two designations. When F is raised by a semitone, it becomes F# – the note between F and G. When G is lowered a semitone, it becomes G♭. The two notes, F# and G♭, are, in fact, the same. Their relationship is termed enharmonic. The correct name for a note between F and G depends on both its relationship to a key and its harmonic context. G♭ is in a flat key and F# is in a sharp key. Scales also overlap. Enharmonic keys are F# /G♭, C# /D♭, and C♭ /B.

The name used depends on the relationship of the scale to other keys, or the ease with which the music can be written.

Using the cycle of keys

The circles show the cycle of keys, demonstrating the relationships between keys in both fifths and fourths. The outer circle, moving clockwise, shows the movement of keys in fifths. The inner circle, moving anti-clockwise, shows the movement of keys in fourths. From any point, a complete cycle of 12 movements in either direction moves through all the keys before returning to the starting-point.

Barre chords

The barre is a chord technique in which the first, or sometimes other, left-hand fingers, hold down adjacent strings across the fingerboard. It enables chords to be built on any fret by providing a base from which the second, third, and fourth fingers can form chord shapes. When the first finger is used to form a barre across the strings, a chord can be moved to every chromatic degree of the scale. Six of the open-string shapes shown on page 118 form the basis for major and minor barre voicings, and their barre versions are shown below.

BARRE TECHNIQUE

Acquiring barre technique is a difficult stage in learning to play the guitar. The strings dig into the joints and the softer parts of the first finger, causing discomfort. With practice, this will soon pass. Keep the barre straight, and ensure that the first finger applies even pressure across the strings. The second, third, and fourth fingers can also form half-barre shapes, thus enabling the player to hold down a wide range of chord voicings on the guitar in all keys.

First barre chords

In this example, an open string chord shape is moved up to the 3rd fret position using the barre. The first finger, forming the barre, becomes the equivalent of the open string chord notes, while the 3rd and 4th fingers hold down the remaining notes. The open-string chord voicing of E minor is moved up to become G minor on the 3rd fret. The chord retains the same overall shape as it is moved to all other fret positions.

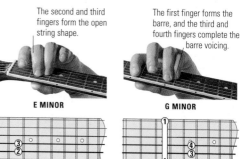

The second and third fingers form the open string shape.

The first finger forms the barre, and the third and fourth fingers complete the barre voicing.

E MINOR

G MINOR

Moving E major to F major

To form F major, the notes in a standard E major voicing are raised by a semitone. The first finger is pressed down across the strings on the first fret, and the second, third, and fourth fingers complete the major chord shape.

E MAJOR

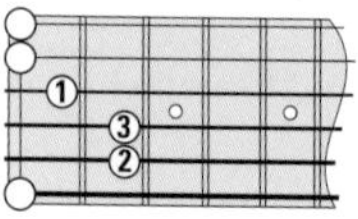

F MAJOR

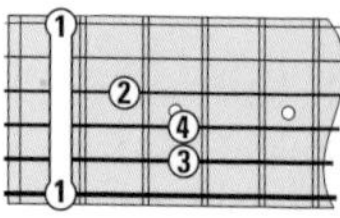

Moving E minor to F minor

To create F minor, the notes from a standard E minor voicing are raised by a semitone. The first finger is pressed down across the strings on the first fret, and the third and fourth fingers complete the minor shape.

E MINOR

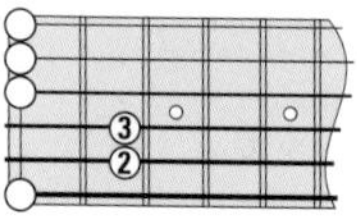

F MINOR

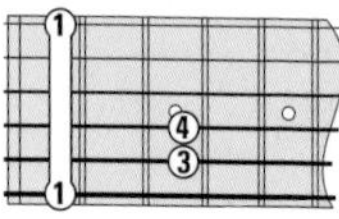

Moving G major to A♭ major

To create A♭ major, the notes from a standard G major voicing are raised by a semitone. The first finger is pressed down across three strings on the first fret and the second, third, and fourth fingers complete the voicing.

G MAJOR

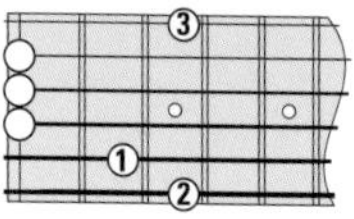

A♭ MAJOR

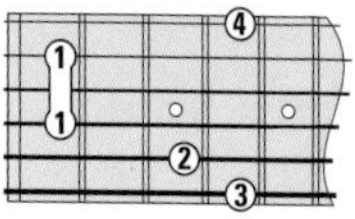

Moving A major to B♭ major

The 5th-string root major chord shape uses five notes, including the note on the 1st string. A number of players use the second finger to hold down both the 4th- and 3rd-string notes, leaving the third finger (instead of the fourth) to hold down the 2nd string. Many electric and steel-string guitars have narrow necks with close string spacing, which makes the full (barre) fingering, including the first string, difficult to play.

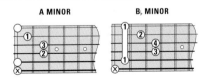

A MAJOR   **B♭ MAJOR**

Alternative fingering The B♭ major chord (*above right*) is played on the four middle strings only. The third finger is used as a half-barre.

Moving A minor to B♭ minor

To create B♭ minor, the A minor open-string shape is moved up by a semitone. The first finger forms a barre on the 1st fret across the first five strings. The second, third, and fourth fingers complete the minor shape.

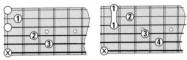

A MINOR   **B♭ MINOR**

Moving C major to D♭ major

To create D♭ major, the C major open-string shape is raised by a semitone. The first finger forms a half-barre on the 1st fret, across the first three strings, and the second, third, and fourth fingers complete the major shape.

C MAJOR   **D♭ MAJOR**

Root positions

Barre chords with 5th- and 6th-string roots can be constructed on the fret positions shown below.

Every major or minor chord can be played in more than one position. Barre chords can be moved above the 12th fret, depending on the type of guitar.

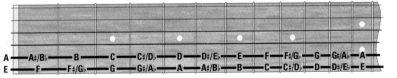

FORMING THE BARRE

Forming barre chords is physically difficult for the beginner. The first finger must be pushed down across the strings, with extra pressure coming from the thumb. Adding the other fingers when completing chord shapes may pull the first finger out of position and strain the left hand. Pressing notes down with the second, third, and fourth fingers might feel awkward, as a certain amount of additional stretching is necessary at first. Keeping the barre stable is also difficult. When moving barre chords around the fingerboard, relax the left hand and release the tension from the thumb and fingers. The half-barre, shown below, is the first of three different ways to develop a good barre technique. Between two and four strings are played across the fingerboard. Start off by holding two strings with the first finger, and add a string at a time until the full barre is achieved.

Barre on the 1st and 2nd strings

Barre on the 1st, 2nd, and 3rd strings

Barre on the 1st, 2nd, 3rd and 4th strings

FURTHER BARRE TECHNIQUES

The second and third methods of forming and practicing barres use the first finger to hold a full barre over all six strings. To begin with, the full barre position can be rather uncomfortable, and differing approaches can assist in the development of this technique. The examples below show how to build the fingering for an F major chord in stages. In the first example, the chord is formed by adding notes to the first finger barre. When the first finger is placed across a whole fret, strumming all the notes clearly is a helpful exercise for checking the position. In the second example, the other fingers are stabilized before the barre is added. It is worth noting that the 1st fret is a difficult position on which to play barre chords. At this position on the fingerboard, fret spacing is at its widest, and there is also considerable string tension next to the nut. Moving the chord shape halfway up the fingerboard can be easier when first practicing barre technique.

Full barre position

Begin by placing the first finger across the whole of the 1st fret of the fingerboard. Strum all six strings as a chord. Gradually add the other three fingers to form the major chord shape, and play all six strings. When you are comfortable with this technique, try playing on other fret positions. At first, the strings will cut into the flesh on the fingers. This can be painful, but eventually the skin hardens up and the joints and muscles become stronger. If you have difficulty holding down the barre, move the first finger up the fingerboard to a higher fret such as the 7th and push the strings down there. The string tension is much lower at this point so therefore it requires much less effort to push the strings against the fingerboard. Once you are used to forming the barre, try to move it back into the 1st fret position.

1 Begin by holding the barre firmly and evenly across the 1st fret of the fingerboard. You must make sure that none of the strings buzz.

2 Start to form the chord shape. While holding the barre across the 1st fret place the second finger on the 2nd fret of the 3rd string.

3 Still holding the barre, continue to build up the chord by placing the third finger on the 3rd fret of the 5th string. Make sure the strings do not buzz.

4 Complete the major chord by placing the fourth finger on the 3rd fret of the 4th string. Notice that the three fingers will take pressure off the barre.

Adding the barre to a chord

The third technique for forming the barre is, first, to play an open E major shape with the second, third, and fourth fingers. This is not the standard fingering for E major. Move the basic shape one fret up the fingerboard. Play this chord movement, which is often used in Spanish flamenco music. When the fingers feel comfortable and stable with the upper chord shape, add the barre to the 1st fret of the first two strings with the first finger. Then move the finger right across to form a barre by pressing down the 1st fret of the 6th string.

1 Begin by playing an E major chord with the second, third, and fourth fingers. Start by placing the second finger on the 1st fret of the 3rd string.

2 Move the shape up a fret and play the chord using the three fretted and three open strings. This chord has a flamenco flavor.

3 Add the barre to the 1st fret, converting the chord to an F major barre shape. Either gradually form the barre, or place the finger across all the strings.

BARRE SEVENTH CHORDS

The major seventh, dominant seventh, and minor seventh chords can also be played on the main barre positions, by adding the seventh note to major and minor chord shapes. Using the barre positions with the root on the 6th string, the major and minor chords are converted to sevenths by removing the fourth finger. The doubled root is replaced by the seventh a semitone below. Using the root on the 5th string, the doubled octave note is removed, and the seventh in the chord is held by the barre. This applies to all of the shapes apart from the first example, where the B♭ major chord is converted to B♭ major 7th and refingered with the seventh held by the second finger. Practising the movement of major and minor chords to sevenths is an effective way to learn new shapes. The standard barre shapes are shown below with their seventh voicings. The last example shows alternative major voicing converted to a major seventh.

F dominant 7th

F major becomes a dominant 7th by taking the fourth finger away from the 4th string. The 7th is held by the barre on the 1st fret of the 4th string.

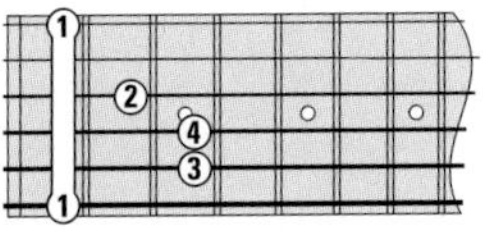

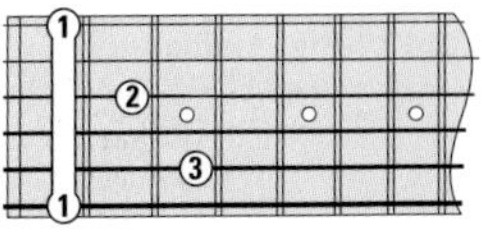

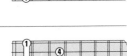

F minor 7th

F minor chord is converted to F minor 7th by removing the fourth finger from the 4th string. The 7th is held by the barre on the 1st fret of the 4th string.

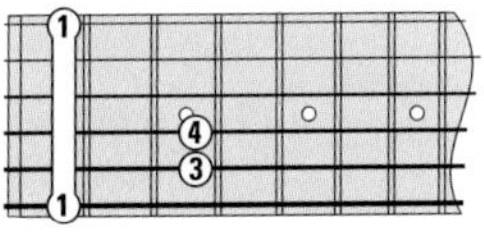

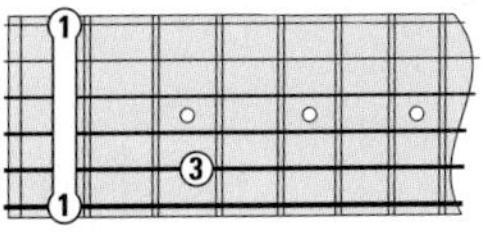

B♭ major 7th

B♭ major is converted to a B♭ major 7th by replacing the second finger with the third, and placing the second finger on the 2nd fret of the 3rd string.

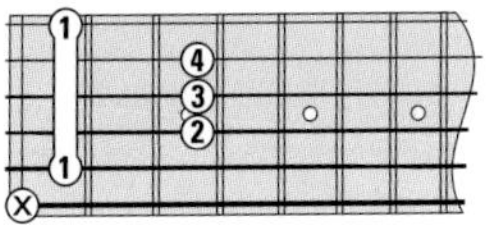

B♭ dominant 7th

B♭ major is converted to a B♭ dominant 7th by placing the third finger on the 3rd fret of the 4th string. The 7th is held by the barre on the 3rd string.

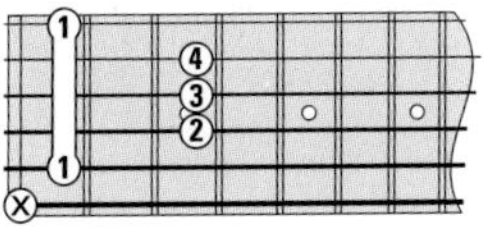

B♭ minor 7th

B♭ minor is converted to a B♭ minor 7th by taking the fourth finger away from the third string. The 7th is held by the barre on the 1st fret of the 3rd string.

D♭ major 7th

D♭ major is converted to a D♭ major 7th by taking the second finger away from the 2nd string. The 7th is held by the barre on the 1st fret of the 2nd string.

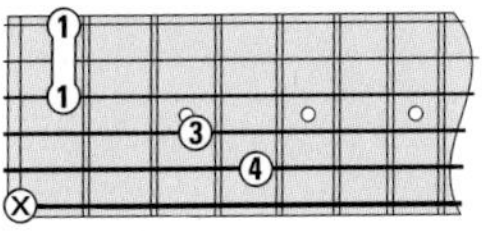

Moving chords

Music is frequently built around a few closely related chords. G major, C major, and D major are the **I**, **IV**, and **V** chords from the key of G. They can be played easily by using open-string voicings, and are commonly found in all styles of music. Combining open-string and fretted barre voicings creates many variations on these chords. Playing the three chord types through the variations below will help develop a basic understanding of primary chord movements.

THE I-IV-V CHORD SEQUENCE

In the major keys, the primary major chords are those built on the tonic (**I**), subdominant (**IV**), and dominant (**V**). They are related to each other by a series of strong musical movements. When combined in a sequence, these chords may be used to create music and melody of considerable variety. A thorough understanding of the primary major chords in every key is a secure foundation on which to build a comprehensive vocabulary for accompanying songs

and for improvisation. There are a number of positions for each chord, and these can be played in many different ways. With the exception of D major in the open-string voicing, the chords in the section below all have their lowest root note on either the 6th or the 5th string. The numbers in circles show the fingers to be used; circles without numbers represent open strings which must be played. Listen to and compare the different shapes, and practise them slowly.

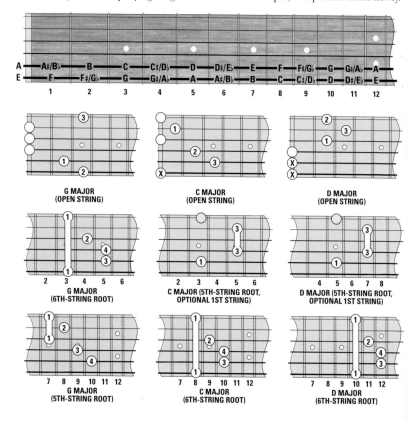

TRANSPOSING G, C AND D

When similar types of standard voicing are used to play a three-chord sequence, the pattern of movements is very easy to remember visually on the fingerboard. A fixed series of the three chords – G, C, and D major – can be transposed to other keys by shifting the shapes to different fret positions. For example, G, C, and D are raised a semitone to the key of A♭, to form A♭, D♭, E♭, by simply moving the entire progression up by one fret. Moving up the fingerboard one fret at a time transposes the sequence in ascending semitones. Moving down the fingerboard transposes the sequence in descending semitones – F♯/G♭, F, and finally E. The **I-IV-V** sequence in a 12-bar blues is one of the most widely used basic structures in rock music. The three chords can be played either as open-string chords or as fretted shapes. Major chords are often simplified to a chord of just roots and fifths – the third is not played. These chords, in a **I-IV-V** sequence in G, are sometimes written as G5, C5, and D5. The root and the fifth for each major chord can be played on the 5th and 6th strings. An additional octave root can be included on the 4th or the 3rd string.

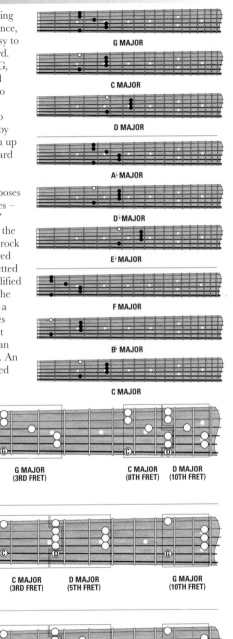

G MAJOR

C MAJOR

D MAJOR

A♭ MAJOR

D♭ MAJOR

E♭ MAJOR

F MAJOR

B♭ MAJOR

C MAJOR

G-C-D on the 6th string
The sequence can be played with a single shape. Starting with G major on the 3rd fret, move the shape to the 8th fret (C major), and then on to the 10th fret (D major).

G MAJOR (3RD FRET)   C MAJOR (8TH FRET)   D MAJOR (10TH FRET)

G-C-D on the 5th string
G-C-D can also be played using one shape based on a 5th-string root. Starting with G major on the 10th fret, moved down to the 3rd fret (C major), and back up to the 5th fret to D major.

C MAJOR (3RD FRET)   D MAJOR (5TH FRET)   G MAJOR (10TH FRET)

5th string sevenths
II-V-I in C major can be played using seventh shapes on the 5th string. Start with D minor 7 on the 5th fret; move to G dominant seventh on the 10th fret; and then C major 7 on the 3rd fret.

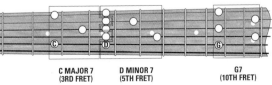

C MAJOR 7 (3RD FRET)   D MINOR 7 (5TH FRET)   G7 (10TH FRET)

Chord finder

Over the following pages is an extensive range of chords built from fifth-, sixth-, and fourth-string roots. All have roots placed on the 3rd fret. Each chord shape may be moved up or down the fingerboard to any of the 12 fret positions, providing hundreds of different chords.

CHORD NOTES

On the fingerboard diagrams throughout the chord finder, numbers inside circles show which left-hand fingers are used. A circle on the fretboard, with no number, shows that the note is optional. A blue bar connecting strings represents a barre or a half-barre. To find a chord type, first select a neighboring string position.

For example, in order to play a B7♭5, find C7♭5 among the 5th-string chords based on C roots on the page opposite. If this shape is then moved down one fret to the B root on the 2nd fret, B7♭5 is formed. Dozens of voicings can be formed from the fifth string root. See the chord dictionary on page 186.

A — A♯/B♭ — B — C — C♯/D♭ — D — D♯/E♭ — E — F — F♯/G♭ — G — G♯/A♭ — A

ROOTS ON THE 5TH STRING

All the chords on these two pages have a C root, on the 3rd fret of the 5th string. From this point, they can be compared harmonically, and the constituent notes can be memorized in relation to the C root. Chords with a 5th-string root often have adjacent outer or inner strings that are not played. Prevent these unused strings from ringing by letting the sides of the fingers rest naturally against them. Some chords can be played either with or without a barre. For example, on C major 7 the first finger barre can hold G.

C major 7th (C△7)
This uses C (root), G (perfect fifth), B (major seventh), and E (major third). Play the 5th, 4th, 3rd, and 2nd strings.

C dominant 7th (C7)
This uses C (root), G (perfect fifth), B♭ (minor seventh), and E (major third). The strings used are the 5th to the 2nd.

C minor 7th (C-7)
Play C (root), G (perfect fifth), B♭ (minor seventh), and E♭ (minor third) on the 5th, 4th, 3rd, and 2nd strings.

C minor 7th flat 5th (C7♭5)
Play C (root), G♭ (diminished fifth), B♭ (minor seventh), and E♭ (minor third).

C diminished 7th (C°7)
The notes are C (root), G♭ (diminished fifth), B♭♭ /A (diminished seventh/major sixth), and E♭ (minor third).

C dominant 7th flat 5th (C7♭5)
Play C (root), G♭ (diminished fifth), B♭ (minor seventh), and E (major third).

C dominant 7th sharp 5th (C7#5)
Play C (root), G♯ (augmented fifth), B♭ (minor seventh), and E (major third).

2   3   4   5   6

C major 7th sharp 11th (C△#11)
Play C (root), F♯ (augmented 4th/11th), B (major seventh), and E (major third).

C minor/major 7th (C-△7)
Play C (root), G (perfect fifth), B (major seventh), and E♭ (minor third) using 5th to 2nd strings.

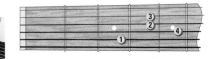

C major 6th (C6)
Play C (root), E (major third), A (major sixth), and C (octave root). Play all the strings from the 5th to the 2nd.

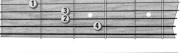

C minor 6th (C-6)
Play C (root), A (major sixth), E♭ (minor third), and G (perfect fifth). Play the 5th, 3rd, 2nd, and 1st strings.

C major 9th (C△9)
Play C (root), E (major third), B (major seventh), and D (major ninth). The 5th to the 2nd strings are used.

C dominant 9th (C9)
Play C (root), E (major third), B♭ (minor seventh), and D (major ninth) using the 5th to the 2nd strings.

C minor 9th (C-9)
The chord is formed using the notes C (root), E♭ (minor third), B♭ (minor seventh), and D (major ninth).

ROOT CHORDS ON THE 6TH STRING

Building chords from a root on the 6th string enables the guitarist to play low-register chords as well as full-sounding five- and six-note voicings. Many of the most complex and attractive harmonies are played using all six strings. Five- and six-note chords are often reduced by not playing the 5th string. This gives a more balanced sound. In these instances, the doubled thirds or fifths are left out.

Altering voicings in this way also enables chords to be moved around with more flexibility. Some of the standard added-note voicings have a rather bottom-heavy and muddy texture when the four lower strings are sounded together. Therefore, voicings without the 5th string are used here. For example, play G major 7, the first chord below. If this is played with a D on the 5th string it sounds less effective.

Chord notes
The intervals shown on the fingerboard are named from the root (in this case, G). The same pattern can run from any fret position on the

6th string. Any of the 12 chromatic semitones can be used as a root for any chord. For example, play the first chord shape G major 7 and move all the fingers up by one fret to form A♭ major 7.

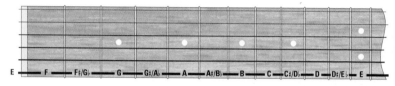

E   F   F♯/G♭   G   G♯/A♭   A   A♯/B♭   B   C   C♯/D♭   D   D♯/E♭   E

G major 7th (G△7)
G (root), F♯ (major 7th), B (major 3rd), and D (perfect 5th) are played on the 6th, 4th, 3rd, and 2nd strings.

G dominant 7th (G7)
This chord is formed from G (root), F (minor 7th), B (major 3rd), and D (perfect 5th).

G minor 7th (G-7)
This chord uses the notes G (root), F (minor 7th), B♭ (minor 3rd), and D (perfect 5th).

G minor 7th flat 5th (G-7♭5)
The notes are G (root), F (minor 7th), B♭ (minor 3rd), and D♭ (diminished 5th).

G diminished 7th (G°7)
Play G (root), F♭/E (diminished 7th/major 6th), B♭ (minor 3rd), and D♭ (diminished 5th).

G dominant 7th flat 5th (G7♭5)
Play the notes G (root), F (minor 7th), B (major 3rd), and D♭ (diminished 5th).

G dominant 7th sharp 5th (G7#5)
Play the notes G (root), F (minor 7th), B (major 3rd), and D# (augmented 5th).

G major 7th sharp 11th (G△7#11)
Play G (root), F# (major 7th), B (major 3rd), and C# (augmented 4th/11th).

ROOT CHORDS ON THE 4TH STRING

On the four upper strings of the guitar the chordal possibilities are more limited. Eleventh chords and others can be formed, but with only four voices—they lack some of the notes that give certain chords their harmonic character. The upper-string chords are ideal for supporting melody. Their bright sound, good separation, and high register lend themselves to chord fills in group playing.

Chord notes
The intervals shown on the fingerboard are named from the root (in this case, F). The same pattern can run from any fret position on the 4th string. Any of the 12 chromatic semitones can be used as a root for any chord.

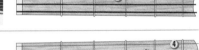

D — D#/E♭ — E — F — F#/G♭ — G — G#/A♭ — A — A#/B♭ — B — C — C#/D♭ — D

F major 7th (F△7)
In this chord, the notes are F, C, E, and A. The voicing order is root, perfect 5th, major 7th, and major 3rd.

F dominant 7th (F7)
The chord is formed from F (root), C (perfect 5th), E♭ (minor 7th), and A (major 3rd).

F minor 7th (F-7)
This chord uses the notes F (root), C (perfect 5th), E♭ (minor 7th), and A♭ (minor 3rd).

F minor 7th flat 5th (F-7♭5)
This chord consists of the notes F (root), C♭/B (dim. 5th), E♭ (minor 7th), and A♭ (minor 3rd).

F diminished 7th (F°7)
Play F (root), C♭/B (diminished 5th), E♭♭/D (diminished 7th/major 6th), and A♭ (minor 3rd).

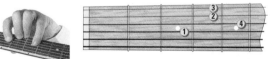

The modal system

Each of the seven degrees of the major scale can be treated as the starting-point for a scale. These scales are known as "modes", and are assigned classical Greek names. Every mode has a distinct series of fixed intervals, with the first note of the scale acting as a principal note for both melody and harmony. Each of the seven modal scales has its own recognizable sound and character.

THE USE OF MODES

Modes break the major system down into seven scales which can be used for composition and improvisation. Because of the precise order of tones and semitones, each mode has its own distinct melodic flavour and pattern.

C Ionian scale
Commonly referred to as the major scale, the Ionian has an order, from the root, of major and perfect intervals.

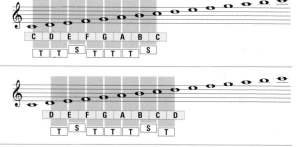

D Dorian scale
The Dorian mode is a minor scale. It is similar to the Aeolian natural minor scale, apart from its major sixth.

E Phrygian scale
This minor scale has a distinctive sound arising from the minor and perfect intervals in relation to the root.

F Lydian scale
This major scale has an augmented fourth in relation to the root, creating an unusual harmonic flavour.

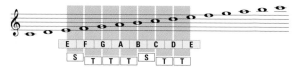

G Mixolydian scale
This major scale has a minor seventh in relation to its root. By raising the seventh by a semitone, it becomes G major.

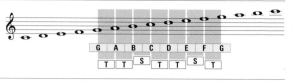

A Aeolian scale
This is usually referred to as the minor scale. It is used as a primary scale for building chordal harmony.

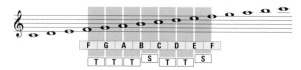

B Locrian scale
This minor mode has a perfect fourth, a diminished fifth, and minor intervals in relation to the root.

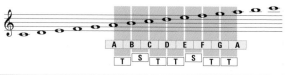
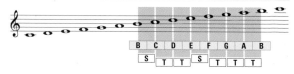

PLAYING AND HEARING MODES

The first note of a mode can be played alongside each of the scale notes as a drone and left to resonate under the modal scales. This sustained note is known as a pedal note. It is one that is heard continuously through a section of music – either repeated or sustained, at one pitch. In the examples below, it is played below the notes of each mode by striking one of the lower strings and letting the note ring out under the mode. The two lowest strings of the guitar – the 6th (E) and 5th (A) – can both be used as open strings under the E Phrygian and A Aeolian

modes. To play a low pedal note under the remaining five modes, the 6th or 5th string must be tuned to one of the notes C, D, F, G, or B. A higher-octave note is played on a fretted or open position as a reference point, and one of the open lower strings is tuned to this note an octave below. For example, the pedal note D is played on the 6th string by tuning the open E down by a tone. The open 4th string, D, is used as a reference note. Strings can be tuned to other modal notes by playing other strings or fretted notes, an octave above, as references for tuning up or down.

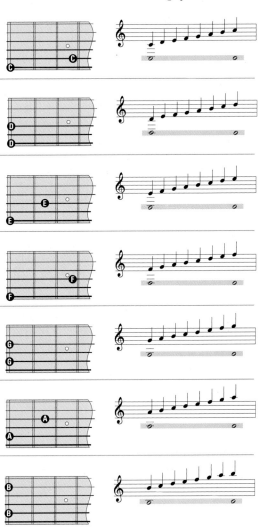

Playing the Ionian scale in C
De-tune the 6th string to a C (an octave below the 3rd fret of the 5th string). Play the open 6th string, and play the Ionian/major scale starting from the 5th string.

Playing the Dorian scale in E
De-tune the 6th string to a D (an octave below the open 4th string). Using the re-tuned 6th string as a low D, play the Dorian scale from the 4th string.

Playing the Phrygian scale in E
Play the open 6th string, E, and play the Phrygian mode ascending from E on the octave above, starting on the 2nd fret of the 4th string.

Playing the Lydian scale in F
Tune the 6th string up to F (an octave below F on the 4th string's 3rd fret). Using the 6th string as a low F, play the Lydian mode ascending from the 4th string.

Playing the Mixolydian scale in G
De-tune the 5th string to the note G (an octave below the G string). Use this to play the Mixolydian mode from the 3rd string.

Playing the Aeolian scale in A
The open 5th string of the guitar is tuned to the note A. Using the 5th string as a low A, play the Aeolian ascending from the 3rd string.

Playing the Locrian scale in B
Tune the 5th string up to B (an octave below the open 2nd string). With the 5th string as a low B, play the Locrian ascending from the 2nd string.

Playing major scales

The capability of playing in all twelve major scales is vital to mastering the guitar. Music modulates and is often transposed from one key to another, changing its mood and colour. The position and structure of different scales must be memorized in order to play them comfortably. Start by taking the basic one-octave positions for each key, and compare them with their closely related scales. The range of each scale can gradually be extended to cover the entire fingerboard in stages.

SINGLE-OCTAVE SCALES

The keynote of each of the major scales shown here is determined by the lowest available note on the fingerboard. The keynotes run from the first note of E major, on the open 6th string, to the first note of Eb major, on the 1st fret of the 4th string. The keynotes E major, F major, F# /Gb major, G major, and Ab major scales start on the 6th string; A major, Bb major, B major, C major, and Db major start on the 5th string; and D major and Eb major start on the 4th string.

C major
The C major scale starts on the 3rd fret of the 5th string. It ascends with D, E, and F on the 4th string; G and A on the 3rd string; and B and C on the 2nd string. It uses the four middle strings.

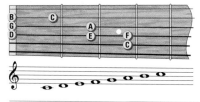

G major (1 sharp)
The G major scale starts on the 3rd fret of the 6th string. It ascends on the 5th string using A, B, and C; continues on the 4th string with D, E and F# and ends with the open G string.

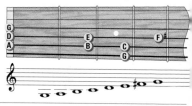

D major (2 sharps)
The D major scale starts on the open 4th string. It ascends on the 4th string with E and F#; moves to the 3rd string with just G and A; and ends on the 2nd string with, B, C#, and D.

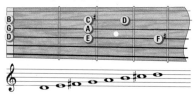

A major (3 sharps)
The A major scale starts on the open 5th string. It scale ascends with B and C# on the 5th string; D, E, and F# on the 4th string; and ends with G# and A on the 3rd string.

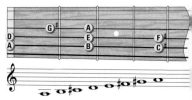

E major (4 sharps)
The E major scale starts on the lowest note E on the open 6th string. It ascends with F# and G# on the 6th string; A, B, and C# on the 5th string; and D# and E on the 4th string.

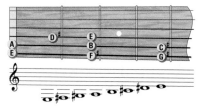

B major (5 sharps)
The B major scale starts on the note B on the 2nd fret of the 5th string. It ascends with C# on the 5th string; D#, E, and F# on the 4th string; G# and A# on the 3rd string; and open B.

ENHARMONIC SCALES

Two major scales consist of the same notes played at the same pitch, but with a different set of note names. They are F#/Gb and C#/Db. For example, the notes in the key of F# are the same as the notes in Gb. The same applies to C# and Db. The term enharmonic is used to describe identical notes, scales, and chords.

F# major (6 sharps)
The F# major scale starts on the 2nd fret of the 6th string, and ascends with G# on the 6th string; A#, B, and C# on the 5th string; and D#, E# and F# on the 4th string. E# is the same as F.

Gb major (6 flats)
The Gb major scale starts on the 2nd fret of the 6th string. It ascends with Ab on the 6th string; Bb, Cb, and Db on the 5th string; and Eb, F, and Gb on the 4th string. Cb is the same as B.

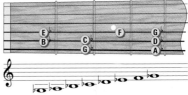

C# major (7 sharps)
The C# major scale starts on the 4th fret of the 5th string. It ascends with D#, E#, and F# on the 4th string; G# and A# on the 3rd string; and B# and C# on the 2nd string. B# is the same note as C.

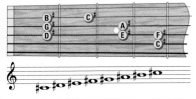

Db major (5 flats)
The Db major scale begins on the 4th fret of the 5th string. It ascends with the notes Eb, F, and Gb. Ab and Bb are played on the 3rd string, and C and Db are played on the 2nd string.

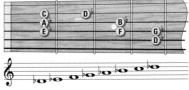

Ab major (4 flats)
The Ab major scale starts on the 4th fret of the 6th string. It scale ascends with Bb, C, and Db on the 5th string; Eb and F on the 4th string; and open G and Ab on the 3rd string.

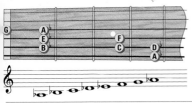

Eb major (3 flats)
The Eb major scale starts on the 1st fret of the 4th string. It ascends with F on the 4th string; open G, Ab, and Bb on the 3rd string; and C, D, and Eb on the 2nd string.

Bb major (2 flats)
The Bb major scale starts on the 1st fret of the 5th string. It ascends with C on the 5th string; open D, Eb, and F on the 4th string; and open G, A, and Bb on the 3rd string.

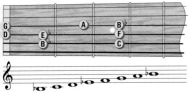

F major (1 flat)
The F major scale starts on the note F on the 1st fret of the 6th string. It ascends with G on the 6th string; open A, Bb, and C on the 5th string; and open D, E, and F on the 4th string.

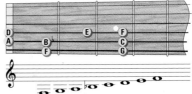

FULL MAJOR SCALES

The full major scales, forming a pattern right across the fingerboard, are shown below in a sequence following the cycle of fifths. Learn each shape and position one key at a time. The diagrams show the fingerboard up to the 15th fret.

C major

The scale uses the notes C, D, E, F, G, A, and B. The pattern from the open string to the 11th fret repeats from the 12th fret upwards. The keynotes (C) are all marked as green dots. It is important to learn the position of all the C major notes.

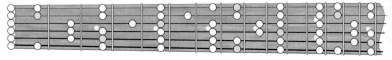

G major

The scale uses the notes G, A, B, C, D, E, and F♯. The pattern from the open string to the 11th fret repeats from the 12th fret. The keynotes (G) are marked as green dots. Compare the fingering patterns of G with its added F♯ with C major.

D major

The scale uses the notes D, E, F♯, G, A, B, and C♯. The pattern from the open string to the 11th fret repeats from the 12th fret. The keynotes (D) are marked as green dots. Compare the fingering patterns of D with its added C♯ with G major.

A major

The scale uses the notes A, B, C♯, D, E, F♯, and G♯. The pattern from the open string to the 11th fret repeats from the 12th fret. The keynotes (A) are marked as green dots. Compare the fingering patterns of A with its added G♯ with D major.

E major

The scale uses the notes E, F♯, G♯, A, B, C♯, and D♯. The pattern from the open string to the 11th fret repeats from the 12th fret. The keynotes (E) are marked as green dots. Compare the fingering patterns of E with its added D♯ with A major.

B major

The scale uses the notes B, C♯, D♯, E, F♯, G♯, and A♯. The pattern from the open string to the 11th fret repeats from the 12th fret. The keynotes (B) are marked as green dots. Compare the fingering patterns of B with its added A♯ with E major.

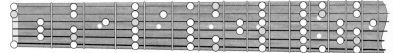

F♯ /G♭ major

This scale uses the notes F♯, G♯, A♭, B, C♯, D♯, E♯, and the enharmonic equivalent, G♭, A♭, B♭, C♭, D♭, E♭, and F. The pattern from the open string to the

11th fret repeats from the 12th fret. The keynotes (F♯/G♭) are marked as green dots. Compare F♯/G♭ major with B major. Try to memorize these fingering patterns with both of their names.

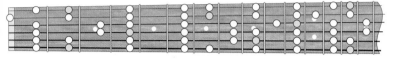

D♭/C♯ major

The notes used in this scale are D♭, E♭, F, G♭, A♭, B♭, and C. They also have an enharmonic equivalent which runs C♯, D♯, E♯, F♯, G♯, A♯ B♯.

They form a pattern from the open string to the 11th fret; this repeats from the 12th fret. The keynotes (D♭) are marked as green dots. Although it is useful to know this scale as C♯, it is not often used.

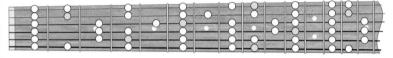

A♭ major

The components of this scale are A♭, B♭, C, D♭, E♭, F, and G. The pattern from the open string to the 11th fret repeats from the 12th fret. The

keynotes (A♭) are marked as green dots. Start to learn these scale positions and patterns by memorizing the position of the root note and double octave A♭ scale starting on the 4th fret.

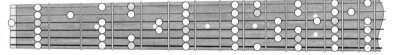

E♭ major

The notes used here are E♭, F, G, A♭, B♭, C, and D. As in the scales above, the pattern from the open string to the 11th fret repeats from the 12th fret.

The keynotes (E♭) are marked as green dots. Start to learn these scale positions and patterns by memorizing the position of the root note and double octave E♭ scale starting on the 11th fret.

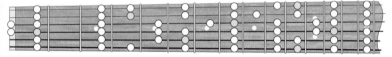

B♭ major

This scale consists of the notes B♭, C, D, E♭, F, G, and A. The pattern from the open string to the 11th fret repeats from the 12th fret, and the

keynotes (B♭) are marked as green dots. Start to learn these scale positions and patterns by memorizing the position of the root note and double octave B♭ scale starting on the 6th fret.

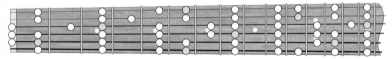

F major

The scale uses the notes F, G, A, B♭, C, D, and E. The pattern from the open string to the 11th fret repeats from the 12th fret. The keynotes (F) are

marked as green dots. Start to learn these scale positions and patterns by memorizing the position of the root note and double octave F scale starting on the 1st fret. Compare with C major.

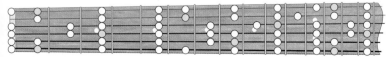

The minor system

All major keys have a relative minor key, with a scale and a group of chords based around a minor keynote. There are three different types of minor scale: the natural (or Aeolian) minor, the harmonic minor, and the melodic minor.

NATURAL AND HARMONIC MINOR

In the key of C major, the related natural minor scale is A, using the notes A-B-C-D-E-F-G. The harmonic minor is formed by adding a sharp, raising the seventh degree by a semitone. The series of notes becomes A-B-C-D-E-F-G♯.

A minor Aeolian scale
The natural Aeolian minor scale has the following intervals from the root: major second, minor third, perfect fourth, perfect fifth, minor sixth, and minor seventh. In A minor, it uses the notes of the C major scale starting from its sixth degree.

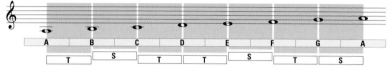

A minor harmonic scale
The harmonic minor scale has a major seventh from the root, which acts as the leading note in the scale. This scale starts on A and uses the notes of the C major scale, except G natural, which is raised a semitone to G♯.

MINOR TRIADS

Natural minor triads starting from the note A are identical to those in C major, but they begin from a different point.

When A Aeolian minor is altered to A minor harmonic, the inclusion of the G♯ alters three of the triads.

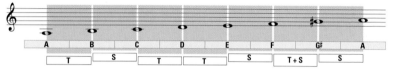

HARMONIC MINOR CHORDS

The harmonic minor system of chords can be extended to sixths, sevenths, diminished sevenths, and ninths.

They appear in sections of minor harmony, and are used for contrasting major and minor chordal movements.

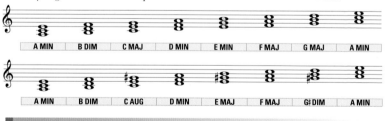

	SIXTH	SEVENTH	DIMINISHED	NINTH	OTHER TYPES		
A		A MIN/MAJ7		A MIN/MAJ9	A MIN/MAJ11		
B		B MIN7♭5	B DIM7		B MIN11♭5		
C		C MAJ7♯5			C MAJ9♯5		C6♯5
D	D MIN6	D MIN7	D DIM7	D MIN9	D MIN7♭5		D MIN11♭5
E		E7		E7♭9	E7♯5	E7♯5♭9	E7
F	F6	F MAJ7	F DIM7		F MIN/MAJ7		F MAJ7♯11
G♯		G♯DIM7	G♯DIM7		G♯DIM7 ADD E		

HARMONIC MINOR SCALE

A one-octave A minor harmonic scale can be played from either the open 5th string or the 5th fret of the 6th string. Memorize the fingering pattern from the open string and the fingering pattern from the 5th fret and try to connect the two patterns together. Another way of getting to know A minor harmonic patterns is to take C major and raise every G to a G#.

Open string position
This position, starting on open A, uses all the open strings apart from G: this is raised to G#. The three-fret jump on the 1st string may be difficult at first.

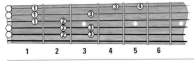

5th-fret position
Starting on the 5th fret of the 6th string, play across the fretboard, shifting down to the 4th fret of the 3rd string. Do not move the thumb position.

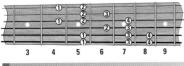

MELODIC MINOR SCALE

A minor melodic scale is played from the open 5th string or the 5th fret of the 6th string. In classical music this scale is played in an ascending form with two sharps and a descending form without sharps. It is exactly the same as the Aeolian mode. For improvising over chords including D7♭5 and G#7♭5, the melodic minor is played with sharps ascending and descending.

Open string position
This pattern starts on the open A string and ascends, with F# and G#, in tone and semitone steps, using all of the open strings aside from G.

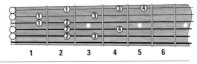

5th-fret stretch position
The A minor melodic scale can be played from the 5th fret. Play C on the 5th string with the first finger. There is a wide stretch to the second finger.

TRANSPOSING MINOR SCALES

The harmonic and melodic minor scales can be played from all keynotes by moving a position along the fingerboard as a block. The harmonic and melodic positions for G minor and C# minor are played using the same shape as A.

Transposing the harmonic minor scale
This fingering position can be moved along the 6th string using each fret as a keynote. The lined blocks show the positions for harmonic minor scales in G and C#. Move from G harmonic minor up seven frets to C# harmonic minor.

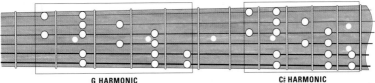

G HARMONIC   **C# HARMONIC**

Transposing the melodic minor scale
Any fingering position can be moved along the 6th string using each fret as a keynote. The lined areas show the positions for melodic minor scales in the keys of G and C#. Move from G melodic minor up seven frets to C# melodic minor.

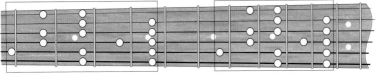

G MELODIC   **C# MELODIC**

Techniques and effects

The guitar has a rich and varied range of tonal colors and sounds. These can be brought out by using a number of techniques such as string bending, slides, hammering, pull-offs, and the use of tremolo arm. Trills, mordants, and other ornaments can also be used to embellish simple melodies.

PRACTICING EFFECTS

Practice sliding up and down the fingerboard as a way of moving from one position to another. Try to play a scale on one string with each finger in turn, sliding from note to note. Make use of all the textures: use vibrato on each note, staccato, and varying degrees of muting and sustain.

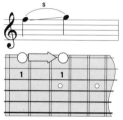

The slide
Strike the note F, and then slide with the first finger up to the note G on the 3rd fret without releasing the pressure.

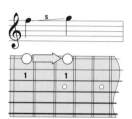

Slide with struck note
Strike the note F, slide the finger up to G, and strike that note. Reverse these movements to play a descending slide.

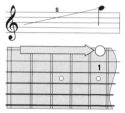

Sliding up to a note
Place the first finger on the 4th fret without playing the note, and slide the finger up to the 5th fret where the note is then played.

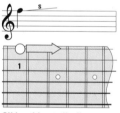

Slide with a trail-off
Strike a note and slide up or down three or four frets, releasing the pressure at any time so that the sound dies away.

Portamento (or "Glissando")
The first and last notes in an ascending or descending slide are struck, the slide being played so that its every "note" is heard.

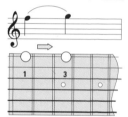

Hammer-on
While F, played with the first finger, is ringing, hit the 3rd fret with the third finger. The hammering action sounds G.

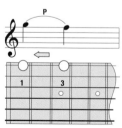

Pull-off
Place the first finger on F. Play G with the third finger, then take it away, pulling the string down. This will sound the note F.

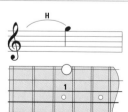

Hammering a note
Notes can be played on the guitar without using the right hand. Try playing G and then pulling it off to sound open G.

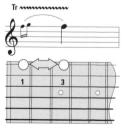

The Trill
Play the note F, then hammer G. Use a pull-off from G to sound F again. Play these notes as one continuous, rapid movement.

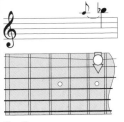

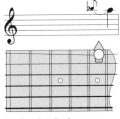

Bending
Strike the note A, on the 5th fret of the 1st string, and bend the string upwards as it rings, to raise the pitch of the note. Try bending A one semitone to B♭.

Pre-bend and release
Hold down A, then bend it up to a B♭ without playing it. Hold it in position and strike the note. While it is ringing, pull the string back to its fret position.

Acciaccatura and Appoggiatura
The acciaccatura is played very quickly just before a principal note. The appoggiatura is similar, but has half the time value of the note that it precedes.

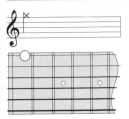

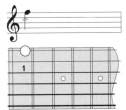

Muted notes
The letter **X**, written as above, is a direction to play the strings percussively. Mute the strings (*see* p.146) and play the notes; this produces a deadened sound.

Tremolo picking
A note written with small bars across the stem is to be repeated rapidly and continuously for its time value. Two bars indicate very fast movement.

Upper and lower mordants
Play a note, then the note above it (or the note below it, if playing a lower mordant), and then the original note again – all as one rapid movement.

Vibrato
Hold E on the 2nd string. Rock the fingertip rapidly from side to side to create wavering sustain.

Using a tremolo arm
A variety of effects can be created by pushing the tremolo arm down, which lowers the pitch, or pulling it up, which raises it. Compare it with bending a note on a fret. Play a phrase, and, on the last note, move the

tremolo arm. Try playing an E on the 12th fret and pulling it up and down by a semitone. Play a note with the tremolo arm pressed down. Let it return to a normal position. This gives a "scooped" effect to the note.

HARMONICS

Open-string natural harmonics occur over certain frets. Three can be played by touching a string lightly over the 5th, 7th, and 12th frets (the 12th fret produces an octave harmonic). A note held on any fret has artificial harmonics between the fret and the bridge. Play F♯ on the 2nd fret and place the finger

lightly over the 14th fret. This gives the octave harmonic. Play by lightly touching the harmonic over the fret with the first finger and plucking the string with the thumb or the second or third finger. This can be played with a pick held between the thumb and the second finger. A diamond indicates a harmonic.

Variations
Play a three-note scale by holding down F♯, G, and A and playing harmonics over the upper frets. Now hold the chord of C major and play the chord with harmonics over the frets. All are played 12 frets higher.

Modal improvising

Single notes that are played with chords tend to function as extensions of the underlying harmonic structure: the melodic quality of a note played over a block chord depends on their relationship to each other. Modal chords have different voicings and structures that determine the sound of related modal notes. Modal scales can be used to enlarge the range of improvising.

MODES WITHIN THE C MAJOR SCALE

The degrees of the C major scale (**I–VII**, and a repeated **I**) are shown in the upper stave of each diagram below. A seventh chord has been used in each bar. The gray shading marks the chord type (Cmaj7 in the first example), which is then varied

in a four-bar sequence (C6, Cmaj9 etc.) shown on the lower stave. Play this and the variations on each degree. Then play the modal scale. To hear the effect of each note in context, it is helpful to record these chord sequences.

C major chords (I)

Chords using the first degree of the C major scale as their keynote are constructed from the notes C, D, E, G, A, and B. The major chord and its common

extensions are C6, C major 7, C major 9, and C6/9. In the standard **I** chord form, the note F is rarely used, but it can be voiced carefully with the notes C, F, B, and E to support single notes.

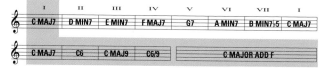

C Ionian

Play the exercises against the standard chords (**I–VII** in the upper stave). The seven-note arpeggio (in the fourth bar) includes the note F,

which sounds dissonant when stressed against some of these chords, although it is perfectly acceptable within passages of notes or if it is not stressed heavily on an accent.

D minor chords (II)

Chords using the second degree of the C major scale as their keynote can be constructed using all of the notes of the Dorian mode: D, E, F, G, A,

B, and C. Minor chords and their common extensions are used in all types of progressions. As a standard **II** chord, all the scale notes can be added to form attractive voicings.

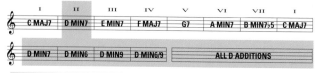

D Dorian

Play the exercises over the standard chords. Try the full seven-note arpeggio against the D minor 7 chord and its extensions. Dorian chords are

extremely important in melody and improvisation. The Dorian mode is the most accessible of all seven modes and can be used over any of the seven modal chords.

E minor chords (III)

Chords using the third degree of the C major scale as their keynote are built from the notes E, G, A, B, and D. The common extensions used are E minor 7, and E minor 11 without a ninth. As a standard **III** chord, not all the scale notes are used.

I	II	III	IV	V	VI	VII	I
C MAJ7	D MIN7	E MIN7	F MAJ7	G7	A MIN7	B MIN7♭5	C MAJ7

E MIN7	E MIN7	E MIN11	E MIN11	E PHRYGIAN CHORDS ADD C(♭6), F(♭9)		

E Phrygian

Play the exercises against the standard chords, and the full seven-note arpeggio with E minor 7 and its extensions. Note that C and F are dissonant. Play the E Phrygian voicings using the entire scale.

F major chords (IV)

Chords using the fourth degree of the C major scale as their keynote are constructed from the notes F, G, A, B, C, D, and E. The common extensions are F6, F major 7, F major 9, F6/9, and F major 7#11. They are used in all types of sequence.

I	II	III	IV	V	VI	VII	I
C MAJ7	D MIN7	E MIN7	F MAJ7	G7	A MIN7	B MIN7♭5	C MAJ7

F6	F MAJ7	F MAJ9	F6/9	F LYDIAN CHORDS, ADD B	

F Lydian

Play the exercises against the standard chords, and the full arpeggio against the F major 7 chord and its extensions. The Lydian scale creates an interesting sound when played against major chords with its augmented fourth degree.

G major chords (V)

Chords using the fifth degree of the C major scale as their keynote are built from the notes G, A, B, C, D, E, and F. The common extensions are G6, G7, G9, G11, and G13. As a standard **V** chord, all the notes of the scale are used.

I	II	III	IV	V	VI	VII	I
C MAJ7	D MIN7	E MIN7	F MAJ7	G7	A MIN7	B MIN7♭5	C MAJ7

G7	G9	G11	G13	ALL G ADDITIONS	

G Mixolydian

Play the exercises against the standard chords, and the full seven-note arpeggio against the G7 chord and its extensions. Mixolydian chords are important for melody and improvisation. The note C can sound wrong if stressed against G7.

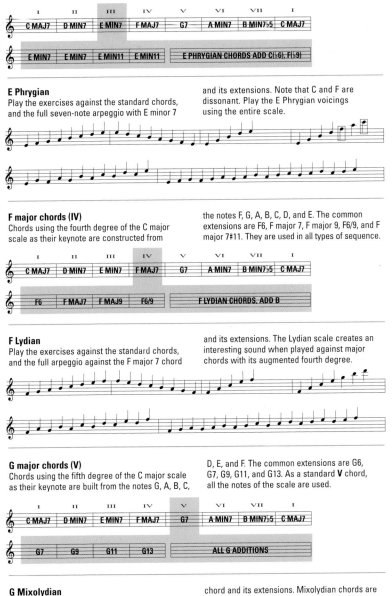

A minor chords (VI)

Chords that use the sixth degree of the C major scale as their keynote are built from the notes

A, B, C, D, E, and G. Common extensions are A minor 7, A minor 9, and A minor 11. Altered Aeolian chords can also include the note F.

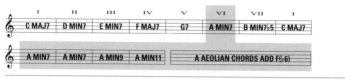

A Aeolian

Play the exercises against the standard chords, and the seven-note arpeggio against the

A minor7 chord and its natural extensions. Notice how the note F sounds dissonant when it is stressed against these chords.

B diminished chords (VII)

Chords taking the seventh degree of the C major scale as their keynote are formed using the notes B,

D, E, F, G, and A. Common extensions are B minor 7♭5, and B minor 11♭5 without a ninth. Altered Locrian voicings can also include the note C.

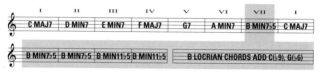

B Locrian

Play the exercise against the standard chords, and the seven-note arpeggio against the B chord

and its natural extensions. Notice how the note C sounds dissonant when it is stressed in the context of these chords.

PLAYING MODAL SCALES AND CHORDS

The sound of each mode over a chord is defined by the relationship of the principal note to structures and voicings. The fingerboard below shows seven

positions for chords, each one on a different modal degree of the scale, running in the key of C—from F on the 1st fret, to E on the 12th fret.

Chords on modal degrees

F Major 7 (1st fret) uses notes from the Lydian mode. G7 (3rd fret) uses notes from the Mixolydian mode. A minor (5th fret) uses the Aeolian mode. B minor 7 flat 5 (7th fret) uses

notes from the Locrian mode. C major 7 (8th fret), uses notes from the Ionian (major) mode. D minor 7 (10th fret), uses notes from the Dorian mode. E minor (10th fret) uses notes from the Phrygian mode. Chords can be revoiced for modes.

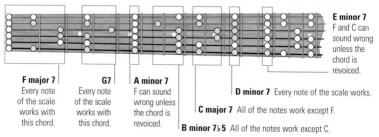

E minor 7 F and C can sound wrong unless the chord is revoiced.

F major 7 Every note of the scale works with this chord.

G7 Every note of the scale works with this chord.

A minor 7 F can sound wrong unless the chord is revoiced.

D minor 7 Every note of the scale works.

C major 7 All of the notes work except F.

B minor 7♭5 All of the notes work except C.

DOUBLE-OCTAVE MODAL POSITIONS

The modal scales can all be played over two octaves across the fingerboard, starting on the 6th string. These scales are marked with green dots on the chart below. The modal scales ascending from the 5th string are marked in blue. These extend by just over an octave in order for them to be played without changing position. When a mode is played from the 6th string, it can be fingered easily as a pattern without requiring a shift in overall position. Modes from the 5th string must be played with either a shift in position or stretch fingering if they are to be extended over two octaves. The positions starting from each string should be memorized and combined into one overall fingering pattern that covers the entire fingerboard. On the seven diagrams below, the notes in C which are not part of each fingering pattern are marked with white circles. Try to include these eventually. The position of each mode in relation to the major keynote and the other modes should be memorized.

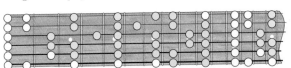

C Ionian (major)
C runs from both the 3rd fret of the 5th string and the 8th fret of the 6th string.

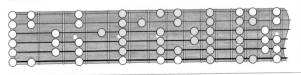

D Dorian
D runs from both the 5th fret of the 5th string and the 10th fret of the 6th string.

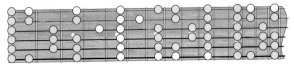

E Phrygian
E runs from both the open 6th string and the 12th fret, and the 7th fret of the 5th string.

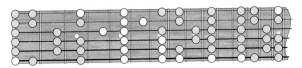

F Lydian
F runs from both the 1st fret of the 6th string and the 8th fret of the 5th string.

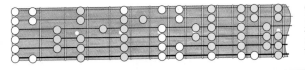

G Mixolydian
G runs from both the 3rd fret of the 6th string and the 10th fret of the 5th string.

A Aeolian
A runs from the open 5th string and the 12th fret, and from the 5th fret of the 6th string.

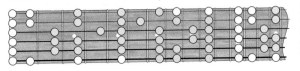

B Locrian
B runs from both the 2nd fret of the 5th string and the 7th fret of the 6th string.

Advanced techniques

Virtuoso electric guitar playing has resulted in innovations and changes in technique. Fast playing, and flowing phrases with extended intervals, both demand skillful coordination. A modern guitarist will be able to play demanding passages across the fingerboard, use stretch fingering over all the strings, and master fret tapping for higher elements.

FRET TAPPING

The right hand can play notes by tapping the string. At first, tap G on the 1st string using the second or third finger of the left hand, and then pull the finger off, sounding the open E string. Using the right hand to tap makes it possible to play phrases with any intervals. A three-note movement can be played by tapping the 7th fret with the second finger of the right hand, pulling the note off to sound fretted G, and then pulling off with the left hand to sound the open E.

Hammer on G on the 3rd fret, and pull off to sound the open E.

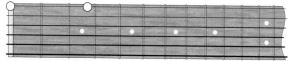

3RD FRET AND OPEN STRING

Tap B on the 7th fret, and pull off to sound G and then E.

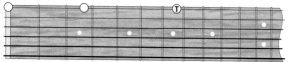

TAPPING THE 7TH FRET

Tap C# on the 9th fret, and pull off to A on the 5th fret. Pull off A to F#.

Tap E on the 12th fret, and pull off to A on the 5th fret. Pull off A to F#.

TAPPING ACROSS THE FINGERBOARD

Play an E minor pentatonic scale across the fretboard. Extend the two notes on each string to a three-note motif by playing a high note with the second finger of the right hand and keep repeating this. Tap across the strings and play repeating ascending and descending variations by pulling off to the open string with the left and right hands. Try cyclical phrases, starting with any note.

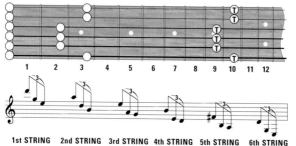

1st STRING   2nd STRING   3rd STRING   4th STRING   5th STRING   6th STRING

The right hand
Some players tap with the first finger while resting the thumb on the neck or the body to give stability. If the second finger is used, it is possible to hold the pick between the thumb and first finger and stabilize the tapping finger with the third and fourth fingers.

STRETCH FINGERING

Fast-flowing passages can be played by using three notes per string. Play a G major two octave scale starting on the 10th fret of the 5th string. Divide the 15-note scale into five groups with three notes on each string. The first note in each group is played with a plectrum downstroke and the two following notes are hammered. Practice the scale in this form, aiming to create a very even legato effect. Move the first finger quickly and accurately onto the fret positions for each of the strings.

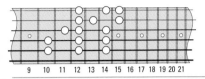

Double-octave position
Using three notes per string, which can either all be picked or played with legato hammer ons and pull offs, memorize this entire two-octave position and practice it as one block of notes.

Legato stretch fingering
Legato fingering removes the percussive effect of picking and creates a smooth, flowing sound. Start by using the fingering pattern of G major starting on the 10th fret and play each group of three notes using an initial pick downstroke. Try to ensure that all the notes ring evenly. This is achieved by hammering the strings firmly onto the frets without too much force. Play a descending pattern using pull-offs and start each group of notes with a picked downstroke. You can also use an upstroke to play the descending pattern.

Extending the positioning
It is possible to play very large stretches by playing four notes on one string. The pattern here starts from the 10th fret and is an extended D Mixolydian fingering block. Stretch gently to include the black notes to form new patterns.

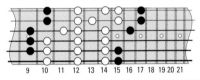

Dorian with stretch fingering
Here is another modal pattern using three notes per string. It is A Aeolian starting on the 12th fret. The diagonal jump from the 3rd string to the 2nd string and the 2nd string to the 1st string is difficult at first. Join this up with the above patterns.

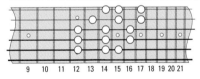

SUBDIVISION OF THE BAR

The diagram below shows a 4/4 bar as a mathematical chart with all the notes in accurate time relationships. The left-hand side represents the first beat of the bar: each crotchet on the top row sustains for a quarter of a bar. The fifth crotchet represents the beginning of the next bar. Compare the different note subdivisions.

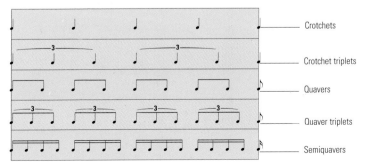

Crotchets

Crotchet triplets

Quavers

Quaver triplets

Semiquavers

Jazz progressions

Learning standard sequences is helpful for improvising within a structure. Standard blues and jazz sequences can be memorized for use as structures on which to base further development. They provide ideal frameworks for chord substitution and creative chord thinking. Progressions can be transposed by converting the main scale-tone chords on each tonal center to Roman numerals. Try to become familiar with these sequences.

JAZZ AND BLUES VARIATIONS

Play the 12-bar blues variations below in E. Compare each sequence with the basic jazz/blues structure in the first example. All the sequences are in 4/4 time. The first sequence is simple and straightforward. The lower sequences use **II-V** movements and substitutions. The last sequence has been transposed to C.

E7	A7	E7	E7	A7	A7	E7	C#7	F#m7	B7	E7	B7
E7	A7	E7	Bm7 E7	A7	A7	E7	C#7	F#m7	B7	E7 C#m7	F#m7 B7
E7	A7	E7	Bm7 Bb7	A7	A7	E7	G#m7 C#9	F#m7	F7	E7 C#7	F#7 B7
E7 Bb7	A7 Bb°7	E7/B	Bm7 Bb7	A7 Bb7	A7 F7	E7 Eb7	D7 C#7	F#m7	D7 Eb7	E7 G7	F#7 B7
E7	Ebm7 D7	Dbm7 C7	Bm7 Bb7	A7	Bb°7	E7/B C7	C#7	F#m7	B7	E7 G7	C7 F7

Em7	Em7	Em7	Em7	Am7	Am7	Em7	Em7	F#m7b5	B7	Em7	Em7
Em7	F#m7	Em7	Em6	Am7 Bm7	Am7 Am6	Em7	Em7	F#m7b5	F7	Em7	B7#9

E7	A7	E7	E7	A7	A7	E7	C#7	F#m7	B7	E7	B7
C7	F7	C7	C7	F7	F7	C7	A7	Dm7	G7	C7	G7

TURNAROUNDS

The term "turnaround" applies to chordal movements that move through a series of variations before returning to the beginning. These are normally based around the use of **II-V-I** movements at the end of a sequence. Develop a two-bar turnaround in stages. Play the chord sequence C major 7, A minor 7, D minor

7, G7, and C major 7 (*below left*). Convert all the chords to dominant sevenths or ninths. Now link each chord to the next using the series of bass notes (*below right*). This creates a bass line with a note on every beat, running C-Bb-A-Db-D-Ab-G-B. The last note, B, leads back to C at the beginning of the two-bar sequence.

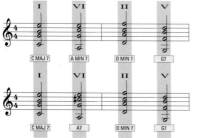

STANDARD JAZZ PROGRESSIONS

This uses **II-V-I** movements with "link chords." The first two bars are **II** and **V** chords, moving to **I** in the third bar and **IV** in the fourth. The fifth bar is a **II** chord of the relative minor; the sixth is the relative minor **V**; the seventh is the relative minor **I**; and the eighth acts as a dominant chord. Bars 17 to 24 are the minor and major chords in reverse. Bars 25 to 32 form a cycle leading to the end.

Dm7	G7	CM7	FM7	Bm7♭5	E7	Am7	A7
Dm7	G7	CM7	FM7	Bm7♭5	E7	Am7	Am7
Bm7♭5	E7	Am7	A7	Dm7	G7	CM7	FM7
Bm7♭5	E7	Am7 G♯7	Gm7 F♯7	FM7	Bm7♭5 E7	Am7	Am7

RHYTHM CHANGES

The sequence below follows a series of standard rhythm changes. The first four bars are a B♭ turnaround, followed by a **II-V-I** movement in E♭, with a link chord leading back to a turnaround. The middle eight section (bars 17 to 24) is a series of **II-V** movements in the cycle of keys running from G major, C major, F major, and B♭ major. The last section is similar to the first eight bars.

B♭7 G7	Cm7 F7	B♭7 G7	Cm7 F7	Fm7 B♭7	E♭E♭m	B♭7 G7	Cm7 F7
B♭B°7	Cm7 C°♯7	Dm7 G7	Cm7 F7	B♭B♭/D	E♭E°	B♭7 G7	Cm7 F7
Am7	D7	Dm7	G7	Gm7	C7	Cm7	F7
B♭G7	Cm F7	B♭G7	Cm7 F7	Fm7 B♭7	E♭E°	B♭	B♭

SIXTEEN BAR MINOR BLUES

A minor 7 (**I**) is played for the first four bars. This is raised by a fourth to D minor 7 for two bars. A **II-V** chord change takes the sequence back to four bars of **I**. Bars 13 to 14 move through related major chords and head to a **V** chord. The movement to the **V** chord at the end of bar 14 takes the sequence back to **I**.

Am7	Am7	Am7	Am7	Dm7	Dm7	Bm7♭5	E7
Am7	Am7	Am7	Am7	CM7 Am7	FM7 E7	Am7	Am7

BASS LINES

This is a bass line for the standard jazz sequence shown at the top of this page. After the root has been played at the beginning of the bar, the remaining notes are played as chord harmonies and link notes. Try inverting the notes.

D E F A	G A G B	C G C E	F E D C	B D F A	G♯E D B	A B C E	C♯B♭A E
D E F A	G A G B	C G C E	F E D C	B D F A	G♯E D B	A B C E	A E C A
F D B G♯	E F♯G G♯	A B C E	B♭G E C♯	D E F A	G F E D	C E A G	F E D C
B F D B	E D C B	A C G♯F♯	G B♭F♯E	F A C B♭	B F E G♯	A B C E	A

Soloing over chords

Each chord type has at least one related scale. One of the best ways to develop skill in playing over chords is to work constantly through chord sequences with a wide range of variations. But lines that fit over chords often use notes that do not occur in the chord structure or the added harmonic extensions.

FITTING MODES TO CHORDS

The chord types below should be transposed to every one of the 12 roots for improvising. Play the suggested scales.

The position of a chord within a sequence will often suggest a particular scale, while the ear may suggest another.

II and V chords

Play the D minor 7 on the second (II) degree, and G7 on the fifth (V) degree of C major. Use the D Dorian scale when playing D minor 7, and the G

Mixolydian when playing G7. Play in C major using the scale all over the fingerboard and experiment with every mode. Try to follow the outline of the chords as well using arpeggios with scales.

Dm7	Dm7	Dm7	Dm7	G7	G7	G7	G7
D DOR	D DOR	D DOR	D DOR	G MIX	G MIX	G MIX	G MIX

II chord

Play D minor 7 on the second (II) of C major, using D Dorian. When the sequence changes to A minor 7, play this as an A Dorian II chord in the key of

G major. Play four bars in C major and four bars in G major. Now play D Dorian and when the chord moves to A minor 7 play A Aeolian. For some people this may be a more pleasing effect.

Dm7	Dm7	Dm7	Dm7	Am7	Am7	Am7	Am7
D DOR	D DOR	D DOR	D DOR	A DOR	A DOR	A DOR	A DOR

V chord

Play the chord G7 on the fifth degree (V) of C major, using the G Mixolydian scale. C7 is the V chord of F major. Play the C Mixolydian mode.

Move from the key of C to the key of F major. Use each tonal centre fully. You may notice that stressing the note C against G7 and the note F against C7 can sound weak.

G7	G7	G7	G7	C7	C7	C7	C7
G MIX	G MIX	G MIX	G MIX	C MIX	C MIX	C MIX	C MIX

The II-V movement

Play A minor 7 and D7 to form the II-V movement of G major, using the A Dorian and D Mixolydian modes. Next, D minor 7 to G7 is in the key of C,

followed by G minor 7 to C7 which is in the key of F, and C minor 7 to F7 which is in the key of B♭ major. This sequence follows the cycle of fourths with the key centres G-C-F-B♭.

Am7	D7	Dm7	G7	Gm7	C7	Cm7	F7
A DOR	D MIX	D DOR	G MIX	G DOR	C MIX	C DOR	F MIX

C scale chords

Play the seventh chords on each degree of the key of C as a chord sequence. Improvise on each chord, using its related mode. If the chord

sequence is played quickly, clash tones, particularly on III and VI, can be used as passing notes. Try the III and VI chords using a Dorian scale, and the I chord using a Lydian scale.

CM7	Dm7	Em7	FM7	G7	Am7	Bm7♭5	CM7
C ION	D DOR	E PHR	F LYD	G MIX	A AEO	B LOC	C ION
C LYD	D DOR	E DOR	F LYD	G MIX	A DOR	B LOC	C LYD

Pentatonic scales

In rock music, many chords are played based on three-note triads with doubled notes, or as "5" chords with roots and fifths. These chords have a pentatonic minor sound when used for soloing, and they can be related to the Dorian mode. Play a "5" chord, then major, minor, minor seventh, and dominant seventh chords.

C5	C5	CM	CM	Cm	Cm	Cm7	C7
C PENT	C PENT	C PENT	C PENT	C PENT	C PENT	C PENT	C PENT
C DOR	C DOR	C DOR	C DOR	C DOR	C DOR	C DOR	C DOR

Minor scales

The sequence of chords below consists of a series of chords from the harmonic minor scale. On each one of these chords it is possible to use either harmonic minor or melodic minor scales or even major modes. Try the different scales and choose the one that sounds best. For example, on Am/M7 play F and G# or F# and G#.

Am/M7	Bm7♭5	CM7#5	Dm7	E7	FM7	G#7	Am/M7
A HAR	A HAR	A HAR	A HAR	A HAR	A HAR	A HAR	A HAR
A MEL	B LOC	A MEL	D DOR	A MEL	F LYD	G# DIM	A MEL

MAJOR AND MINOR II-V-I

The **II-V-I** movement may occur in a large range of variations. For example, a major **II-V** movement can be used to approach a major or minor **I** chord, and a minor **II-V** can be used to approach a minor or major **I** chord.

II-V-I in C

Play the major **II-V** movement in the key of C, using the Dorian and Mixolydian modes. Play the minor **II-V** movement in the key of C; use modes and minor scales. When a **II-V** resolves to the C Minor **I** chord, play Aeolian or Dorian.

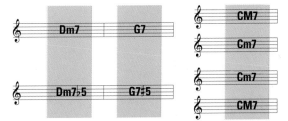

The II-♭V-I

The **II-♭V-I** movement occurs frequently in chord sequences. It may be approached in a number of different ways. On the ♭V play D melodic minor.

Also try playing G# melodic minor as a variation. This can run from the C# (D♭). When D♭ 13 is used as a full chord, try playing D♭ Mixolydian in G♭ major. Try to find notes that sound right.

Dm11	D♭7♭5	CM7	C6	D♭13	CM7	G7♭5	CM7
D DOR	D MEL	C ION	C ION	D♭ MIX	C ION	G# MEL	C ION
C MAJ	G# MEL	C LYD	C LYD	G♭ MAJ	C LYD	D MEL	C LYD

Modulations

Take one chord type, and play a sequence based on a series of modulations on different roots. For example, play the minor seventh with a different chord in each bar. Relate the chord to the mode from the first note and the primary tonal centre. Make up chord sequences with different types of chords including major and dominant sevenths.

Dm7	Fm7	Am7	Cm7	E♭m7	F#m7	Gm7	Em7
D DOR	F DOR	A DOR	C DOR	E♭ DOR	F# DOR	G DOR	E DOR
C MAJ	E♭ MAJ	G MAJ	B♭ MAJ	D♭ MAJ	E MAJ	F MAJ	D MAJ

Chord dictionary

It is essential to learn chords on the guitar. They are fundamental to all types of music. Chords form shapes on specific frets and the best way to learn them is to memorize their shape and overall position. Every chord type has a number of different shapes and positions and it is important to choose the right one for a song or a sequence.

ADVICE FOR PLAYERS

There are thousands of chords on the guitar and this chord dictionary represents a small but important part of them. Use the following pages as a dictionary. For example, if you want to find a chord such as E7#9, first go to the letter name E on page 195 and then go through all the chords until you come to E7#9—the second chord on page 196. Compare the same chord type as a shape under different letter name roots and you will see that they are simply the same chord on a higher or lower fret.

Over the next 24 pages 492 chords are split into 12 roots running from C and ascending in 12 semitones to B. One major chord shape on the middle strings has been shown with an alternative fingering for guitars with narrow necks or players with big fingers. Chords higher up the fingerboard shown under the bass note letter names A and E use the appropriate open lower bass string as their root note, so therefore there is no "X" in a circle on these strings. In some cases chords have also been shown with an open top E string.

Playing songs and sequences

Many songs just use majors, minors, sixths and sevenths. Very often the chords for a popular song look difficult simply because they are in an unusual key or because they start in a simple key such as C that modulates to a distant key. Jazz is more harmonically sophisticated and it requires rich chordal harmonies. It starts with seventh chords as the basic chord type.

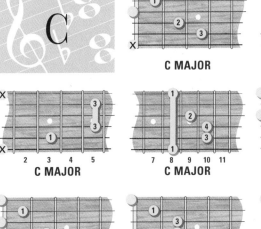

C MAJOR

C MAJOR

C MAJOR

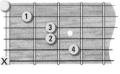

C MAJOR

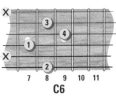

C/G

C/E

C6

C6

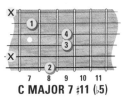

C MAJOR 7

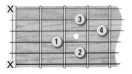

C MAJOR 7

C MAJOR 7

C MAJOR 7 ♯11 (♭5)

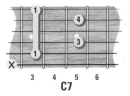

C MAJOR 9

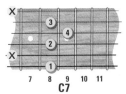

C6/9

C7

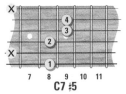

C7

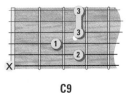

C7

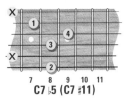

C7 ♭5 (C7 ♯11)

C7 ♯5

C9

C7 ♭9

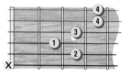

C7 ♯9

C7 ♯5 ♯9

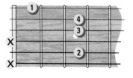

C11

C13

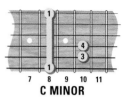

C SUS4

C AUG (C+)

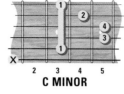

C MINOR

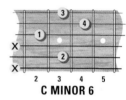

C MINOR

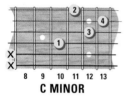

C MINOR

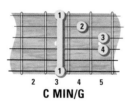

C MIN/G

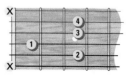

C MINOR 6

C MINOR 7

C MINOR 7

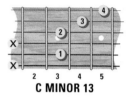

C MINOR 9

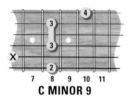

C MINOR 9

C MINOR 11

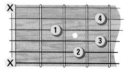

C MINOR 13

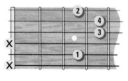

C MINOR/MAJOR 7

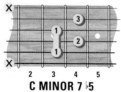

C MINOR 7 ♭5

C DIMINISHED 7 (C°7)

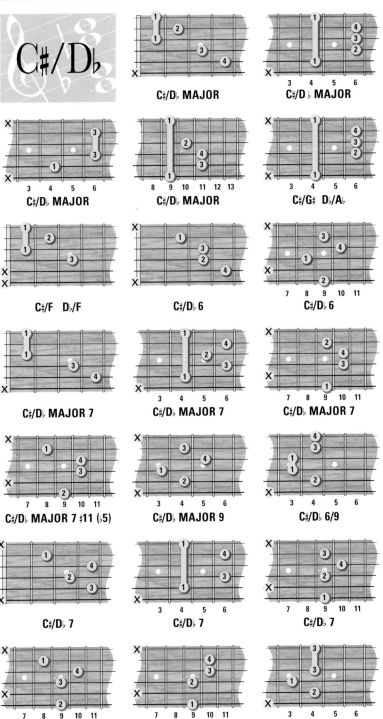

C♯/D♭

C♯/D♭ MAJOR

C♯/D♭ MAJOR

C♯/D♭ MAJOR

C♯/D♭ MAJOR

C♯/G♯ D♭/A♭

C♯/F D♭/F

C♯/D♭ 6

C♯/D♭ 6

C♯/D♭ MAJOR 7

C♯/D♭ MAJOR 7

C♯/D♭ MAJOR 7

C♯/D♭ MAJOR 7 ♯11 (♭5)

C♯/D♭ MAJOR 9

C♯/D♭ 6/9

C♯/D♭ 7

C♯/D♭ 7

C♯/D♭ 7

C♯/D♭ 7 ♭5 (♯11)

C♯/D♭ 7 ♯5

C♯/D♭ 9

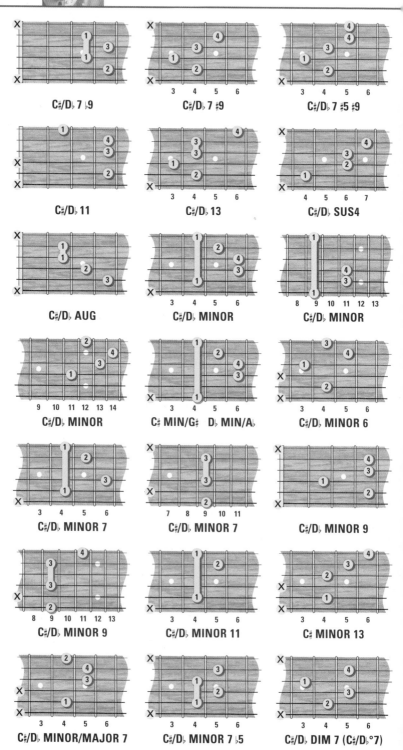

C#/Db 7 b9

C#/Db 7 #9

C#/Db 7 #5 #9

C#/Db 11

C#/Db 13

C#/Db SUS4

C#/Db AUG

C#/Db MINOR

C#/Db MINOR

C#/Db MINOR

C# MIN/G#   Db MIN/Ab

C#/Db MINOR 6

C#/Db MINOR 7

C#/Db MINOR 7

C#/Db MINOR 9

C#/Db MINOR 9

C#/Db MINOR 11

C# MINOR 13

C#/Db MINOR/MAJOR 7

C#/Db MINOR 7 b5

C#/Db DIM 7 (C#/Db°7)

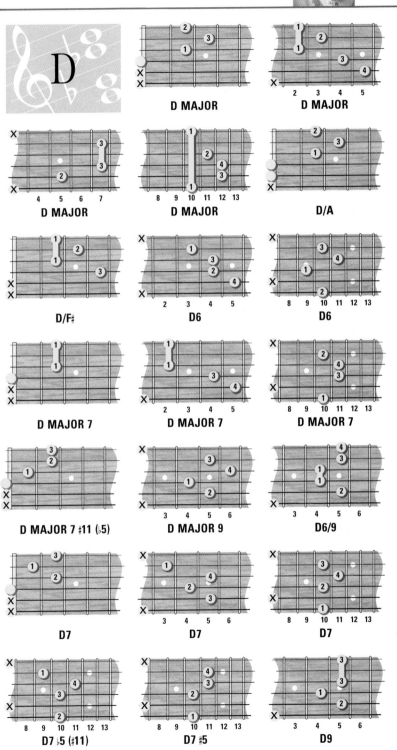

D

D MAJOR

D MAJOR

D MAJOR

D MAJOR

D/A

D/F♯

D6

D6

D MAJOR 7

D MAJOR 7

D MAJOR 7

D MAJOR 7 ♯11 (♭5)

D MAJOR 9

D6/9

D7

D7

D7

D7 ♭5 (♯11)

D7 ♯5

D9

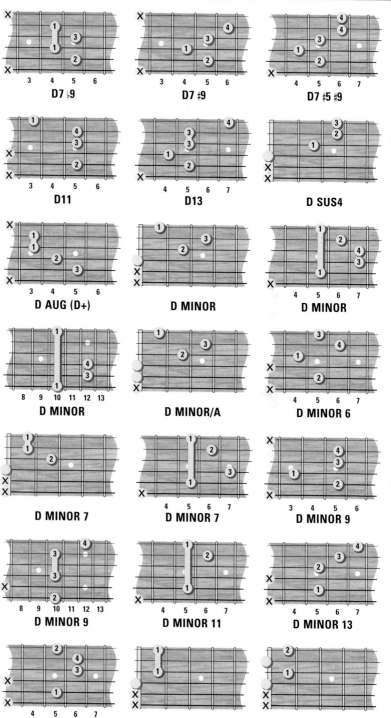

D7 ♭9

D7 ♯9

D7 ♯5 ♯9

D11

D13

D SUS4

D AUG (D+)

D MINOR

D MINOR

D MINOR

D MINOR/A

D MINOR 6

D MINOR 7

D MINOR 7

D MINOR 9

D MINOR 9

D MINOR 11

D MINOR 13

D MINOR/MAJOR 7

D MINOR 7 ♭5

D DIMINISHED 7 (D°7)

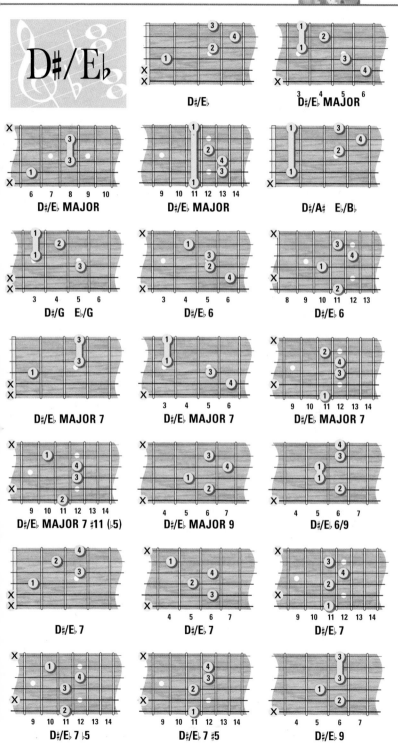

D#/Eb

D#/Eb

D#/Eb MAJOR

D#/Eb MAJOR

D#/Eb MAJOR

D#/A# Eb/Bb

D#/G Eb/G

D#/Eb 6

D#/Eb 6

D#/Eb MAJOR 7

D#/Eb MAJOR 7

D#/Eb MAJOR 7

D#/Eb MAJOR 7 #11 (b5)

D#/Eb MAJOR 9

D#/Eb 6/9

D#/Eb 7

D#/Eb 7

D#/Eb 7

D#/Eb 7 b5

D#/Eb 7 #5

D#/Eb 9

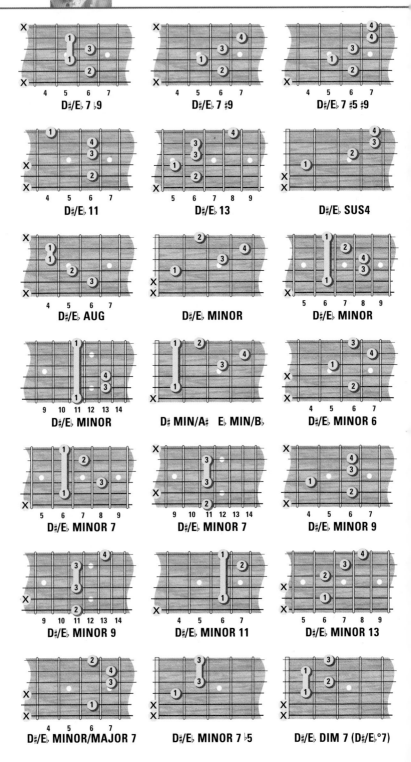

D#/E♭ 7 ♭9

D#/E♭ 7 #9

D#/E♭ 7 #5 #9

D#/E♭ 11

D#/E♭ 13

D#/E♭ SUS4

D#/E♭ AUG

D#/E♭ MINOR

D#/E♭ MINOR

D#/E♭ MINOR

D# MIN/A#   E♭ MIN/B♭

D#/E♭ MINOR 6

D#/E♭ MINOR 7

D#/E♭ MINOR 7

D#/E♭ MINOR 9

D#/E♭ MINOR 9

D#/E♭ MINOR 11

D#/E♭ MINOR 13

D#/E♭ MINOR/MAJOR 7

D#/E♭ MINOR 7 ♭5

D#/E♭ DIM 7 (D#/E♭°7)

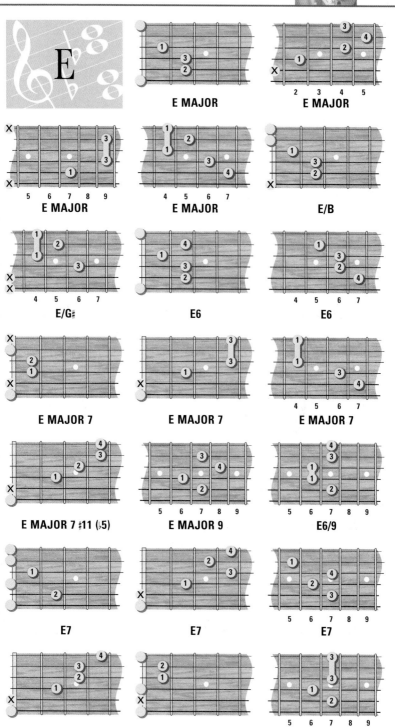

E

E MAJOR

E MAJOR

E MAJOR

E MAJOR

E/B

E/G♯

E6

E6

E MAJOR 7

E MAJOR 7

E MAJOR 7

E MAJOR 7 ♯11 (♭5)

E MAJOR 9

E6/9

E7

E7

E7

E7 ♭5 (♯11)

E7 ♯5

E9

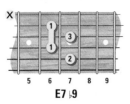

E7 ♭9

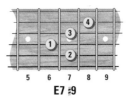

E7 ♯9

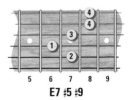

E7 ♯5 ♯9

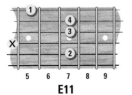

E11

E13

E SUS4

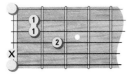

E AUG

E MINOR

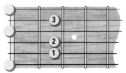

E MINOR

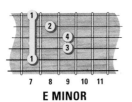

E MINOR

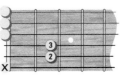

E MINOR/B

E MINOR 6

E MINOR 7

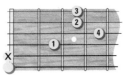

E MINOR 7

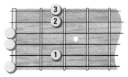

E MINOR 9

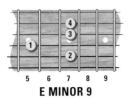

E MINOR 9

E MINOR 11

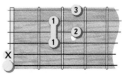

E MINOR 13

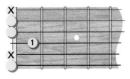

E MINOR/MAJOR 7

E MINOR 7 ♭5

E DIMINISHED 7 (E°7)

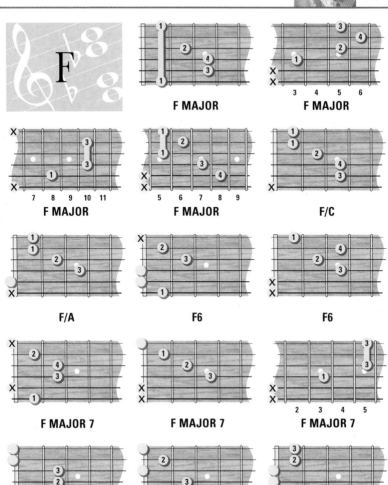

F

F MAJOR

F MAJOR

F MAJOR

F MAJOR

F/C

F/A

F6

F6

F MAJOR 7

F MAJOR 7

F MAJOR 7

F MAJOR 7 #11 (♭5)

F MAJOR 9

F6/9

F7

F7

F7

F7 ♭5 (#11)

F7 #5

F9

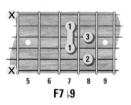

F7 ♭9

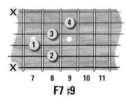

F7 ♯9

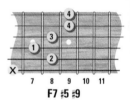

F7 ♯5 ♯9

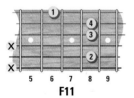

F11

F13

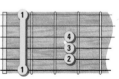

F SUS4

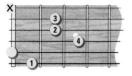

F AUG

F MINOR

F MINOR

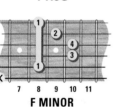

F MINOR

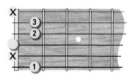

F MINOR/C

F MINOR 6

F MINOR 7

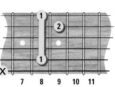

F MINOR 7

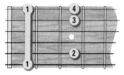

F MINOR 9

F MINOR 9

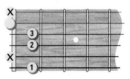

F MINOR 11

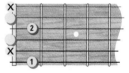

F MINOR 13

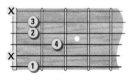

F MINOR/MAJOR 7

F MINOR 7 ♭5

F DIMINISHED 7 (F°7)

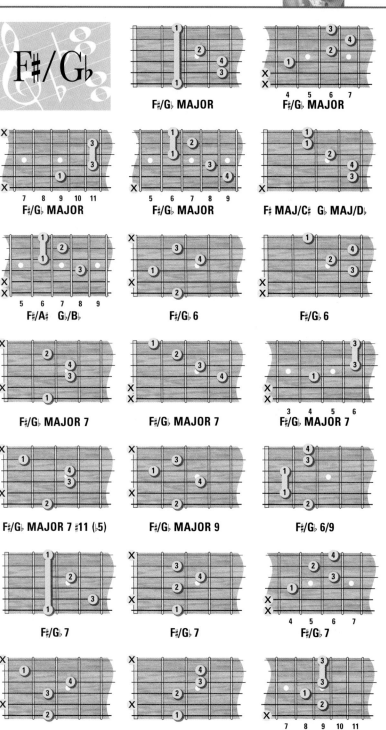

F#/G♭

F#/G♭ MAJOR

F#/G♭ MAJOR
4 5 6 7

F#/G♭ MAJOR
7 8 9 10 11

F#/G♭ MAJOR
5 6 7 8 9

F# MAJ/C# G♭ MAJ/D♭

F#/A# G♭/B♭
5 6 7 8 9

F#/G♭ 6

F#/G♭ 6

F#/G♭ MAJOR 7

F#/G♭ MAJOR 7

F#/G♭ MAJOR 7
3 4 5 6

F#/G♭ MAJOR 7 #11 (♭5)

F#/G♭ MAJOR 9

F#/G♭ 6/9

F#/G♭ 7

F#/G♭ 7

F#/G♭ 7
4 5 6 7

F#/G♭ 7 ♭5

F#/G♭ 7 #5

F#/G♭ 9
7 8 9 10 11

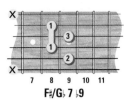

F#/G♭ 7 ♭9

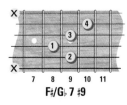

F#/G♭ 7 #9

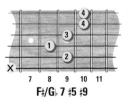

F#/G♭ 7 #5 #9

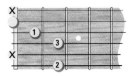

F#/G♭ 11

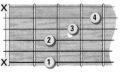

F#/G♭ 13

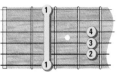

F#/G♭ SUS4

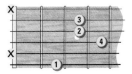

F#/G♭ AUG

F#/G♭ MINOR

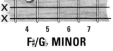

F#/G♭ MINOR

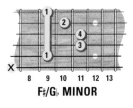

F#/G♭ MINOR

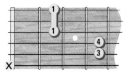

F# MIN/C#   G♭ MIN/D♭

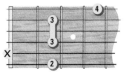

F#/G♭ MINOR 6

F#/G♭ MINOR 7

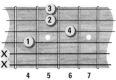

F#/G♭ MINOR 7

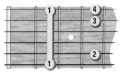

F#/G♭ MINOR 9

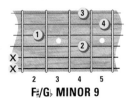

F#/G♭ MINOR 9

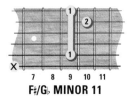

F#/G♭ MINOR 11

F#/G♭ MINOR 13

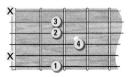

F#/G♭ MINOR/MAJOR 7

F#/G♭ MINOR 7 ♭5

F#/G♭ DIM 7 (F#/G♭°7)

G

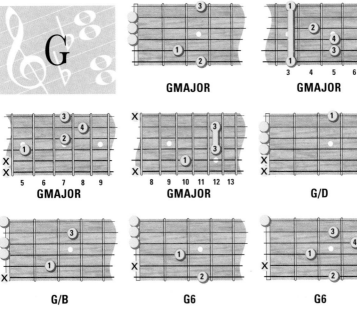

GMAJOR   **GMAJOR**

GMAJOR   **GMAJOR**   **G/D**

G/B   **G6**   **G6**

G MAJOR 7   **G MAJOR 7**   **G MAJOR 7**

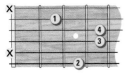

G MAJOR 7 #11 (♭5)   **G MAJOR 9**   **G6/9**

G7   **G7**   **G7**

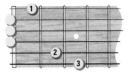

G7 ♭5 (#11)   **G7 #5**   **G9**

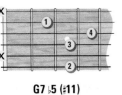

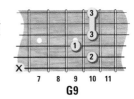

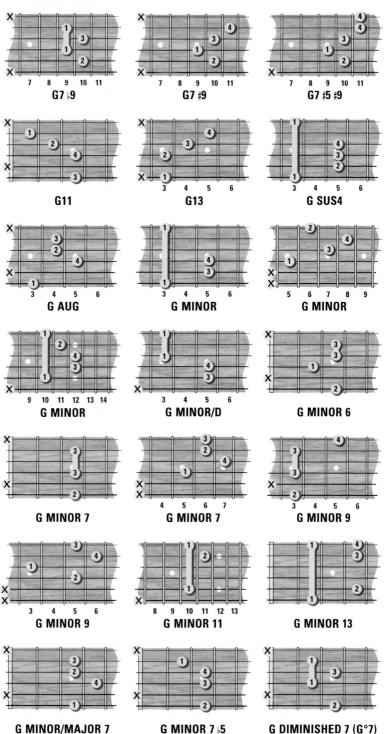

G7 ♭9

G7 ♯9

G7 ♯5 ♯9

G11

G13

G SUS4

G AUG

G MINOR

G MINOR

G MINOR

G MINOR/D

G MINOR 6

G MINOR 7

G MINOR 7

G MINOR 9

G MINOR 9

G MINOR 11

G MINOR 13

G MINOR/MAJOR 7

G MINOR 7 ♭5

G DIMINISHED 7 (G°7)

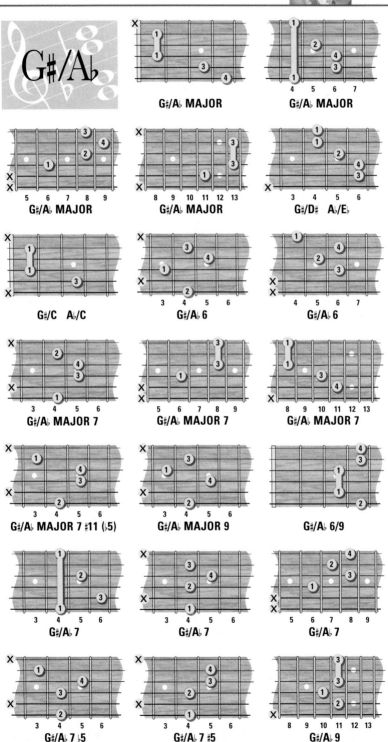

G♯/A♭

G♯/A♭ MAJOR

G♯/A♭ MAJOR

G♯/A♭ MAJOR

G♯/A♭ MAJOR

G♯/D♯   A♭/E♭

G♯/C   A♭/C

G♯/A♭ 6

G♯/A♭ 6

G♯/A♭ MAJOR 7

G♯/A♭ MAJOR 7

G♯/A♭ MAJOR 7

G♯/A♭ MAJOR 7 #11 (♭5)

G♯/A♭ MAJOR 9

G♯/A♭ 6/9

G♯/A♭ 7

G♯/A♭ 7

G♯/A♭ 7

G♯/A♭ 7 ♭5

G♯/A♭ 7 #5

G♯/A♭ 9

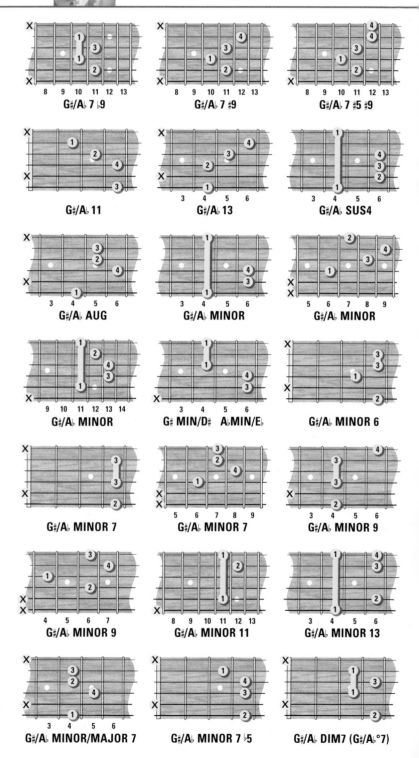

G#/A♭ 7 ♭9

G#/A♭ 7 #9

G#/A♭ 7 #5 #9

G#/A♭ 11

G#/A♭ 13

G#/A♭ SUS4

G#/A♭ AUG

G#/A♭ MINOR

G#/A♭ MINOR

G#/A♭ MINOR

G# MIN/D#   A♭MIN/E♭

G#/A♭ MINOR 6

G#/A♭ MINOR 7

G#/A♭ MINOR 7

G#/A♭ MINOR 9

G#/A♭ MINOR 9

G#/A♭ MINOR 11

G#/A♭ MINOR 13

G#/A♭ MINOR/MAJOR 7

G#/A♭ MINOR 7 ♭5

G#/A♭ DIM7 (G#/A♭°7)

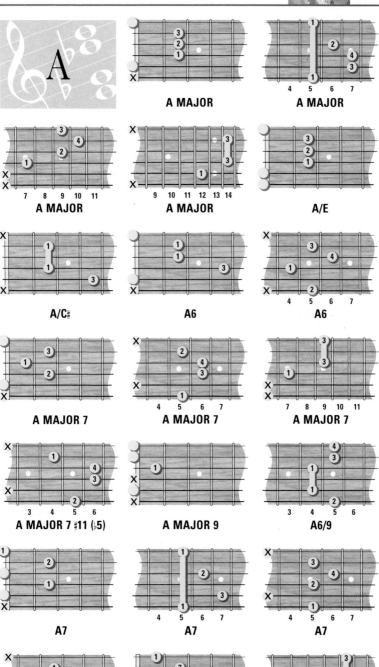

A

A MAJOR

A MAJOR

A MAJOR

A MAJOR

A/E

A/C♯

A6

A6

A MAJOR 7

A MAJOR 7

A MAJOR 7

A MAJOR 7 ♯11 (♭5)

A MAJOR 9

A6/9

A7

A7

A7

A7 ♭5 (♯11)

A7 ♯5

A9

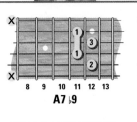

A7 ♭9

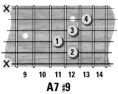

A7 ♯9

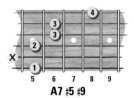

A7 ♯5 ♯9

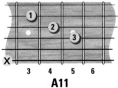

A11

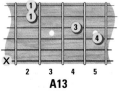

A13

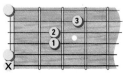

A SUS4

A AUG

A MINOR

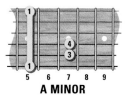

A MINOR

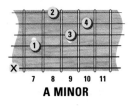

A MINOR

A MINOR/E

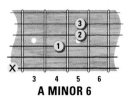

A MINOR 6

A MINOR 7

A MINOR 7

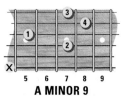

A MINOR 9

A MINOR 9

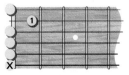

A MINOR 11

A MINOR 13

A MINOR/MAJOR 7

A MINOR 7 ♭5

A DIMINISHED 7 (A°7)

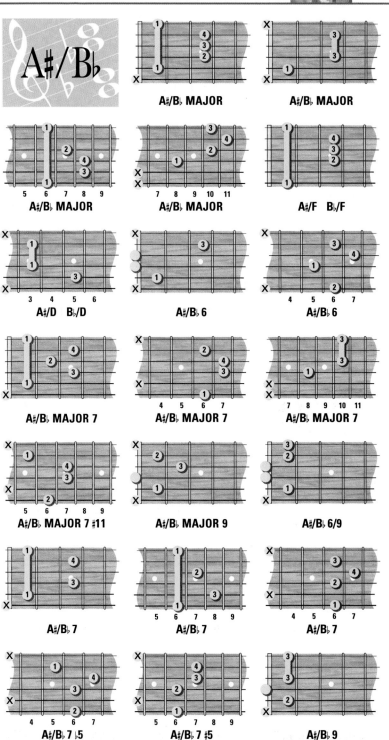

A#/B♭

A#/B♭ MAJOR

A#/B♭ MAJOR

A#/B♭ MAJOR

A#/B♭ MAJOR

A#/F   B♭/F

A#/D   B♭/D

A#/B♭ 6

A#/B♭ 6

A#/B♭ MAJOR 7

A#/B♭ MAJOR 7

A#/B♭ MAJOR 7

A#/B♭ MAJOR 7 #11

A#/B♭ MAJOR 9

A#/B♭ 6/9

A#/B♭ 7

A#/B♭ 7

A#/B♭ 7

A#/B♭ 7 ♭5

A#/B♭ 7 #5

A#/B♭ 9

A#/B♭ 7 ♭9

A#/B♭ 7 #9

A#/B♭ 7 #5 #9

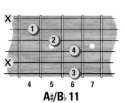

A#/B♭ 11

A#/B♭ 13

A#/B♭ SUS4

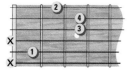

A#/B♭ AUG

A#/B♭ MINOR

A#/B♭ MINOR

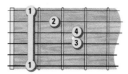

A#/B♭ MINOR

A# MINOR/F   B♭ MINOR/F

A#/B♭ MINOR 6

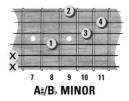

A#/B♭ MINOR 7

A#/B♭ MINOR 7

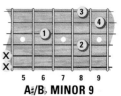

A#/B♭ MINOR 9

A#/B♭ MINOR 9

A#/B♭ MINOR 11

A#/B♭ MINOR 13

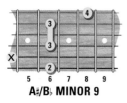

A#/B♭ MINOR/MAJOR 7

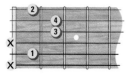

A#/B♭ MINOR 7 ♭5

A#/B♭ DIM 7 (A#/B♭°7)

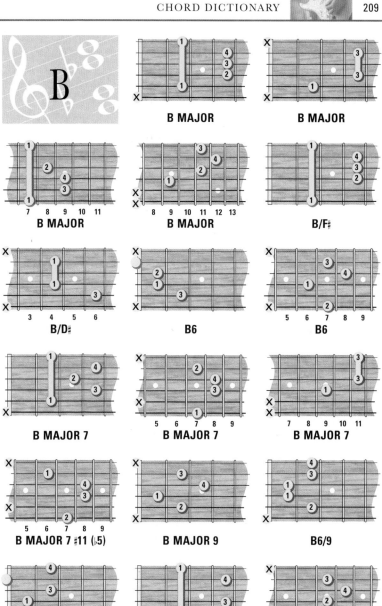

B MAJOR

B MAJOR

B MAJOR

B MAJOR

B/F♯

B/D♯

B6

B6

B MAJOR 7

B MAJOR 7

B MAJOR 7

B MAJOR 7 ♯11 (♭5)

B MAJOR 9

B6/9

B7

B7

B7

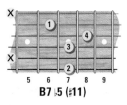

B7 ♭5 (♯11)

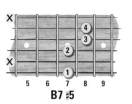

B7 ♯5

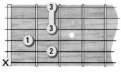

B9

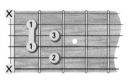

B7♭9

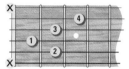

B7♯9

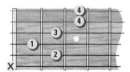

B7♯5♯9

B11

B13

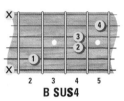

B SUS4

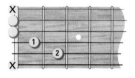

B AUG

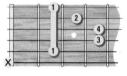

B MINOR

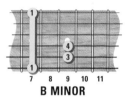

B MINOR

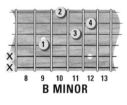

B MINOR

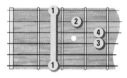

B MINOR/F♯

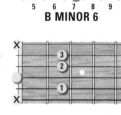

B MINOR 6

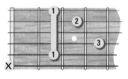

B MINOR 7

B MINOR 7

B MINOR 9

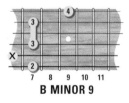

B MINOR 9

B MINOR 11

B MINOR 13

B MINOR/MAJOR 7

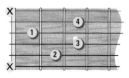

B MINOR 7♭5

B DIMINISHED 7 (B°7)

Care and Maintenance

In terms of its sound, playability, and appearance, a properly setup, well-maintained guitar can be an inspiration to the player. To keep a guitar in good order it is advisable to consult a reputable repairer to undertake any work that you do not feel is within your capabilities.

String care

Strings must be in good condition and correctly fitted. Problems, such as tuning difficulties, buzzes, and loss of volume, can be attributed to playing with strings that are old.

Strings should be renewed regularly. Sweat and dirt will rapidly shorten string life. Cleaning strings with a dry, lint-free cloth will help prolong the life of the frets and fingerboard.

RESTRINGING

You will need a wire-cutter, a string winder, and a tuner. You can remove one string at a time or all of them at once. New strings always take a little time to settle; gently pull the tuned string away from the fingerboard to help tuning stability. On the following pages are tips to help players string their guitars.

String winder
The slot is placed over the end of the tuner (machinehead). This allows the string to be wound on evenly with greater speed.

RESTRINGING SOLID-BODY GUITARS

The method of attaching the ball-end of the string varies. One way of attaching the string to the tuner capstan is shown below – the strings can simply be threaded through and wound downward on the capstan. One type of capstan has a hole in the top (*right*). Locking tuners enable the strings to be locked to the capstan. The string is drawn through the capstan, leaving virtually no slack. It is then locked and can be tuned to pitch with less than one full turn of the capstan. You should always remember to de-tune the strings fully before unlocking this type of mechanism.

String ends
The winding around the capstan traps the end of the string in place.

Vertical capstan hole
Cut the string in length and insert into the hole. Bend to one side and wind on. With this method the string ends are kept neatly out of the way.

RESTRINGING SOLID-BODY GUITARS WITH TREMELO

With guitars with tremolo systems, if all the strings are removed they should be detuned gradually in turn. Remember that altering the tuning of one string will affect the others. Locking tremolo systems are different: they often require the strings to be clamped at the nut and the bridge, so the ball-end of the string must be cut off before the string is clamped to the bridge saddle. Place the string in the bridge and tighten the clamp securely. Before clamping the nut, set the fine-tuners on the tremolo to a midway position, stretch-in the strings, and tune to pitch.

Supporting with shims
When tuning, use shims such as a pile of cards to bring the tremolo system to the correct position. Once tuned, the shims fall away.

String types

There are two types of strings: nylon and steel. Steel strings have different string-wraps. Roundwound strings are used on acoustic and electric guitars. Flatwound strings are designed to eliminate finger noise. Attention should be given to the gauge and tension of strings. Consider volume (heavier gauges produce more volume), tone, and ease of playing.

Nylon strings
These are used only on classical and flamenco guitars. The three treble strings are made from monofilament nylon. The lower strings are made from a multifilament nylon core and are invariably roundwound, with different types of metal wrap. Nylons strings are available in low, medium, high, and extrahigh tensions.

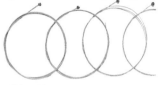

Nylon strings

Steel strings
These are used for acoustic and electric guitars are all made with steel cores. For electric guitars the wrap is made from a nickel/iron alloy, nickel-plated steel, stainless or other metal, or alloy. The various materials used for the wrap will give different tonal responses and slightly different levels of output when amplified. On steel strings for acoustic guitars, the wrap is usually made from bronze, brass, or similar alloys. "Phosphor bronze" strings produce a rich tone with strong bass response. "Bronze" or brass strings are brighter and more "bell-like" in tone. Sometimes these strings are labeled with the "copper/zinc or tin" alloy ratio. Roundwound strings are used for both acoustic and electric guitars. They are characterized by their tonal response, sustain, and brightness. Flatwound strings are designed to eliminate finger noise and have a perfectly smooth feel, but are duller in sound, with a pronounced mid-range response and less sustain.

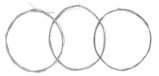

Bronze wound strings

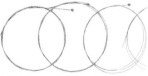

Nickel wound electric guitar strings

STRING INSTALLATION TIPS

- Never put metal strings on a guitar designed for nylon strings.
- Wind the string turns on the capstan downward toward the headstock.
- Where the string needs to be cut to length before fitting, make a 90-degree bend and cut the excess string off about ½in (1.2cm) from the bend. This prevents string wrap slippage.
- Changing string gauges may necessitate adjustments to the guitar.
- A string that breaks can be dangerous. When bringing strings to pitch, keep your eyes shielded.

FITTING NYLON STRINGS

It is useful to make a small knot at the very end of the treble strings when fitting nylon strings, after the tie at the bridge. This stops the string slipping through the bridge if the string-tie fails: the "whipping" effect of a tensioned string slipping can cause damage. Some wound strings have an inch or two of loose winding at one end: this section should not be used at any of the string-ties. The plain treble strings improve with age, becoming brighter and louder as the nylon hardens under tension. They can last a long time before being needing to be replaced. Wound strings deteriorate and lose tone more rapidly; for this reason players change bass strings more frequently.

Stringing the capstan
Turn the machine head until the capstan hole is at 90 degrees to the headstock face and thread the string down through the capstan hole. Bring the string-end around the back of the capstan and thread the string beneath itself, forming a knot. This prevents string slippage at the headstock.

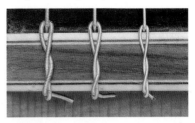

String-ties at the bridge
Pass approximately 2⅘in (7cm) of the string through the front of the tie-block. Pull the end of the string back over, passing it under the string's original point of entry. Wrap the end around itself to hold the string. This should be done twice for wound strings and four times for treble strings.

FLATTOP ACOUSTICS

There are two types of bridge pins on a flattop guitar. One has a recess running down one side to accommodate the string. The second has no recess: instead there is a slot cut at the leading side of the pin hole in the bridge where the string sits. Always fully detune a string before removing the bridge pin. Bend the ball end of the new string slightly to one side to fit (*right*). Refit the bridge pin and ensure that it remains properly seated when tuning to pitch. Here the ball-ends are retained at the back edge of the bridge.

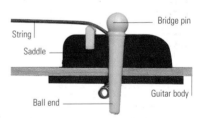

Bridge pin cross-section
This cross-section shows the type of bridge used on a flattop acoustic guitar. Note that the purpose of the bridge pin is to hold the ball end in position under the bridge plate, not to take the string tension. Pins should fit snugly in their holes.

FLAMENCO GUITARS

Today, many older flamenco guitars and a few traditional instruments are fitted with friction pegs rather than geared tuners (machineheads). If the pegs do not fit tightly enough, accurate tuning becomes difficult. Peg paste used by violinists can be applied to improve grip. Stringing at the headstock is the same as for a nylon-string guitar (*above*). Fortunately, slotted headstocks with tuners are commonly used today.

ARCHTOP GUITARS

Traditionally, a tailpiece retains the strings on archtop guitars. The bridge is not usually attached to the top but instead is held in position by the string tension. As the position and seating of the bridge is critical, it is essential that it is relocated correctly when restringing. Changing the strings individually is advisable as this avoids bridge movement. When tuning to pitch, check that there is no forward tilting on the bridge.

Cleaning

It is important that a guitar is kept clean. Any agents used should be compatible with the type of body finish. Prevent dirt build-up by wiping after use. This is the best way to keep a guitar in good condition. For all wiping and polishing, use a clean, 100 percent cotton cloth.

THE BODY

Cleaning may be carried out with a cloth moistened with warm water. The finish should then be buffed with a dry cloth. Cellulose and synthetic finishes can be cleaned with special guitar polish. Do not use cleaning agents that contain silicone. Wax polish may also have an adverse effect. French polish finishes, commonly found on high-quality classical guitars, are delicate and should be cleaned by wiping lightly with a barely damp cloth or chamois, followed by buffing with a dry cloth. Never use any type of abrasive cleaner.

Cleaning fluids
A wide variety of specialized cleaning and polishing fluids are available for the body and strings. Use a separate cleaning and buffing cloth.

Body cleaner   **String cleaner**   **Cleaning cloth**   **Buffing cloth**

Routine cleaning
Clean the dirt from under the strings regularly.

CLEANING STRINGS

Strings must be clean in order to produce a good tone and accurate tuning. Dirt and sweat can cause corrosion. Clean the strings after use with a dry, lint-free cloth. This can be wrapped under the strings (left) and drawn along their entire length a few times. Some players prefer to clean each string individually. String lubricants can prevent corrosion and will keep the strings in good condition. If used, be sure to remove any surplus. Do not use string lubricants with nylon strings.

THE FINGERBOARD

On ebony or rosewood fingerboards, a little lemon oil can be applied to help loosen grease and dirt. This also "feeds" the wood, preventing it from becoming too dry. The oil should be left on for a few minutes, then cleaned off with a dry cloth. Then vigorously polish the whole of the fingerboard with a clean, dry cloth. Lacquered maple fingerboards can be cleaned in a similar way. Steel wool should be used with great caution. On electric guitars, cover the pickups to protect them from steel particles.

Use a clean dry cloth

Setting up

The term setting up describes adjustments made to achieve the best possible sound and playing action. There is no definitive setup; ultimately the goal should be to accommodate the individual player's style and technique within the adjustment limitations of the instrument. Setting-up should be carried out by a specialist, although many players may wish to make simple adjustments themselves.

ACTION

The term action refers to the playability of the guitar. Many factors contribute to the action, but essentially it is determined by the height of the strings above the frets. This is usually measured between the top of the 12th fret and the bottom of the string: for electric guitars the average figure ranges from $\frac{1}{20}$ to $\frac{1}{16}$in (0.13 to 0.2cm), and for acoustics, $\frac{1}{16}$ to $\frac{1}{10}$in 0.2 to 0.28cm().

On electric guitars, the bridge saddles and/or bridge are adjustable, and can simply be raised or lowered to alter the action. On flattop acoustic guitars the saddle is usually preformed from bone or synthetic material, and the action can be lowered by accurately filing the bottom of the saddle.

Adjusting the action
Action is changed by altering the height of the saddles on the bridge. Turning the saddle screws clockwise usually raises the height of the saddle, and so increases the space between the string and the fret.

Use a small screwdriver

NUT

The nut governs the height of the open strings above the 1st fret. Measurements are taken from the top of the 1st fret to the bottom of the string: for electric guitars these range on average from $\frac{1}{100}$ to $\frac{1}{50}$in (0.025 to 0.05cm), and for acoustics, $\frac{1}{64}$ to $\frac{1}{32}$in (0.035 to 0.065cm). Adjustments are made by either refiling the nut slots or replacing the nut. It is essential that the string slots in the nut are filed at a precise angle, to provide the string with a clean "takeoff" point, and that each slot is proportional to the string diameter. The material used for the nut affects the sound quality of the open strings. Bone or hard synthetic materials are commonly used. Teflon or graphite-based materials are recommended when using a nonlocking tremolo system.

CAMBER

The setting of the individual string heights at the bridge and nut must conform with the camber, or the radius of the fingerboard. This is checked by measuring the height of each string at the 12th fret and the 1st fret. You will notice that the action is set highest on the bass side. This is because the heavier strings need greater clearance to vibrate freely. The camber of the bridge and nut should be set so that the action of each string gradually increases from the 1st to the 6th strings. On electric guitars with individually adjustable saddles this can easily be set. On flattop acoustic guitars the saddle crown can be carefully reworked or, if necessary, a new saddle can be made for the guitar. Classical and Flamenco guitars normally have no bridge and fingerboard camber.

INTONATION

For the intonation to be accurate, the vibrating length of the string must be set proportionally to scale length, action, and string gauge. Without correct intonation, accurate tuning over the entire fingerboard cannot be achieved. It is important to install new strings before adjusting the intonation, as well as checking that nut height, relief, and action are correctly adjusted and that the frets are in a reasonable condition. On most electric guitars, adjustable saddles allow each string to be intonated individually. Tune to pitch and compare the note produced by the open string with that produced at the 12th fret. If the 12th-fret note is flat, the string length must be shortened by moving the saddle closer to the nut. If the 12th-fret note is sharp, the

opposite adjustment must be made. The adjustments are continued until the two notes are in tune. An electronic tuner is essential and for comparison harmonics on the 12th fret can be used.

Fender saddles
When tuning the saddles on a Fender or similar type of guitar, their position in relation to overall string length can be adjusted using a screwdriver.

FRET CONDITION

Frets should ideally be of uniform height and properly fitted; however, as frets constantly become worn, maintenance will be necessary. Frets can be reprofiled several times, but will eventually need replacing by a specialist. Fret height can be checked by holding a string down on

two adjacent frets and using a feeler gauge to measure the gap between the fingerboard and the bottom of the string. Measurements should be taken where fret wear is most apparent on the fingerboard. Refretting may be needed if this reading is less than 0.6mm.

TRUSS ROD

The truss rod reinforces the neck against string tension. Most rods are adjusted by means of a hex, or slotted nut, situated at the heel or headstock end of the neck. Slackening it by turning the nut counterclockwise increases relief; tightening it decreases relief. The many different types of truss rod, together with

the quality and types of timber used for the neck and fingerboard, will produce varying results from adjustment. Even the necks of two apparently identical instruments may behave in different ways when similar adjustments are made. With this in mind, you may wish to attempt some adjustments to improve the action or test different string gauges. If so, first check the relief. If there is no relief, the neck may be convex and the rod should be slackened until relief is obtained. Adjustments should be made in increments of a half-turn of the hex/slotted nut, and the relief rechecked. Adjustments greater than a full turn in either direction are not recommended. Finally, remember that the action at the nut and bridge will be affected by truss-rod adjustment. It is better if a specialist adjusts the truss rod.

Headstock end
Truss rods with adjustment at the headstock end are often made with allen wrenches. Turn it gradually with great care and attention.

GUITAR DIRECTORY

There is a wide range of resources available for guitarists in the US and Canada. This directory aims to give you a starting point for obtaining information on both local and national levels. Wherever possible, additional information about particular entries has been given.

WEBLINKS

GENERAL SITES

A1 Guitar

members.aol.com/mikeyjake/guitar/guitar.html

This site has suggestions and information on how to write songs, form a band, get gigs, and even start your own label.

Better Guitar

www.betterguitar.com

Features news and reviews of equipment and helpful instructions.

Electric-Guitars.Net

www.electric-guitars.net

Information on how to choose and care for an electric guitar, with helpful pictures and diagrams.

Guitar Notes

www.guitarnotes.com

Links to anything and everything about guitars.

Guitar Stuff

www.guitarstuff.com

An online guitar magazine featuring reviews, classifieds, and lessons.

Guitar.com

www.guitar.com

An extensive site for guitar enthusiasts from around the globe, featuring discussions, interviews, special deals, and more.

Guitar-Guitar.com

www.guitar-guitar.com

An internet guitar guide featuring forums, chats, private messaging, and a newsletter. Registration is free.

Guitarists.net

www.guitarists.net

An online community of guitarists from all backgrounds exchanging ideas, experiences, and more.

GuitarSite.com

www.guitarsite.com

A constantly updated database of online guitar resources. Also features weekly online magazine.

Harmony Central

www.harmony-central.com

Includes instruction, discussion groups, tablatures, and product review databases.

The Musical Instrument Exchange

www.mixchange.net

An online marketplace for people looking to buy or sell guitars and other instruments.

WholeNote

www.wholenote.com

A popular online guitar community, offering something for everyone, from the beginner to the seasoned professional. Features online lesson-authoring tools so guitarists can pass their knowledge on to others.

GUITAR TYPES

Acoustic-Guitars.net

www.Acoustic-Guitars.Net

Offers advice on choosing an acoustic guitar, plus lessons and care instructions.

The Bluegrass Guitar Home Page

www.bluegrassguitar.com

A convenient source of information about the acoustic flat-top guitar and its use in bluegrass music.

BunnyBass

www.bunnybass.com

An obsessive virtual showcase of exotic and unusual basses and guitars.

The Dobro Pages

ourworld.compuserve.com/homepages/GMaass

A resource for players of lap-style wood-bodied resophonic guitars.

GuitarNuts

www.guitarnuts.com/index.php

A popular electric guitar page with an emphasis on shielding and wiring.

Lunatics Lounge

users.adelphia.net/~cygnusx_1

Includes detailed technical information about modifying and adjusting your electric and acoustic guitars.

The Museum of Musical Instruments

www.themomi.org
contact@themomi.org

A virtual online museum featuring exhibits of 19th- and 20th-century guitars and other instruments.

The Scalloped Fretboard Guitar

www.ancient-future.com/guitar/scallop.html

An introduction to an unusual instrument that combines qualities of the South Indian vina and the steel string guitar.

Vintage Guitars Info

www.provide.net/~cfh

Pictures and text focusing on the history of vintage guitars, along with information for collectors.

Vintage Rocker

www.vintagerocker.com

A resource for collectors and owners of vintage guitars. Includes classified ads.

EQUIPMENT

GuitarGeek

www.guitargeek.com

An online database of the electric guitar rigs used by famous guitarists, using diagrams to show what gear is used and how it is all connected.

Music Gear Review

www.musicgearreview.com/guitar

Provides consumer reviews of electric and acoustic guitars as well as equipment and accessories.

Sterner Capo Museum

w1.865.telia.com/~u86505074/capomuseum

An online museum dedicated to the capo (a movable bar attached to the fretboard of a guitar).

The Tremolo Page

www.electricguitar.50megs.com/tremolo.htm

Offers a history of the vibrato bar (also known as the tremolo unit or whammy bar), along with reviews of various models.

STYLES OF PLAYING

Celtic Fingerstyle Guitar

www.win.net/~mainstring/celtic.html

A helpful introduction to the playing of Celtic, Irish, and Scottish music on solo guitar.

The Guitar Effects Oriented Web Page

www.geofex.com

Instructional information on how to achieve a variety of electric guitar effects.

Guitar & Lute

home.earthlink.net/~guitarandlute

Historic information on the guitar and lute. Includes free tablature and sheet music.

Jazz Guitar Discussion Group

www.jazzguitargroup.com

Features discussions on the theory, practice, and history of the jazz guitar.

Perso Flamenco and Classic

perso.flamenco.free.fr/english/indexe.htm

Offers free tablature and sheet music for flamenco and classical guitars.

CHORD DICTIONARIES, TABS, AND TUITION

Absolute Tabs

www.tabs.co.za

Contains alphabetical tablature archive, online guitar tutorial, and links.

Chord House

www.looknohands.com/chordhouse

Provides detailed chord and scale finger settings for both left-handed and right-handed players.

Gootar

www.gootar.com

Features a wide variety of chord generators and chord name finders.

Guitar Inferno

home.tiscali.be/ guido.vanspranghe

Includes recorded riffs and tabs by amateur guitarists.

GuitarLounge.com

www.guitarlounge.com

Features online guitar lessons delivered through streaming audio and video.

Online Guitar Chord Dictionary

hatbox.lib.virginia.edu/ gtrchord/gtrchord

A chord dictionary searchable by root, type, bass note, and position.

Ultimate Chord Book

www.ultimatechordbook.com

An online chord book which uses a unique algorithmic approach to generate chords on the fly.

Web Riffs

www.webriffs.net

A site where musicians can post their original riffs and songs.

MANUFACTURERS

Brownsville Guitars Samson Technologies Corp.

575 Underhill Blvd., Syosset, NY 11791

www.Samsontech.com
T: (516) 364-2244

Manufacturers of the Thug, Choir Boy, and other electric guitars

Carvin Corporation

12340 World Trade Drive
San Diego, CA 92128-3742

T: (800) 854-2235
www.carvin.com

Makers of custom electric guitars and basses, as well as the Cobalt series of acoustic guitars.

Dean Guitars

15251 Roosevelt Blvd.,
Suite 206 Clearwater,
FL 33760

T: (717) 519-9669
www.deanguitars.com

Makers of a broad range of electric, bass, and acoustic guitars.

Gibson Original Acoustic Instruments

The Gibson Bluegrass Showcase
161 Opry Mills Drive
Nashville, TN 37214

www.Gibson.com
T: (800) 4-GIBSON

Makers of banjos, mandolins, dobros, and other acoustic stringed instruments.

Epiphone

645 Massman Drive
Nashville, TN 37210

T: (615) 871-4500
www.gibson.com

Epiphone introduced the first solid-body electric guitar in 1941 and continues to produce quality products today.

The ESP Guitar Company

10903 Vanowen Street, Unit A
North Hollywood, CA 91605

T: (800) 423-8388
F: (818) 506-1378
www.espguitars.com

Makers of electric guitars and basses with a heavy-metal edge.

Fender Musical Instruments Corporation

8860 E. Chaparral Road, Suite 100, Scottsdale, AZ 85250

T: (480) 596-9690
F: (480) 596-1384
www.fender.com

An American icon for over 50 years. Makers of the Telecaster, Stratocaster, and other electric and acoustic guitars.

Fernandes Guitars International, Inc.

8163 Lankershim Blvd.
North Hollywood, CA 91605

T: (800) 318-8599
F: (818) 252-6790
www.fernandesguitars.com
info@fernandesguitars.com

Japan's leading guitar manufacturer now produces a full range of electric guitars and basses for the American market.

Gibson

T: (615) 871-4500

relations@gibson.com /
www.gibson.com

*An American icon, Gibson
manufactures acoustic,
electric, and custom guitars.*

G.M.P. Guitars

510 E. Arrow Highway
San Dimas, CA 91773-3341

T: (909) 592-5144
F: (909) 599-0798
www.gmpguitars.com

*Makers of the Roxie, G.M.P.
strives to combine the best
aspects of guitars by Gibson,
Fender, and P.R.S. to provide
innovative alternatives to the
old standards.*

Guild

**Fender Musical Instruments
Corporation**

8860 E. Chaparral Road, Suite
100, Scottsdale, AZ 85250

T: (602) 596-9690
www.fender.com

*One of the oldest American
manufacturers, Guild makes
high-quality acoustic and
electric guitars.*

Hamer

Kaman Music Corporation
PO Box 507
Bloomfield, CT 06002-0507

www.KamanMusic.com
T: 860-509-8888
askus@hamerguitars.com

*Founded in Chicago in 1974,
Hamer makes modern electric
guitars with a vintage soul.*

Hartke

Samson Technologies Corp.
575 Underhill Blvd.
Syosset, NY 11791

T: (516) 364-2244
F: (516) 364-3888 F
www.samsontech.com
hartke@samsontech.com

*Hartke is known for its bass
amplifiers, strings, and
accessories. They have
recently begun making bass
guitars of their own.*

Ibanez

Ibanez Guitar Catalog
Dept. JDWS Box 886
Bensalem PA 19020

T: (215) 638-8670
www.ibanez.com

*Ibanez makes electric and
acoustic guitars, as well as
mandolins, amplifiers, and
accessories.*

Jackson

T: (800) 433-5627

www.jacksonguitars.com

*Creators of the Dinky, the
Rhoads, and the Warrior,
Jackson makes electric
guitars that are meant to
be played hard.*

Kramer

www.MusicYo.com

*Kramer guitars are designed
and built specifically for hard
rock guitar players.*

Kellar Bass Systems

101 First Street, #231
Los Altos, CA 94022

T: (866) 364-2021
F: (408) 725-7939
www.jambass.com
bkellar@jambass.com

*Keller Bass Systems created
the Jam Bass (tm), a panel
that attaches to the back of
the guitar neck and simulates
the bass sound so you can
play both guitar and bass
together.*

Martin

C. F. Martin & Co., Inc.
510 Sycamore Street
P. O. Box 329
Nazareth, PA 18064-0329

T: (610) 759-2837 or
(800) 633-2060
F: (610) 759-5757
www.mguitar.com
info@martinguitar.com

*Martin has been crafting
acoustic guitars since 1839
and has a reputation as one
of the world's finest guitar
makers.*

Modulus Guitars

8 Digital Drive, Suite 101
Novato, CA 94949

T: (415) 884-2300 or
(800) 758-2918
F: (415) 884.2373
www.Modulusguitars.com
custserv@modulusguitars.com

*Home of the Flea Bass,
inspired by Red Hot Chili
Peppers bassist Flea, Modulus
specializes in bass guitars, but
also offers a selection of
Genesis electric guitars.*

MusicVox

T: (609) 667-0444 or (877) Musicvx
www.MusicVox.com
Guitar@musicvox.com

MusicVox makes the unique Spaceranger and Spacecadet electric guitars. The Spaceranger was featured in Austin Powers' "Goldmember".

Ovation

Kaman Music Corporation
PO Box 507
Bloomfield, CT 06002-0507

T: (860) 509-8888
www.KamanMusic.com
askus@ovationguitars.com

Ovation specializes in acoustic/electric guitars since 1966.

Parker Guitars

444 E. Courtland Street
Mundelein, IL 60060

T: (978) 988-0102 or (800) 687-6863
www.parkerguitars.com

Ken Parker is the creator of the Parker Fly electric guitar. Many models are available, or you can have one made custom to your specs.

Paul Reed Smith Guitars

380 Log Canoe Circle
Stevensville, MD 21666 USA

T: (410) 643-9970
F: (410) 643-9980
www.prsguitars.com
custserv@prsguitars.com

Inspired by the great electric guitars of the 1950s and '60s, PRS is known for its attention to quality.

Reverend Instruments

27300 Gloede, Unit D
Warren, MI 48088

T: (586) 775-1025
www.reverenddirect.com
catalog@reverenddirect.com

Joe Naylor and his small, highly skilled staff combine vintage sensibilities with design innovation to produce electric guitars known for their tone.

Rickenbacker International Corporation

3895 South Main Street
Santa Ana, CA 92707

T: (714) 545-5574
F: (714) 754-0135
www.rickenbacker.com
info@rickenbacker.com

Founded in 1931, the Rickenbacker International Corporation (R.I.C.) made the first modern electric guitars.

Samick
Greg Bennett Guitars

18521 Railroad Street
City of Industry, CA 91748

T: (626) 964-4700
samickmusic@earthlink.net /
http://www.samickguitar.com/

Greg Bennett has designed a new line of acoustic, electric, and bass guitars for Samick.

Schecter Guitars

1840 Valpreda Street
Burbank, CA 91504

T: (323) 469-8900
www.schecterguitars.com

Known for their nu-metal drop-tuned guitars, Schecter also makes basses and custom guitars.

Takamine
Kaman Music Corporation

PO Box 507
Bloomfield, CT 06002-0507

T: (860) 509-8888
www.kamanmusic.com
askus@takamine.com

Located in Japan, Takamine specializes in acoustic/ electric guitars. Takamine pioneered the slider control preamp style and set the industry standard with their palethetic pickup.

Taylor

1980 Gillespie Way
El Cajon, CA 92020

T: (619) 258-1207 or (800) 943-6782
www.taylorguitars.com

For over 25 years, Taylor has been making acoustic and acoustic/electric guitars.

ToneSmith Guitars

19817 Jackie Lane
Rogers, MN 55374

T: (763) 428-8907
www.tonesmith.com

ToneSmith makes electric and bass guitars, as well as left handed guitars at no extra charge.

Transperformance

T: (970) 482-9132
www.selftuning.com
sales@transperformance.com

TransPerformance makes an automated tuning system called the Performer™, a small computer that can be mounted inside a guitar to easily control tuning while performing.

Yamaha

T: (714) 522-9011 or
(800) 879-1131
www.yamahaguitars.com
guitarguru@yamaha.com

*Yamaha produces a wide
variety of acoustic, electric,
and bass guitars. They offer
the EZ – Learning Guitar, a
self-teaching guitar with guide
lights.*

RETAIL STORES

Guitar Center

www.guitarcenter.com

*Guitar Center carries every
top name, as well as a wide
selection of classic vintage
instruments. They have over
100 stores in 34 states (see
website for individual location
information).*

Musician's Friend

T: (800) 391-8762
www.musicansfriend.com

*Musician's Friend is an
online/mail-order store. It is an
authorized dealer for more
than 900 manufacturers.*

Sam Ash Music Stores

T: (888) 615-5904

www.samashmusic.com (store
locations, events, and history)
www.samash.com (online
store

*Sam Ash has over 40 locations
in 14 states and has been in
business since 1924. Shop
online at www.samash.com
or call 1-800-4-SAMASH.*

PUBLICATIONS

Alfred Publishing

www.alfred.com

*Alfred Publishing is the
world's largest educational
music publisher, offering
instructional print, software
and DVD titles.*

Acoustic Guitar

www.acousticguitar.com

Bass Guitar Magazine

www.guitarworld.com

Fingerstyle Guitar Magazine

MI Media, LLC
21143 Hawthorne Blvd. #508
Torrance, CA 90503

T: (888) 223-3340
www.fingerstyleguitar.com

*Fingerstyle Guitar Magazine
caters to fingerstyle guitar
players at all levels of playing
ability.*

Flatpicking Guitar Magazine

High View Publications
P.O. Box 2160
Pulaski, VA. 24301

T: (800) 413-8296
www.flatpick.com
info@flatpick.com

*Flatpicking Guitar Magazine
specializes in all aspects of
flatpicking the acoustic guitar.*

Guitar Player Magazine

Box 58590
Boulder, CO 80322-8590
T: (800) 289-9839

www.guitarplayer.com
guitplyr@musicplayer.com

*Guitar Player provides stories
on artists, gear, and
workshops, as well as
instructional articles.*

Guitar World Magazine

www.guitarworld.com

Guitar World Acoustic Magazine

www.guitarworld.com

Just Jazz Guitar Magazine

T: (404) 250-9298
F: (404) 250-9951
www.justjazzguitar.com
justjazzguitar@mindspring.com

*Just Jazz Guitar features the
greatest players, educators
and writers in the field of jazz
guitar.*

songxpress.com

www.songxpress.com

*Website of Warner Bros.
Publications, a division of the
Warner Music Group, one of
the world's largest publishers
of music. Site contains a wide
area of multimedia instructional
and educational material.*

20th Century Guitar

T: (631) 273-1674
F: (631) 434-9057
www.tcguitar.com
tcguitar@tcguitar.com

*T.C.G. Magazine specializes in
collectible & vintage
American guitars.*

Vintage Guitar Magazine

PO Box 7301
Bismarck, ND 58507

T: (701) 255-1197 or
(800) 844-1197
F: (701) 255-0250

www.vintageguitar.com
vguitar@vguitar.com

*Vintage Guitar is the largest
magazine dedicated to vintage
guitars and the guitarists who
made them famous.*

EVENTS

Listings of events can be found in the above magazines, in addition to the suggested sites below.

Dr. Duck's Events & Shows

www.ducksdeluxe.com/ddevents.html

A comprehensive listing of events and shows around the country.

Guitar Digest

www.guitardigest.com

An online site that lists, and regularly updates, upcoming events.

Guitar Foundation of America

http://www.guitarfoundation.org/events.asp

Lists both international and national guitar events.

Harmony Central

http://www.harmony-central.com/MarketPlace/events.html

Features a search engine to find music events near you.

Indie-Music.com

www.indie-music.com

Both amateur and veteran musicians regularly log on to Indie-Music.com for the latest news, CD reviews, articles, and contact directory updates.

TUITION/TEACHING ORGANIZATIONS

American Institute of Guitar

250 West 54th St., Room 615
New York, NY 10019

(212) 757-3255
www.aiguitar.com

Founded in 1975, the American Institute of Guitar teaches students of all ages and skill levels, from beginner to advanced, in guitar, piano and keyboards, bass, voice, violin, cello, brass and winds, classical, jazz, rock, blues, flamenco, Brazilian, R&B, funk, world beat, metal, pop, fingerstyle, and country.

Austin Guitar School

5400 North Lamar, Suite 102
Austin, TX 78751

T: (512) 442-2880
www.austinguitarschool.com

Since 1987, this school has specialized in private instruction for all styles of guitar. Private lessons are available for electric bass, mandolin, classical, lap steel, 4 and 5 string banjo.

Berklee College of Music

1140 Boylston Street
Boston, MA 02215

T: (617) 266-1400
www.berklee.edu
admissions@berklee.edu

Founded in 1945, Berklee College of Music is the world's largest independent music college specializing in the study of contemporary music. They also have an online extension school at www.berkleemusic.com.

Indiana University

School of Music
Bloomington, IN 47405-2200

T: (812) 855-7998
F: (812) 856-6086

www.music.indiana.edu/som/guitar/guitarhomepage.htm
musicadm@indiana.edu

The prize-winning Guitar Department at the Indiana University opened in 1989, and offers bachelor, master, doctoral, performer, and artist programs.

The Julliard School

60 Lincoln Center Plaza
New York, NY 10023-6588

T: (212) 799-5000
www.juilliard.edu
admissions@julliard.edu

Julliard specializes in classical music training and offers higher education to students with a strong music background.

Learnguitar.net

http://www.learnguitar.net

Personalized Online Guitar Lessons, where you can choose your own online guitar instructor.

Mannes College of Music

50 West 85th Street
New York, NY 10024

T: (212) 580-0210
www.mannes.edu

A renowned college of music, offering full college programs in music or adult classes; focus is on classical guitar.

Musician's Institute
1655 McCadden Place
Hollywood, CA 90028-6115

T: (323) 462-1384 or
(800) 255-7529
/www.mi.edu

One of the top schools in the country, a comprehensive, hands-on education in contemporary music performance, recording, guitar making, and music business.

National Guitar Workshop (NGW)
Box 222
Lakeside, CT 06758

800-234-6479 or 860-567-3736
emily@guitarworkshop.com /
www.guitarworkshop.com

The National Guitar Workshop offers outstanding summer music classes in Guitar, Bass, Keyboards, Drums, Mandolin, Banjo, Songwriting, and Voice. They have workshops on college campuses in Los Angeles, San Francisco, Austin, Nashville, Seattle, New Orleans, Chicago and New Milford; check their website for current listings.

Phillip and Patricia Frost School of Music at the University of Miami
PO Box 248165
Coral Gables, FL 33124-7610

T: (305) 284-2241
F: (305) 284-6475
www.music.miami.edu/

A first class music program that has attracted some of the finest musicians in the world to become instructors there. Jazz and Latin are the big topics but there are other opportunities as well. They also have a guitar summer camp.

The American Music School
4319 Fremont Ave. N.
Seattle, WA 98103

T: (206) 545-2908
www.americanmusic.com

Offers private individual instruction, group classes, and master classes, and workshops, in a range of guitar styles.

EXHIBITIONS/ MUSEUMS

Guitar Fox
www.guitarfox.com/guitarshows.htm

Guitar Fox provides comprehensive lists of guitar shows around the country.

The American Guitar Museum
1810 New Hyde Park Road
New Hyde Park, New York 11040

516.488.5000
www.americanguitarmuseum.com/

Located in a charming three-story colonial farmhouse, the American Guitar Museum is full of vintage guitars and is a monument to the world's greatest guitar makers. Admission is free.

Country Music Hall of Fame® and Museum
222 Fifth Ave. S.
Nashville, TN 37203

T: (615) 416-2001 or
(800) 852-6437
www.countrymusichalloffame.com
eblast@countrymusichalloffame.com

The Country Music Hall of Fame® presents the history of country music and memorializes country music masters.

Georgia Music Hall of Fame
200 Martin Luther King, Jr. Blvd. Macon, GA 31201

T: (478) 750-8555 or (888) GA-ROCKS
www.gamusichall.com

Over 450 artists are represented at the Georgia Music Hall of Fame, including Little Richard, James Brown, Otis Redding, and the Allman Brothers Band. The museum features music, video, memorabilia, instruments, performance costumes, and more.

Kenneth G. Fiske Museum of The Claremont Colleges Bridges Auditorium
450 North College Way
Claremont, CA 91711-4491

T: (909) 621-8307
www.cuc.claremont.edu/fiske/index.asp
arrice@rocketmail.com

The Fiske Museum is an eclectic museum of instruments dating from the 17th century through the 20th century, includings antique guitars, mandolins, lutes, and banjos. Admission is free.

Museum of Making Music

5790 Armada Drive
Carlsbad, CA 92008

T: (760) 438-5996 or
(877) 551-9976
F: (760) 438-8964
www.museumofmakingmusic.org

The Museum of Making Music is an interactive museum tracing American Popular Music from the 1890s to the present. It houses over 500 vintage instruments— including an authentic guitar-making workshop—hundreds of audio/video examples, and a hands-on area.

Museum of Musical Instruments

PO Box 8447
Santa Cruz, Ca 95061

877-30-Music
www.TheMoMI.org
contact@themomi.org

The Museum of Musical Instruments is an online museum.

National Music Museum

The University of South Dakota
414 East Clark Street
Vermillion, SD 57069

T: (605) 677-530
F: (605) 677-6995
www.usd.edu/smm
smm@usd.edu

The National Music Museum houses more than 10,000 American, European, and non-Western instruments, including many rare guitars. It is recognized as "A Landmark of American Music" by the National Music Council.

GUITAR SOCIETIES BY REGION

Guitar Foundation of America

PO Box 1240
Claremont, CA 91711

www.guitarfoundation.org
info@guitarfoundation.org

The G.F.A. is an organization founded in 1973 to provide guitarists with a full range of educational, literary, and performance resources and opportunities.

ARIZONA

Arizona Classic Guitar Society

P.O. Box 25766
Tempe, AZ 85285-5766

Bluewater Guitar Society

John Del Quadro
P.O. Box 518
Bullhead City, AZ 86442

Tucson Guitar Society

6662 E Paseo San Andres
Tucson, AZ 85718

www.tucsongs.org/tucsongs
info@tucsongs.org

CALIFORNIA

American Guitar Society

Gregory Newton, President
20752 San Jose St.
Chatsworth, CA 91311

T: (818) 349-7960
www.csun.edu/~igra/ags/index.html
newtonguitar@earthlink.net

Carmel Classic Guitar Society

Terrence Farrell
P.O. Box 6543
Carmel, CA 93921

www.starrsites.com/CarmelClassicGuitar/index.html

The Cuesta Guitar Circle

Cuesta College Community
Programs
P.O. Box 8106
San Luis Obispo, CA 93403

http://home.earthlink.net/~reedandchic/index.html

Fresno Guitar Society

Leng Widjaja
P.O. Box 25972
Fresno CA 93729

Orange County Guitar Circle

Lee Zimmer
P.O. Box 3102
Costa Mesa, CA 92626

www.ocgc.org

Sacramento Guitar Society

www.sacguitar.org

San Francisco Classical Guitar Society

Ernest Culver
560 Nineteenth Street
San Francisco, CA 94107

T: (415) 731-7336
www.sfcgs.org
SFCGS@aol.com

San Joaquin Valley Guitar Society

David Schramm
2470 Polson Avenue
Clovis, CA 93611

T: (559) 325-8057
www.sjvgs.org
dave@schrammguitars.com

South Bay Guitar Society

Tom Ingalz, Vice President
19 N. 2nd St., Suite 102
San Jose, CA 95113

T: (408) 294-0400
www.sbgs.org

Ventura County Classical Guitar Society

www.vccgs.com/guitar.htm

COLORADO

Boulder Guitar Society
Richard Comly
1011 N. Cedarbrook
Boulder, CO 80302

Colorado Springs Guitar Society
Email:
President@ColoradoSpringsGu
itarSociety.org

www.coloradospringsguitarso
ciety.org

Classical Guitar Society of Northern Colorado
1445 Wakerobin Court
Fort Collins, CO 80526

www.coloradoguitar.com

Denver Classical Guitar Society
Rochelle A. Chartier, President
7881 Oak St.
Arvada, CO 80005
T: (303) 940-7097

www.denverclassicalguitarsoc
iety.org
denverclassicalgs@yahoo.com

South Colorado Classic Guitar Society
Jim Bosse
930 Harrison Ave.
Canon City, CO 81212

tuttdb@msn.com

Western Colorado Classical Guitar Society
Bill Kain
P.O. Box 1981
Grand Junction, CO 81502

bkain@acsol.net

CONNECTICUT

Connecticut Classical Guitar Society
Penny Phillips
P.O. Box 1528
Hartford, CT 06144

FLORIDA

Miami Classic Guitar Society
Carlos Molina
P.O. Box 0725
Miami, FL 33265

Central Florida Classical Guitar Society
Jesse Tan, President
14644 Quail Trail Circle
Orlando, FL 32837

T: (407) 857-8312
wbeckeroags@earthlink.net

Classical Guitar Society of Tallahassee
Tim Atkinson
326 Meadow Ridge Drive
Tallahassee, FL 32312

T: (850) 668-1643 evenings
T: (850) 521-0700 day
www.istal.com/cgst/
www.istal.com/cgst/
mdxguitar@yahoo.com

North Florida Classical Guitar Society
Sharon Ketts
4405 S.W. 98th Place
Gainesville, FL 32608

T: (352) 378-0659

Florida East Coast Classical Guitar Society
Dale Predovic
1710 Canterbury Dr.
Indialantic, FL 32903

http://home.earthlink.net/~dale
31/

Orlando Acoustic Guitar Society
Will Becker, President
3508 Manitou Dr.
Orlando, FL 32839

T: (407) 835-9867
wbeckeroags@earthlink.net

Pensacola Guitar Society
Joe Stallings
Pensacola Jr. College Music
Dept. 1000 College Blvd.
Pensacola, FL 32504

Tampa Bay Guitar Society
Thomas Coffey
15913 Country Place
Tampa, FL 33624

GEORGIA

Guitar Atlanta
Eddie Minjarez
PO Box 8475
Atlanta, GA 31106

www.guitaratlanta.org
guitaratlanta@hotmail.com

IDAHO

Idaho Classic Guitar Society
Steve Trott
550 W. Fort St.
Boise, ID 83754 Illinois

ILLINOIS

Chicago Classic Guitar Society
Pamela Kimmel
P.O. Box 4485
Skokie, IL 60076-4485

www.chicagoclassicalguitarso
ciety.org
p.kimmel@comcast.net

INDIANA

The Bloomington Classical Guitar Society
Mark Bisesi, President
PO Box 6181
Bloomington, IN 47407-6181

Classical Guitar Society of Evansville
James Doane
105 South Willard St.
Fort Branch, IN 47648

www.cgse.org

Indiana Society of the Classic Guitar
6516 N. Cornell Ave.
Indianapolis, IN 46220

KANSAS

The Kansas City Guitar Society
John Jenab
110 S. Cherry, Suite 200
Olathe, Kansas 66061

jjenab@mindspring.com

Wichita Guitar Society
John Francis
1221 W. 17th N
Wichita, KS 67203

T: (316) 263-7561
http://sologuitarist.net/wichita
_guitar.html
wichitaguitar@sologuitarist.net

MAINE

Downeast Classical Guitar Society
P.O. Box 232
Bangor, ME 04402

Seacoast Guitar Society
PO Box 790
York, ME 03909

T: (207) 363-1886
F: (207) 363-7263

www.seacoastguitar.org

MARYLAND

Baltimore Classical Guitar Society
Michael Oliver, President
4607 Maple Ave.
Baltimore, MD 21227

www.bcgs.org
president@bcgs.org

MASSACHUSETTS

Boston Classical Guitar Society
Sharon Wayne, President
147 Grant St.
Framingham, MA 01702

www.bostonguitar.org
sharon@sharonwayne.net

MICHIGAN

Ann Arbor Classical Guitar Society
Brian and Mary Lou Roberts
1451 Bemidji Dr
Ann Arbor, MI 48103

www.society.arborguitar.org
society@brianroberts.org

Classical Guitar Society of Michigan
Lawrence M. Laub
30542 Charmaine
Roseville, MI 48066-4048

Michigan Fingerstyle Guitar Society
JB Davies
180 High Oak Road, Suite 100
Bloomfield Hills, MI 48304

T: (248) 646-4030
www.fingerstyle.org
info@fingerstyle.org

MINNESOTA

Minnesota Guitar Society
P.O. Box 14986
Minneapolis, MN 55414

www.mnguitar.org

MISSOURI

St. Louis Classical Guitar Society
P.O. Box 11425
St. Louis, MO 63105

T: (314) 567-5566

MONTANA

Western Montana Classical Guitarists
937 S 5th St W.
Missoula, MT 59801-2429

T: (406) 721-6256

NEBRASKA

Omaha Classical Guitar Guild
Box 87
6001 Dodge Street
Omaha, NE 68182

www.omahaguitar.org

NEVADA

Guitar Society of Las Vegas
Dave Carroll, President
P. O. Box 70781
Las Vegas, NV 89170.

gslv@gslv.org
www.gslv.org

Lake Tahoe Classic Guitar Society
Larry Aynesmith
Incline Village, NV 89450

tahoeguitarsociety@hotmail.com
www.tahoeguitarsociety.com/

NEW JERSEY

New Jersey Guitar and Mandolin Society
Michael Lemma, Director
Bergen County Academies
200 Hackensack Ave.
Hackensack, NJ 07601

T: (201) 343-6000 x2313
www.bergen.org/njgms
njgms@bergen.org

NEW MEXICO

Albuquerque Guitar Alliance
Neil Martinez
4816 McMahon, NW A-18
Albuquerque, NM 87114

New Mexico Guitar Society
3316 Lafayette Dr. NE
Albuquerque, NM 87106

NEW YORK

Buffalo Guitar Society
Mir Ali, P.O. Box 1034
Williamsville, NY 14231-1034

T: (716) 810-0549
mirali@sprynet.com

Capital District Guitar Society
Tony Grieco
962 Myrtle Avenue
Albany, NY 12203

T: (518) 489-4323

Classic Guitar Society of Brooklyn
Claudia Block
4750 Bedford Ave., Suite 5F
Brooklyn, NY 11235

The Classical Guitar Society of Upstate New York
Gail Hamilton, Vice President
134 Delaware St
Walton, NY 13856

T: (607) 865-8775
www.cgsuny.org
musicalm@hancock.net

Long Island Classical Guitar Society
Dennis M. Rief, Executive Director
182 Parkside Ave.
Miller Place, NY 11764

www.licgs.us/index.php
New York City Classical Guitar Society
www.nyccgs.com

New York Classic Guitar Society
Seth Himmelhoch
217 Haven Ave, #2D
New York, NY 10033

Rochester Guitar Society
John Wiesenthal
50 N. Plymouth Ave.
Rochester, NY 14614

NORTH CAROLINA

Piedmont Classical Guitar Society
920 Shuman St.
Winston-Salem, NC 27107

T: (910) 775-0844
ncnatural.com/PCGS/guitar.html

Triangle Guitar Society
Randy Reed, President
T: (919) 490-1920

www.triangleguitar.org

OHIO

Columbus Guitar Society
Karl Wohlwend
Capital University
Conservatory of Music
Columbus, OH 43209

T: (614) 236-6240
www.columbusguitarsociety.org
info@columbusguitarsociety.org

Dayton Classic Guitar Society
Jim McCutcheon
8530 Cherrycreek Dr.
Centerville, OH 45458

mccutcheon@udayton.edu

Greater Cincinnati Classic Guitar Society
Christopher Hubbard
386 Misty Dawn Drive
Maineville, OH 45039

T: 513-677-1293
www.cincinnatiguitarsociety.org
hubbardguitar@fuse.net

OKLAHOMA

Bartlesville Guitar Society
Rob Chirico
2817 Redhowe Ct.
Bartlesville, OK 74006

OREGON

Jefferson Classical Guitar Society (formerly Acoustic Guitar Society of Ashland)
Joseph Thompson, Secretary
349 Tudor St.
Ashland, OR 97520

T: (541) 552-9515
www.jeffersonguitar.org
info@jeffersonguitar.org

Portland Guitar Society
P.O. Box 15253
Portland, OR 97293

PENNSYLVANIA

Delaware Valley Fingerstyle Guitar Association
Joe Willson, Founder
PO Box 8115
Radnor, PA 19087

T: (610) 547-3835
www.dvfga.com
joe@dvfga.com

Erie Classical Guitar Society
P.O. Box 9051
Erie, PA 16505-9051

www.angelfire.com/pa/flefebr
e/society.html

The Guitar Society of Fine Art
Michael Chapman, Executive Director
Pittsburgh, PA

www.gsfapittsburgh.org/

LeHigh Valley Guitar And Ensemble Society
Marvin Falcon
1740 W. Livingston St.
Allentown, PA 18104

Philadelphia Classical Guitar Society
Michael Simmons, President
2038 Sansom St.
Philadelphia, PA 19103

T: (215) 567-2972
www.phillyguitar.com

Pittsburgh-Tri-State Classical Guitar Society
106 Brookside Blvd.
Pittsburgh, PA 15241

RHODE ISLAND

Rhode Island Classical Guitar Society
PO Box 1125
Providence, RI 02901-1125

SOUTH CAROLINA

Columbia Guitar Society
PO box 8031
Columbia, SC 29202

jefdeb@usit.net

TENNESSEE

University of Memphis Classical Guitar Society
President, Dept. of Music
University of Memphis
Memphis, TN 38152

Nashville Guitar Society
Byron Fogo
492 Page Dr.
Mt. Juliet TN 37122

TEXAS

Austin Classical Guitar Society
Matthew Hinsley
P.O. Box 49704
Austin, TX 78765

T: (512) 899-1118
www.austinclassicalguitar.org
hinsley@mail.utexas.edu

Guitar Houston
4149 Bellaire Blvd., #229
Houston, TX 77025

E-Mail:
mail@guitarhouston.org
www.guitarhouston.org

Dallas Classic Guitar Society
Mitch Weverka, Executive Director
P.O. Box 190823
Dallas, TX 75219

T: (214) 528-3733
www.dallasguitar.org
dcgs@dallasguitar.org

Fort Worth Classic Guitar Society
Christopher McGuire, Artistic Director

www.guitarsociety.org/Home.
html
chris@guitarsociety.org

UTAH

Utah Guitar Society
Peter Choles
476 E. South Temple
P.O. Box 193
Salt Lake City, UT 84102

VIRGINIA

Charlottesville Classical Guitar Society
Dave Edwards, President
4685 Pelham Dr.
Earlysville, VA 22936

T: (434) 973-0115
F: (434) 975-3935
http://monticello.avenue.org/c
cgs/
dave@rediscov.com

South-West Virginia Classical Guitar Society
Dr. Robert Trent
Radford University
Radford, VA 24141

T: (540) 831-5117
www.radford.edu/~arts/music/
guitar_performance/GuitarFest
/GuitarFest.htm
rstrent@radford.edu

Tidewater Classical Guitar Society
Sam Dorsey
P.O. Box 1171
Norfolk, VA 23501

T: (757) 627-6229
www.tcgs.cx
tcgs@mac.com

WASHINGTON STATE

Guild of American Luthiers
8222 S. Park Ave.
Tacoma, WA 98408-5226

T: (253) 472-7853
www.luth.org

A non-profit educational membership organization, formed in 1972 to advance the craft of string instrument making and repair through a free exchange of information

Northwest Classical Guitar Society
David Feingold
1809 Summit St.
Bellingham, WA 98225

Rosewood Guitar Society
8402 Greenwood Ave.
N Seattle, WA 98103

T: (206) 297-8788
www.halcyon.com/rosewood/page2.html

Seattle Classic Guitar Society
P.O. Box 31256
Seattle, WA 98103-1256.

F: (206) 270-9342
www.seattleguitar.org
SeattleCGS@halcyon.com

The Classical Guitar Society of the Tri-Cities
Adolfo Reparaz
811 W. Margaret
Pasco, WA 99301

T: (509) 542-8180
www.3-cities.com/~cgstc/guitar.html
cgstc@bossig.com

Yakima Valley Classical Guitar Society
James Durkee
2505 W. Chestnut
Yakima, WA 98902

T: (509) 453-7234

WASHINGTON, DC

Washington Guitar Society
John Rodgers, President
4500 Connecticut Ave., NW #605
Washington, DC 20008

www.dcguitar.org/wgs/

WISCONSIN

Madison Classical Guitar Society
http://userpage.chemie.fu-berlin.de/~kastow/mcgs/index.html

Milwaukee Guitar Society
John Stropes
1132 Lake Avenue
Racine, WI 53403-1925

T: (414) 636-9910
F: (414) 636-9911
stropes@execpc.com

WYOMING

Cheyenne Guitar Society
www.worldguitarist.com/cheyenne.html
guitarlj2@attbi.com

CANADIAN MANUFACTURERS

Beneteau Guitars
109 Forest Street
St. Thomas, ON
N5R 2J8

T: (519) 633-6994
www.beneteauguitars.com

Acoustic guitar maker since 1974.

Dingwall Designer Guitars
P.O. Box 9194
Saskatoon, SK
S7K 7E8

T: (306) 242-6201
www.dingwallguitars.com

Manufacturer of designer electric and bass guitars.

F Bass
16 McKinstry Street
Hamilton, ON
L8L 6C1

T: (905) 522-1582

www.fbass.com

Custom built basses and exotic tops.

Fury Guitar Manufactures Ltd.
902 Avenue J North
Saskatoon, SK
S7L 2L2

T: (306) 244-4063
www.furyguitar.com

Fury Guitars has manufactured electric guitars since 1962.

Garrison Guitars
P.O. Bos 13096
St. John's, NL
A1B 3V8

T: (709) 745-6677
www.garrisonguitars.com

*Garrison's is one of Canada's
largest acoustic guitar
manufacturers.*

Godin Guitars

www.godinguitars.com

*Godin guitars are built in four
locations, three in Quebec and
one in New Hampshire. Godin
are best known for their
acoustic guitar brands:
Seagull, Simon & Patrick,
Norman, LaPatrie and Art &
Lutherie.*

Jean Larrivee Guitars
780 E. Cordova Street
Vancouver, BC
V6A 1M3

T: (604) 253-7111
www.larrivee.com

*Larrivee Guitars produces
steel string guitars and have
plants in British Columbia and
southern California.*

Lado Musical Inc.
205 St, David Street
Lindsay, ON
K9V 5K7

(705) 328-2005
www.lado-guitars.com

*Unique custom made acoustic,
electric and bass guitars.*

Northwood Guitars
#308-20445 62nd Avenue
Langley, BC
V3A 5E6

T: (604) 515-7576
www.northwoodguitars.com

*Specialize in hand-built guitars
with exotic woods and design
options.*

Sawchyn Guitars
2048 Montague Street
Regina, SK
S4T 3J7

T: (306) 522-3134
www.sawchyn.com

*Sawchyn Guitars has been the
maker of acoustic guitars and
mandolins since 1972.*

Timtone Custom Guitars
7742 – 22nd Street
Grand Forks, BC
V0H 1H2

www.timtone.com

*A small company that custom
builds 10-12 electric, electric-
acoustic guitars and basses
each year. Each instrument is
build to the specifications of
the eventual owner.*

CANADIAN PUBLICATIONS

Canadian Music Network
604-111 Peter Street
Toronto, ON
M5V 2H1

T: (416) 979-2228
www.canadianmusicnetwork.
com

*Weekly national trade
magazine.*

Chart Magazine
#200-41 Britain Street
Toronto, ON
M5A 1R7

www.chartattack.com

*Semi-monthly national
magazine.*

Country Music News
P.O. Box 7323 Vanier Terminal
Ottawa, ON
K1L 8E4

T: (613) 745-6006
www.countrymusicnews.ca

*National country music
magazine.*

Exclaim!
7-B Pleasant Blvd.
Unit #966
Toronto, ON
M4T 1K2

T: (416) 535-9735
www.exclaim.ca

*Garrison's is one of Canada's
largest acoustic guitar
manufacturers.*

MOTE Magazine
North Hill Postal Outlet
P.O. Box 65026
Calgary, AB
T2N 4T6

T: (403) 241-5453
www.moregoatthangoose.com

Online indie music magazine.

Soul Shine Magazine
200 Gilroy Drive
Scarborough, ON
M1P 1Z9

T: (416) 751-3884
www.soulshine.ca

Monthly online music
magazine.

CANADIAN SOCIETIES AND ASSOCIATIONS BY REGION

BRITISH COLUMBIA

Coastal Jazz & Blues Society
316 West 6th Avenue
Vancouver, BC
V5Y 1K9

T: (604) 872-5200
www.coastaljazz.ca

Victoria Jazz Society
250–727 Johnson Street
Victoria, BC
V8W 1M9

T: (250) 388-4423
www.vicjazz.bc.ca/vjs/

MANITOBA

Manitoba Blues Society
P.O. Box 52
355 Henderson Highway
Winnipeg, MB
R2L 1Mo

T: (204) 667-3491
www.mbblues.mb.ca

NOVA SCOTIA

East Coast Blues Society
6958 Ward Avenue
Halifax, NS
B3L 2K4

T: 9902) 454-4283
www.eastcoastblues.ca

ONTARIO

Canada South Blues Society
1185 Argyle Road
Windsor, ON
N8Y 3K2

T: (519) 977-9631
www.bluessociety.ca

Toronto Blues Society
910 Queen Street West
Suite B04
Toronto, ON
M6J 1G6

T:(416) 538-3885
www.torontobluessociety.com

SASKATOON

Saskatoon Blues Society Inc
P.O. Box 21035
Saskatoon, SK
S7H 5N9

members.shaw.ca/saskblues/

GLOSSARY

Music is full of terms for describing everything from styles to musical structure and effects. It is important to understand and memorize certain definitions that apply to the guitar and guitar playing.

accent An emphasized note or chord.

accidental A symbol such as a sharp, flat, or natural, placed in front of a note to raise or lower its pitch.

Aeolian mode The mode starting on the sixth degree of the major scale.

arpeggiated Literally, played "like a harp," i.e. the notes of a chord played one after the other rather than together.

atonal Not part of the tonal system of major and minor keys or modes.

augmented A major chord with the fifth raised a semitone.

bar A section of music that groups note values over a given length of time.

bass note The lowest pitched note in a chord or harmonic movement.

bending *see* string bending

blues An African-American style of music that uses its own type of scale and often has a 12-bar form.

blues scale A pentatonic minor scale with added notes. These can be a flattened fifth and a major third and a second and sixth.

bossa nova Brazilian rhythmic style with jazz influences.

bottleneck A guitar technique using a glass or metal tube to play and slide notes and chords. Also called slide.

bout The rounded upper and lower parts of a guitar body on each side of the waist.

break A short solo passage.

bridge Section for fixing and supporting the strings on an guitar.

capo A device that has a bar that can be fixed or clamped on a fret to hold the strings.

changes The sequence of chords used as a basis for improvisation in jazz.

chord Any combination of more than one note played together.

chromatic Chromatic notes are those that fall outside the notes of a key. The chromatic scale is a 12-note scale moving in semitones.

classical A range of different types of formal composition from the medieval period to the present day.

counterpoint The playing of two or more independent parts at the same time.

country A rural popular music originally from the US.

diatonic Using the notes of the major scale and its modes, including the minor in an unaltered form.

diminished A chord based on intervals of a minor third. The diminished scale consists of alternating tones and semitones.

dominant The note or chord on the fifth degree of a diatonic scale. This is often marked with the Roman numeral V.

Dorian mode The mode starting on the second degree of the major scale.

double-stopping Stopping two or more strings with the left hand on the frets.

drone, drone strings One or more strings that can be played so that they sustain underneath chords or linear passages as a pedal tone. Added strings can also be played or tuned to vibrate in sympathy with the main strings.

effects Numerous special effects are available. They include:
chorus Simulates the effect of more than one instrument playing the same note.
compressor (compression) Boosts the volume of quieter notes and reduces that of louder ones, evening out the sound of fast passages.
delay (echo) Mimics the echo effect by playing a delayed copy of the original sound.
distortion Change of tone quality, with a harsh sound achieved by overdriving an amplifier, or the use of a distortion pedal, fuzz box, or overdriver.
enhancer Device to improve definition of a sound.
expander The opposite of compressor, this increases

the range of volume.

flanger Chorus-type effect that uses a delayed signal with a slight pitch variation.

fuzz A form of distortion, operated by a fuzz pedal.

harmonizer A chorus-type effect adding a sound in harmony with the original signal.

Leslie The Leslie cabinet, originally for use with electronic organs, contains a rotating speaker that gives a swirling effect.

octave divider An early form of harmonizer, adding a sound an octave above or below the original signal.

overdriving This produces a form of distortion.

panning Moving the source of the sound within the stereo field.

phasing Playing two identical sounds slightly out-of-phase with one another.

pre-amp A pre-amplifier can be used as a form of tone control or to boost the signal.

reverb Mimics the echo effect, either by a built-in spring reverb or a digital electronic emulation.

tremolo (tremolo bar) Small and rapid variation in the volume of a note. This effect is often confused with vibrato, and the tremolo arm or bar is used to bend the pitch of notes on electric guitars.

Uni-Vibe Swirling effect, similar to Leslie.

vibrato Small and rapid variation in the pitch of a note.

volume pedal Means of altering the volume of sound, useful in creating the "fade-in" effect or as a "swell" pedal.

wah wah The wah-wah pedal controls the relative bass and treble response of a sound. Fully down it has a high treble tone, fully up it emphasizes the bass, and the characteristic "wah-wah" sound is achieved by rocking the pedal back and forth.

feedback The loud whine produced by a microphone or pickup receiving and amplifying its own signal from a loudspeaker.

flamenco A style of playing, singing, and dancing based on Spanish and Moorish influences.

flat Symbol (♭) used for lowering a note by a semitone.

frequency The number of cycles per second, which determines pitch.

glissando A slide from one note to another.

groove A repeated rhythmic pattern in jazz and rock.

hammer-on Notes played by hammering the strings down with the fingers.

harmonic minor An Aeolian mode with a raised seventh.

harmonics Notes with an ethereal tone higher than the pitch of the string, produced by lightly touching the string at certain points.

head In jazz, the statement of the tune before and after the improvised solos.

improvisation Creative process of making music or soloing ad lib.

interval The distance between two notes.

Ionian mode Another term for the major scale.

inversion Chord voicings where the root is not in the bass.

jazz Music characterized by the use of improvisation.

key The reference pitch for a diatonic system.

Latin Music of Latin-American origin, including dance rhythms such as the habañera, samba, rhumba, and bossa nova.

ledger line Small line for placing notes above and below the stave.

legato A smooth, even approach to playing consecutive notes.

licks In jazz and rock, short, almost clichéd phrases inserted into a solo or used as fills.

ligado Term for hammering and pulling off notes.

Locrian mode The mode starting on the seventh degree of the major scale.

Lydian mode The mode starting on the fourth degree of the major scale.

machine head (tuner) Mechanical device for adjusting pitch.

major Chord with a major third between the root and the third. Scale predominantly with major and perfect intervals.

melodic minor An Aeolian mode with a raised sixth and seventh.

microtone Interval of less than a semitone.

MIDI Musical Instrument Digital Interface—allows instruments such as electric guitars and synthesizers to communicate with computers.

minor Chord with a minor third between the root and the third.

Mixolydian mode The mode starting on the fifth degree of the major scale.

modes, modal Scales using the notes of the diatonic scale, other than the major and minor scales. The modes, such as Dorian, Phrygian, and Aeolian, originated in medieval music, but were adopted by jazz players in the 1950s.

modulate Move from one key to another.

motif, motivic A short, recognizable melodic phrase.

natural Symbol (♮) used to cancel the effect of a sharp or flat.

octave The same note at higher and lower frequencies.

open tuning Tuning the strings of the guitar to a specific chord, rather than the conventional EADGBE. There are also other nonconventional tunings such as DADGAD.

pedal note A repeated bass note that supports a sequence of changing harmonies.

pentatonic A scale of five, rather than the more usual seven, notes.

Phrygian mode The mode starting on the third degree of the major scale.

pick Object for striking the strings held by the right hand. Also known as a plectrum.

pickguard A protective plate on the body of the guitar.

pickup The device on electric guitars that picks up and transmits the sound of the strings to the amplifier.

pitch The frequency of a note.

plectrum see pick.

pull-off A note played by pulling the string with the fingers of the left hand.

raga A scale used in Indian music often using microtones.

relative minor The minor system starting on the sixth degree of the major scale.

rest A period of silence.

rhythm A pattern of notes and accents.

riff In popular music, a repeated motif or phrase.

root The note from which a chord takes its name and the lowest note (bass note) in the standard voicing of the chord. In an inversion the root is no longer the bass note.

rubato Not strictly in tempo—played freely and expressively.

scales A series of ascending or descending notes in a specific key, the basis for compositions in the tonal system.

segue Moving without a break to the next movement, section, or piece.

sequence Often a term for a song or a chordal pattern.

sharp Symbol (♯) for raising a note by a semitone.

soh-fah A system of one-syllable abbreviations for scale notes. The notes are Doh-Ray-Me-Fah-Soh-Lah-Te-Doh.

solo An improvised passage over music.

staccato Notes or chords that are short and clipped.

stave Five horizontal lines and spaces on which music is written.

string-bending Using the fingers of the left hand to pull a string to one side, "bending" the pitch of the note.

subdominant The note or chord on the fourth degree (IV) of the major scale.

syncopation Shifting the accent of a melody off the main beat of the bar.

tempo The speed of a piece of music.

timbre The tone quality of a sound.

time signature The two numbers showing the metrical subdivision of a bar.

tonal A system primarily of major and minor keys.

tonic The note or chord on the first degree of a diatonic scale. Often marked with the Roman numeral I.

transposition To move a section or a piece of music to a key with a new pitch.

triad A three-note chord with intervals of thirds.

trill Rapid alternation between one note and the note above.

tuners see machine head.

unison The same note added. For example, on a 12-string guitar, the pairs of strings are tuned in unison, i.e. to the same note.

vamps Repeated accompanying figures in jazz and popular music.

vibrato A technique where a note is moved rapidly (a minor fluctuation in pitch) to create an effect or enhance tone.

voicing The spacing of the notes in a chord.

X-bracing A pair of large wooden braces positioned in the shape of an X inside an acoustic guitar to suppport the top and enhance the sound.

INDEX

Author's acknowledgments

The author would like to thank his agent Julian
Alexander, and Corinne Roberts and Linda Martin at
DK for keeping the project on track.

He would particularly like to thank Ted Kinsey and Mark
Cavanagh for the design; the editors Angela Baynham
and Matthew Milton; Jenisa Patel and Karen Self at DK
for their design guidance; and Trevor Bounford for the
music illustrations. His thanks also to the managing editor,
Miranda Smith, who worked to a really high standard.

He would also like to thank Bill Puplett for the
maintenance section, and the following people for their
help and advice: Rob Aylward, Dave Brewis, Karen
Brock, Clive Brown, Dave Burrlock, Carol Chapman,
Stuart Cumberpatch, Christopher Dean, Keith Dunnell,

Michael Gee, Steve Hart, Andy Holdsworth, Steve
Hoyland, Max Kay, Barry Mason, Charles Measures,
Michael Messer, John Monteleone, Nigel Moyse, Dave
Noble, Bill Pupplet, Clive Russell, Saiichi Sugiyama,
Ced Thorose, Mike Tamborino, Jim Westbrook, David
Weston, Larry Wexer, David Whiteman, Andreas Young.

Publisher's acknowledgments

DK would like to thank Trevor Bounford for the illustrations;
Rachael Swann and Cecilia McKay for picture research;
Mark Cavanagh for design; Richard Dabb and Lucy
Claxton in the DK Image Library; Gary Ombler for
photography; Lette Luff, Richard Gilbert, and Marion
Davies for editorial assistance; Christine Bernstein for the
index; Margaret Parrish for US translation; and Barbara
Berger, John Searci, and Jennifer Crake for the directory.